Just A Basketball

A Comprehensive Guide to Ball Handling and Dribbling Drills

Andy Hart

Order this book online at www.trafford.com/03-2036
or email orders@trafford.com

Most Trafford titles are also available at major online book retailers.

© Copyright 2008 Andrew N. Hart.

All rights reserved. No part of this publication may be reproduced, stored in a retrieval system, or transmitted, in any form or by any means, electronic, mechanical, photocopying, recording, or otherwise, without the written prior permission of the author.

Note for Librarians: A cataloguing record for this book is available from Library and Archives Canada at www.collectionscanada.ca/amicus/index-e.html

Printed in Victoria, BC, Canada.

ISBN: 978-1-4120-1659-9

We at Trafford believe that it is the responsibility of us all, as both individuals and corporations, to make choices that are environmentally and socially sound. You, in turn, are supporting this responsible conduct each time you purchase a Trafford book, or make use of our publishing services. To find out how you are helping, please visit www.trafford.com/responsiblepublishing.html

Our mission is to efficiently provide the world's finest, most comprehensive book publishing service, enabling every author to experience success. To find out how to publish your book, your way, and have it available worldwide, visit us online at www.trafford.com/10510

 www.trafford.com

North America & international
toll-free: 1 888 232 4444 (USA & Canada)
phone: 250 383 6864 ♦ fax: 250 383 6804 ♦ email: info@trafford.com

The United Kingdom & Europe
phone: +44 (0)1865 487 395 ♦ local rate: 0845 230 9601
facsimile: +44 (0)1865 481 507 ♦ email: info.uk@trafford.com

10 9 8 7 6 5 4 3 2

Acknowledgments

One of the greatest components in the game of basketball is the ability to play a "team" game. It is a wonderful sight to watch a team play in harmony and share their success together. We often take for granted the contributions and insight others provide to help us succeed. With that, I would like to thank those who have made this book possible. My wife, Candy, was gracious, supportive, and patient, as this project became bigger and more time consuming than originally thought. Next, my mom and dad were instrumental in providing guidance, suggestions, and picture-taking for the book. To my oldest son, Ryan, for taking many of the pictures and adding his insight for making this book fit many different levels of players. To my youngest son, Kyle, for his sense of humor and encouragement throughout this project. To Max and Jean Smith for their editing and proofreading expertise, which allowed this book to flow better and have a more professional look. To all my former coaches for teaching the fundamentals of basketball and pushing me to become a better player.

Dedication

This book is dedicated to anyone who loves the game of basketball.

Disclaimer

As with any exercise or workout program, consult with your doctor or trainer before starting these exercises and drills. The author does not assume liability (or loss) due to the information contained in this book.

Table of Contents

	Page
Introduction	1
The "World" of Basketball	2
How This Book Is Organized	3
Why Should I Work on Ball Handling and Dribbling?	5
Setting Goals	6
Helpful Hints	7
Warm-up and Stretching	11
Outline of Drills	16
Part I — Basic Ball Handling	**29**
A. Wake Up Drills	29
B. Fingertips	32
C. Ball Around Body – Basic	35
D. Ball Rolls	39
Part II — Basic Dribbling	**41**
A. Stationary Dribbling	41
B. Dribbling Around Body – Basic	47
C. Sitting Dribbling	51
D. Lying On Side	55
Part III — Intermediate Ball Handling	**58**
A. Ball Around Body – Intermediate	58
B. Down On One Knee	61
C. Cradle Drills	63
D. Spider Tap	67
E. Scissors – Pass Through Drill	71

		Page
Part IV	**Intermediate Dribbling**	**73**
	A. Dribbling Around Body – Intermediate	73
	B. Down On One Knee	78
	C. Behind Body	81
	D. Spider Dribble	86
	E. Scissors – Dribble Through Drill	90
	F. Moving Dribbling Drills	95
	G. Wall Dribbling	101
Part V	**Advanced Ball Handling**	**104**
	A. Flip Drills	104
	B. Coordination Drills	111
	C. Quickness Drills	117
	D. One Hand Cradles	121
	E. Ricochet	126
	F. Miscellaneous Drills and Tricks	130
Part VI	**Advanced Dribbling**	**136**
	A. Speed Dribbling – Low Dribbling	136
	B. Crab Dribbling	142
	C. Dribble Lying Down On Back	144
	D. Dribble Lying Down On Stomach	148
	E. Leg Dribbling	151
	F. Miscellaneous Advanced Dribbling Drills	154
Part VII	**Two-Ball Workout**	**160**
	A. Two-Ball Dribbling – Stationary	160
	B. Two-Ball Dribbling – Around Body	168
	C. Two-Ball Dribbling – Moving	172
	D. Ball Handling With Two Balls	175
Part VIII	**Spinning**	**179**
	A. One Ball	179
	B. Two Balls	188
Conclusion		**191**
About the Author		**192**

Introduction

What is *Just A Basketball* all about? Hopefully your ultimate goal for reading this book is to improve your ball handling and dribbling abilities and to learn new drills. *Just A Basketball* is a comprehensive step-by-step guide of ball handling and dribbling drills (with detailed descriptions), beginning with basic ball handling and dribbling fundamentals and then progressing towards more complex drills. The drills in this book were derived from the numerous basketball camps and clinics I attended as a player, coach, and instructor, plus spending countless hours in gymnasiums and backyards learning and creating new drills. I have chosen drills for this book that I found to be enjoyable, beneficial, and challenging for any basketball player. This book is intended for players seeking to increase their basketball skills, from beginners all the way up to the college player. Coaches at all levels, parents, physical education teachers, and recreation employees can also benefit from *Just A Basketball* because teaching and encouraging ball handling drills and fundamentals are a crucial part of a player's development. No matter what your playing, coaching, or teaching experience is, I hope you find this book an invaluable resource for learning, developing, and teaching ball handling and dribbling skills.

Some unique features of *Just A Basketball* :

- a progressive, detailed, and fun how-to guide for ball handling and dribbling drills
- can be used for any skill level (the grouping of drills into skill levels provides you the opportunity to select the appropriate starting or continuing point relative to your individual abilities)
- over 450 ball handling and dribbling drills
- almost every drill can be done individually and requires very little space
- an outline of all the drills and tricks described throughout the book is included to provide a good method for you to develop your own workout and take notes
- each drill has a goal associated with it: a certain number of repetitions, a particular distance, or a specific amount of time
- hundreds of pictures to assist with the drill descriptions
- as a plus, the book includes descriptions for fun basketball tricks related to ball handling and dribbling (such as spinning)

Introduction

The "World" of Basketball

Basketball is undoubtedly one of the fastest growing sports for watching and participating, not only in the United States but all over the world. International competition has given the game a big boost in the last fifteen years, particularly in Europe. The United States Olympic "Dream Team" in 1992 made an extraordinary impact on international competition by showing off their superior skills. In addition, international players are included on most college and NBA rosters. The intense marketing of the NBA, WNBA, and the men's and women's NCAA tournament has generated enthusiasm around the globe. Fans like the action and excitement of a basketball game because of the fast pace and the many abilities that are required. Excellent ball handling and dribbling skills make basketball an entertaining sport to watch. College, WNBA and NBA "superstars" have given basketball celebrity status and brought the game to a higher level. Older, popular players get most of the attention, but the "world" of basketball includes players of both sexes, all ages, all sizes, and all countries. The popularity of basketball continues to grow in all categories, particularly at the high school and college levels, for both male and female.

What makes basketball special is that it covers many different demographics and it is inexpensive in comparison to other sports. Numerous pieces of equipment and expensive gear are not necessary to play. Basketball can be played by male or female of all age groups and income levels. Size is irrelevant because short, tall, big, and little players all enjoy the game. Basketball is played year-round because it is both an indoor and outdoor sport. You see basketball hoops everywhere: on playgrounds, in driveways, in backyards, on garages, hooked onto barns, trees and telephone poles, and, of course, in every gymnasium across the United States. **A number of pictures have been inserted throughout this book to illustrate the variety of places where basketball hoops can be found.** Basketball is unique because it can be played individually, against an opponent (one-on-one), in small groups (e.g., three-on-three) and at the team level (five-on-five). Individual skill development can easily

be improved on your own because all one needs are a ball and a small space in which to work. The improvement of individual skills depends on how hard you want to work and how your skills blend in with the other members of your team. Team play is exciting because it requires contributions from every player in the areas of dribbling, passing, shooting, rebounding, team offense, and team defense.

Introduction

How This Book Is Organized

Following this introduction, you will find a short piece called **Setting Goals**. This goal information is valuable because it provides ideas for improving your ball handling workouts by setting realistic and achievable goals. The importance of setting goals cannot be ignored because of the increasing challenges you will face as you progress through the book. Next you will learn some **Helpful Hints** to make the ball handling and dribbling drills and tricks presented in this book easier. There are more than forty hints to assist you with your workouts, and it is strongly recommended that you refer to them frequently. The last segment prior to the actual drills is **Warm-up and Stretching**. These warm-up activities and stretches are an excellent way to prepare your body for the drills and tricks you will be performing, although they can be used for any basketball situation.

What exactly is a "drill"? Webster's Dictionary defines a drill as "the process of training or teaching by the continued repetition of an exercise." The key word in this definition is "repetition" because each drill in this book must be repeated regularly to develop a good routine and improve your skill level. *Just A Basketball* has been structured based on the **Outline of Drills** preceding the eight main parts of the book. This comprehensive outline lists all the drills and tricks described throughout the book. This is not an exhaustive list of every ball handling and dribbling drill and trick ever invented, but it is an extremely thorough listing. These outline pages will also provide a good method for taking notes and developing your own workouts. Listing the drills in this organized manner allows you to view a complete drill listing without having to sort through the entire text, which is beneficial to those players who have already learned the specific drills they are seeking. The following example shows you the three different portions of the outline and the format used in this book. The main chapters of the book are called "Parts" (shown with Roman numerals), and each part is divided into subgroups called "Sections" (shown with capital letters). The sections are then further divided into the individual "Drills" (shown with numbers).

    III. **Advanced Ball Handling**   (Part)
          A. Cradle Drills   (Section)
              1. Front to back   (Drill)
              2. Side to side   (Drill)
              3. Front to back with clap   (Drill)
              4. Side to side with clap   (Drill)

Introduction

The eight main parts are **Basic Ball Handling**, **Basic Dribbling**, **Intermediate Ball Handling**, **Intermediate Dribbling**, **Advanced Ball Handling**, **Advanced Dribbling**, **Two-Ball Workout**, and **Spinning**. Because each of these main parts has numerous sections, there will be many drills for you to learn and complete. There is a short conclusion at the end of each part summarizing what you learned and emphasizing key points before moving on to the next part. As you progress into the book, each part (or level) becomes more challenging. Progression is a key element in *Just A Basketball*. To become a successful player, you must first learn and develop the basic fundamentals before progressing to the advanced drills. Basic ball handling and dribbling fundamentals do not change regardless of your ability level. Use the first two parts, Basic Ball Handling and Basic Dribbling, as building blocks for the rest of *Just A Basketball*.

As previously mentioned, each part is divided into sections. These sections group similar drills to help you develop certain skills. This grouping of drills into skill levels provides readers the opportunity to select the appropriate starting or continuing point relative to their individual abilities. At the beginning of each section is a brief introduction leading you into the drills for that particular section. Every section is then separated into individual drills. Each drill is clearly identified in bold type. Most drills are explained in detail, allowing you to progress through each one step-by-step. Since many of the drills are similar, detailed descriptions are not necessary for each one. Some of the drills have specific names (e.g., "teeter-totter"); others are identified by a description of the drill (e.g., "ball behind back, throw over head, catch in front"). It is important to realize that the words "drill" and "exercise" are interchangeable in this book; there is absolutely no difference between the two words. Also, the majority of the drills start with the right hand or on the right side before switching to the left hand or left side.

Introduction 5

Why Should I Work on Ball Handling and Dribbling?

Many players ask themselves this same question! Almost every player dreams of scoring the winning basket, hearing the fans cheer, seeing the cheerleaders jump and scream, and bringing a smile from mom and dad. Who wouldn't? The importance of handling the ball in game situations without making mistakes is crucial. It is impossible to score points without the ball; you must learn to take care of it. You have probably seen players lose the ball due to lack of quickness, hand speed, strength, and keeping their heads down, unaware of what is happening around them. Most coaches have the impression that ball handling and dribbling drills are only useful if they can be used in game situations; of course, this statement is completely false! The game of basketball requires you to develop certain attributes before being able to perform at a high level in game situations. *Just A Basketball* provides fun and challenging drills to help your quickness, speed, eye-hand coordination, balance, endurance, agility, and strength. This strength would apply to the arms, legs, forearms, wrists, hands, and fingers. Also, the recent increase in "fast break" basketball has changed the pace of the game, which has resulted in a greater need for exceptional ball handling and dribbling skills. The drills and hints in this book will increase your skill level and help boost your confidence. Making yourself a better player will improve the success of your team. After a few weeks of *Just A Basketball*, your coaches and teammates will be astounded by your ball handling progress.

In today's game you have to be able to handle the ball regardless of the position you play. The drills in this book are not only for point guards or smaller players; they are for all players, male, female, short, tall, young, or old. No matter what category you fit in, be positive about your ball handling abilities. Ball handling can make you a better dribbler, passer, shooter, rebounder, and all-around player. *Just A Basketball* was designed for you to reach your potential and have fun in the process. Many of the drills in this book are highly creative; this is intentionally done to keep the exercises interesting and entertaining. Like it or not, creativity is a large part of basketball today. Just as in music and art, in basketball it is always important to learn the basic fundamentals first and then expand on them by developing new, improved, and creative ideas and methods.

Yes, gaining success from the drills in this book requires a lot of dedication and effort. What makes ball handling and dribbling so unique is that a basket is not required; all you need are a basketball and a strong desire to become a better player. With the exception of a few drills, the entire book is made up of individual drills for you to develop your ball handling and dribbling skills. You may wish to work with a partner to assist you with the drills or to help encourage you throughout your workouts. Either individually or with a partner, it is imperative to have a great deal of confidence and motivation to complete the drills successfully. You will certainly feel some frustration along the way, but you will also experience satisfaction as you begin to develop your abilities. Try to learn all the techniques and be enthusiastic in your daily routine. Of course you cannot do all the drills at one time because that would take you several days. Try to work on a few drills or sections at a time so you are not overwhelmed. Keep in mind that there are over 450 drills in this book! These drills can be done anywhere, such as at your home or a neighborhood court; most of them require very little space. Believe in yourself and take pride in your work, because you are capable of doing much more than you can possibly imagine. **You can become a very good basketball player if you can master *Just A Basketball*. Now let's get started!**

Setting Goals

Just A Basketball is not an easy program to master; it is crucial to learn and practice each drill with a purpose or goal in mind. For any endeavor involving setting goals, there are two questions you must always consider. First, what goals do you want to accomplish? Second, how are you going to accomplish them? For example, tell yourself that you can do better by increasing speed, accuracy, or repetitions, and then determine what dedication is necessary to achieve these goals. If you have the determination, motivation, and proper work ethic, you can attain the goals that you have set.

Just A Basketball starts out with the basic fundamentals but gets more difficult as you continue with the program and develop your own routine. Keeping your goals in mind will boost your confidence and give you the determination to master these exercises. Are you willing to work at becoming a better player and achieving your goals? If you can answer this question with an enthusiastic "yes," then you have the proper attitude to jump right into this book. It will help you to push yourself harder and stay motivated by remembering the inspirational phrase, "right now someone else is practicing and someday I will play against him/her." In addition to the goals you set for this book, be a dreamer and set long-range goals to enhance your future in basketball. These long-range goals could include starting on the JV or varsity teams, helping your team win the city or state championship, or even playing at the college level.

Each drill in *Just A Basketball* has a specific goal such as a certain number of repetitions, a particular distance, or a specific amount of time. The goal stated for each exercise is only an example because players have different skill levels; this is why creating some of your own goals is highly recommended. Set goals for yourself that are clear, realistic, competitive, attainable, and easily measured. Create goals that will challenge and push you to become a complete basketball player. Be persistent and make a strong commitment to reach the goals you have established. Do not change your goals just because you were not successful on the first few tries. It is important to record your goals and results for easy and regular reference. After listing your goals, visualize them by imagining what it is like to do the drills perfectly. This visualization will help achieve the targets you have set for yourself.

Keep a chart of your workout program to help you reach your goals and to monitor your progress. Here are some examples of possible goals:
- Be able to learn and complete a certain drill or set of drills
- Be able to increase the repetitions of a drill within a certain time frame
- Be able to do a drill perfectly every time
- Be able to develop your own ball handling and dribbling routine and perform it correctly

Helpful Hints

The drills in *Just A Basketball* are not easy to achieve and it will require many hours of practice and effort to fully understand and master the drills. This list of helpful hints was designed to assist you in developing your workout and increasing your skills. Consider them as "tools for success." Many of these ideas can be used in other sports and activities in which you participate. These hints need to be read often because they are beneficial when used with the hundreds of drills listed in this book.

- Practice and perform the exercises as closely as possible to the way they are outlined and described in the book. This will help you in learning other drills which are related.

- Do not work on all the difficult drills the same day. Try to mix the easy, hard, and fun exercises to give yourself variety. Execute some basic drills to stay fundamentally sound and do some creative ones to make it exciting.

- At first do not be afraid of making mistakes. It will take time to completely understand how to do the drills. Begin practicing slowly and work your way to faster speeds and more repetitions. Aim for improvement every time you pick up a basketball.

- Do not continue the same drill over and over if you are struggling, because this will only make you frustrated. Go to another one and come back to the drill the next day.

- When you first start a drill, concentrate on the fundamentals and the basic movements. Understand what each exercise is trying to accomplish. Properly execute all the steps the first time so you do not have to retrain yourself a few days later.

- The more drills you learn and master in the beginning, the easier the rest of the drills will become. Many drills are similar, and many refer to the first two parts, Basic Ball Handling and Basic Dribbling.

- Work on both your strengths and weaknesses; this is true in all aspects of basketball. In fact, concentrate on your weaknesses to avoid limitations in your game.

- How long should your workout last? That question depends on you! Aim for thirty minutes at first and see how that works. Make these drills fun for yourself, but do not allow them to wear you down or discourage you.

Helpful Hints

- Eventually, develop your own program that you can execute each day. If you have any desire to become an excellent ball handler and complete player, following a set program regularly is a must.

- Quality practice, not quantity, makes a basketball player. Make the most of each workout.

- Yes, these exercises can be frustrating at times, but do not become discouraged. Do not be impatient because it takes a great deal of practice to master these drills.

- Repetition is important. Come back and do drills that you have done in previous days to make these exercises become automatic.

- Practice the proper execution repeatedly. This cannot be overstated. You will be wasting valuable time and effort by performing the drills incorrectly. Bad habits are hard to break.

- Choose someone to evaluate your progress and techniques, such as a coach, parent, or teammate. This assessment will provide a good indication of your ball handling development. Also do not be timid about asking other players or coaches for advice; a few tips and helpful suggestions can make a big improvement in your game.

- As mentioned in Setting Goals, use the suggested goal(s) for each drill to improve your abilities. Also, create some of your own goals to further challenge yourself.

- Concentration will increase your performance; learn to focus on the task at hand. To help you concentrate and remain focused, pretend you are in a game situation and taking care of the basketball is your number one priority.

- Keep the ball under control because losing the ball continuously is a sign for you to slow down. Also do not "fight" the ball; be as relaxed as possible. Being able to keep the ball under control will help you when you start doing the drills at a much quicker pace.

- When you begin, it is all right to look at the ball to understand the techniques and what the exercise is asking you to do. As your ball handling and dribbling skills increase, being able not to look at the ball will show how much you have progressed (see next hint).

- Make an effort to keep your head up as much as possible to help simulate game conditions. Since you will not be looking down at the ball during a game, try to make it a habit to keep your head up. Also, keeping your head up allows you to get a good feel for the ball without being able to see it.

- Use your finger pads and fingertips to give yourself good ball control, especially with the dribbling exercises.

Helpful Hints 9

- Keep the ball from entering the palms of your hands; this aspect is used in every part of the game but particularly with ball handling and dribbling.

- A complete player must be able to make the weak hand as effective as the strong hand. Learn the importance of using both hands equally well. Make the ball do what you want it to do with both the left <u>and</u> right hands.

- Quickness is a skill that can be developed through hard work and practice. These drills will make your hands move very quickly and with exceptional precision.

- Maintain good body balance and proper footwork, a key to effective ball handling and dribbling. This will aid you in learning the drills faster and can make you feel more relaxed.

- For the exercises that involve a timed goal, find a clock that is easily read and also displays seconds. It is helpful if you can clearly determine how much time you have left to complete a drill.

- Find two or three good basketballs to use in your workouts. Basketballs that have an excellent grip make it much easier for you to handle, dribble, and also spin. Balls with a slick surface are extremely difficult to control.

- Pick a spot to work out where you feel comfortable. Garages, driveways, backyards, basements, gymnasiums, and playgrounds are wonderful locations for your ball handling workout. Most importantly, find a place and a time that is right for you.

- Make sure you have plenty of room to complete the drills, especially room above you since the ball will be thrown and tossed around in some of the exercises.

- Drink a lot of water to maintain your fluid level to prevent dehydration. Consume even more water during and after intense workouts and on very hot days.

- Do not take for granted the need for conditioning, proper rest, and good eating habits. This will help you to be focused and give you the energy needed to complete your ball handling workouts. In basketball, keeping your body in top condition will allow you to compete at a higher level because you will be able to outlast your opponent both physically and mentally.

- Take a day off if you need to. If you happen to miss a workout, just start where you left off and begin there.

- Do not give up because your muscles are sore. Of course you will be sore at first; you are using different muscles than you normally do. This soreness should last only a few days and will go away as your body gets used to a set routine. Performing the warm-up activities and stretching exercises discussed in the next section will help to prevent muscle soreness.

Helpful Hints

- Watch basketball games to study and learn other players' ball handling and dribbling moves. This is a great idea if you are sick or injured. You can learn a lot by observing different techniques and how players move with and without the ball.

- Play your favorite music as you are doing your ball handling workout. This can be a great motivational tool for some players.

- To make the drills more enjoyable, try doing your workout with a partner. Working with a partner can help motivate you, and he/she can also show you new ways to make the drills successful.

- If possible, take video to analyze your strengths and weaknesses. Using the "slow" button on the DVD/VCR allows you to break down your movements. Taking video at different times will give you an idea of how you are progressing.

- Because basketball is played year-round, use the spring and summer as key training times to improve your skills, stamina, and strength. Individual skill development is rarely stressed during the winter season so you must prepare yourself in the off season.

- Be enthusiastic while performing the drills. Make your workouts as enjoyable and exciting as you can.

- You can overcome obstacles by being dedicated, disciplined, and determined. Your attitude, commitment, and work ethic are very important to your ball handling success. Approach each workout with a positive attitude. *Just A Basketball* provides you with the necessary information to become a great ball handler and dribbler; <u>you</u> have to make it happen.

- While other players are saying "can't," be the one who says "can."

- Practice with a purpose and be confident in your ball handling and dribbling skills. Create a positive self-image by inspiring yourself to be an outstanding basketball player.

- **Most important: have fun!**

Warm-up and Stretching

An excellent warm-up and stretching routine is an outstanding way to make your body feel good and relaxed before you start your *Just A Basketball* workout. For optimal performance, flexibility, and reduced soreness, it is also a good idea to repeat these warm-up activities and stretches after your workout.

Warm-up exercises are vital before and after your ball handling workout. A good warm-up prepares your body for a more strenuous workout, much like warming-up an engine in a car or truck before taking off at full speed.

Warm-ups are important for three reasons:
1) they increase flexibility by loosening joints
2) they increase body temperature and heart rate to provide more energy to avoid tiring quickly
3) they prevent injury

Jumping jacks, jumping rope, and push-ups are three warm-up activities that have been suggested. If you are in a gym or outside on a court, some jogging around the court (forward and backward) and some "high knee" running are also recommended. As a good way to prepare for your ball handling workout, try dribbling during your jogging time. A warm-up should last approximately five minutes.

Jumping Jacks – This warm-up is a great way to get the cardiovascular system going and to loosen stiff muscles. Jumping jacks will also get your arms and legs loose to start doing some ball handling and dribbling. Do at least twenty jumping jacks to loosen up, but do not allow yourself to become tired.

Jumping Rope – This exercise is an excellent conditioning warm-up for jump shooters and rebounders, especially for the fourth quarter of a game when you need that extra energy. Ball handlers can benefit from jumping rope because it increases their quickness, endurance, and jumping height, plus helping to develop their balance and coordination. In addition, jumping rope strengthens the knees, calves, thighs, forearms, wrists, and hands.

First, find a rope that is suitable for you. To determine this, the rope should barely touch the floor when it comes underneath your feet. If the rope is hitting the ground really hard instead of just ticking the floor, a shorter rope is needed. While you are turning the rope, keep your elbows close to the body. Turn the rope with your hands and wrists, but do not move your arms around in a circular fashion. Keep your feet close together when jumping, and only bend the knees slightly so you will feel comfortable. Only let your toes touch the floor when jumping by keeping the heels lifted. Using the balls of your feet will strengthen the calves and legs, plus increasing your jumping speed. When jumping, look straight ahead and keep your head level.

After a few days you will be amazed how quickly and how long you can jump. Learn to do jumps on each foot to further develop your balance and coordination. When you become really advanced, teach yourself "double" jumps (<u>two</u> turns of the rope on each single jump) and also try turning the rope backwards instead of forwards. Your overall goal is to develop a smooth jumping rhythm and to jump without any errors for at least two minutes.

<u>**Push-Ups**</u> – To get the upper body ready before starting, do a few push-ups (ten to twenty) to strengthen your arms and chest. A key point is to keep your body parallel to the floor. This means keeping your head, back, butt, and legs in a straight line throughout this warm-up. As

you come down during each push-up, do not let your body touch the floor. If you cannot complete at least ten, try starting the push-ups on your knees and then eventually switch to the regular way. In addition, attempt some "on the ball" push-ups to build up the strength in your hands, wrists, and arms. Simply place both hands on top of the basketball and complete ten push-ups using this "on the ball" method.

After your warm-up, a stretching routine of at least five minutes is necessary before beginning the ball handling drills. Do not overlook this part of your workout because stretching will improve your performance. Stretching promotes a full range of motion and increases flexibility, which is very important in the *Just A Basketball* drills. Stretching also reduces the risk of injury, soreness, and stiffness and should not be an uncomfortable activity. Do not force stretches for extra flexibility if they are causing you pain. The following stretches are recommended, although you may have some of your own that you would like to use. Read the descriptions carefully and follow them as written.

<u>**Neck Stretch**</u> – While standing, stretch your neck by slowly placing your chin on your chest and holding for ten seconds. Next, place your chin on the right shoulder for ten seconds and then put the chin on the left shoulder for ten more seconds. All three of these positions should give your neck a good stretch. In addition, try dropping your right ear slowly towards your right shoulder (move your head as far as you can comfortably go). Hold this position for ten seconds and then repeat the same movement on the left side by dropping the left ear.

Warm-up and Stretching 13

Side Bends – Stand with your feet a little more than shoulder width apart and make sure your back is straight. Put your right arm straight up in the air (next to the right ear) and then slowly lean your upper body to the left stretching out your right side. As you are leaning, place the left arm along your left side and stretch it down by your knee. Hold this stretch for ten seconds. Next, raise the left arm and lean your upper body towards the right to stretch out the left side (for ten seconds). Do not forget to extend the right arm down along your right side near the knee area.

Arm/Shoulder Loops – While still standing, bring your arms up and straight out to your sides. Next, slowly make short loops (circles) with both arms, going in a forward direction at first and then switching to backward loops. Try shrugging your shoulders at the same time to loosen them. Complete ten arm/shoulder loops in each direction.

Tricep Stretch – This stretch will work the muscle on the back of the upper arm called the tricep. While keeping the neck and back straight, extend the right arm behind your head and reach down the middle of your back as far as you can reach. Now put a small amount of pressure on the right elbow by pushing down on it with the left hand. You should feel a good stretch in your right tricep and also the right shoulder. Hold the stretch for ten seconds. Repeat the same steps on the other side by reaching down your back with the left hand and then applying pressure on the left elbow with your right hand.

Chest/Abdominal Stretch – Stand with your knees slightly bent and your feet shoulder width apart. Place your hands on the lower back (just above the hips) and slowly push your elbows toward one another behind your back. This elbow movement will help stretch your chest, abdomen, and also the arms. Hold this stretch for at least ten seconds. It is necessary to keep your shoulders back to maximize this stretch.

Quadricep Stretch – The quadricep is the large muscle at the front of the thigh. It is an important muscle to stretch because many movements in your workout will involve the quadricep. While standing, reach back and grab your right ankle with your right hand. Pull the right foot near your buttocks so the right knee is pointing down and not out to the side. For support and better balance, use a wall or hold a chair with your left hand. Hold this stretch for fifteen seconds to loosen your right quadricep. Repeat the steps on the other side by grabbing the left ankle with the left hand.

14 Warm-up and Stretching

Leg Stretch – To begin, stand with your knees very slightly bent and your feet together. Now bend at the hips and reach down with your hands toward the floor until you feel a stretch in the back of your legs. Depending on your flexibility, some of you may have no problem stretching to the floor. You will feel the entire back of your legs being stretched. Make sure your knees stay slightly bent to avoid placing stress on your lower back. Once you are in a position where the legs feel good, hold the stretch for fifteen seconds. <u>Do not</u> bounce during this stretch.

Knee Bends (Squats) – This stretch is a good way to loosen up the knee area and also to strengthen your legs. Begin with your feet shoulder width apart and your arms extended straight out in front of you for balance. With your back straight and the knees slightly bent, slowly crouch down until you feel like you are almost sitting in a chair. As you bend down, do not let your knees extend past your toes. Once you come to a complete stop, slowly return to your starting position. <u>Do not</u> squat really low to the ground; use the chair method or your knees will become sore. Keep your arms extended throughout this stretch and look straight ahead the entire time. Five knee bends should be sufficient at first, but increase that number to ten as your legs and knees develop more strength.

Ankle Rolls – Lift your right foot off the floor and rotate it slowly in a clockwise fashion five times to loosen the ankle. Once you have done that, rotate it five more times in a counterclockwise direction. Next, switch to the left foot and repeat the same steps, rotating the foot five times in each direction to loosen the left ankle. If you need to, use a chair or a wall for support to maintain balance.

Toe Raises – Toe raises are a good way to strengthen and stretch your ankles, feet, and especially the calves. First, start with your feet shoulder width apart and then slowly raise up on your toes by lifting your heels off the floor as high as you can. Now put your heels almost back to the floor and then slowly raise yourself on your toes again. Ten toe raises is adequate to begin with, but at least twenty raises should be your goal after a few days. As your calves become stronger, hold on to something in front of you and complete the toe raises with only one foot at a time (ten raises on each foot). This exercise is a good warm-up for the next one.

Calf Stretch – Begin by positioning your hands at chest level against a wall or an immovable object such as a pole. Now bend the left leg in front of you and put the right leg behind you (away from the wall). Keep the right leg straight (toes pointed straight ahead) and make sure the right heel stays on the floor. Next, lean forward at the hips so you feel the calf in the right

Warm-up and Stretching 15

leg stretching. Stretch this right calf for fifteen seconds; then reverse your stance so the left leg is behind you (straight) and the right leg is in the front (bent). Repeat the same steps as just described to stretch the left calf.

Back Stretch – Here is a good stretch for both your upper and lower back, plus hips. Begin seated on the floor and extend your right leg. Now cross the left foot over the right leg so it rests to the outside of the right knee. The right elbow should be positioned on the outside of

the left knee. Next, place your left hand behind you on the floor for balance. Last, twist your upper body (trunk) to the left to begin feeling the stretch in your back. Once you feel a good stretch, hold it for fifteen seconds. Repeat the same procedures on the other side by crossing the right foot over the left leg, positioning the left elbow to the outside of the right knee, placing the right hand behind you, and twisting your upper body to the right.

Butterfly (Groin) Stretch – This is probably the most common way to stretch the groin area and the inner thighs. First, sit on the floor with your back straight and put the bottoms of your feet together so the knees are out to the sides. Next, hold your feet with the hands and rest your elbows on the knees for balance. Now place your feet close to your body and lean slightly forward at the hips. You should feel the groin muscles stretching and also the upper portion of your buttocks. Hold this stretch for fifteen seconds. <u>Do not</u> bounce during the stretch and make sure to keep your back straight and your head up the entire time.

Hamstring Stretch – While still sitting on the floor, extend your right leg out and put the left leg in close to your body. Do this by placing the bottom of the left foot against the inner thigh of your right leg. Now bend forward from the hips and reach out towards your right foot with

both hands (without bouncing). Reach forward as far as you can to really stretch the right hamstring (if possible, grab your foot). Hold the stretch for fifteen seconds while keeping your head up and your back straight. Make sure the right foot remains upright and it stays in a straight line with the hip and the knee. Repeat the same procedures as just described on the other side to stretch the left hamstring. Simply extend the left leg out, put the right leg in close to your body, and reach towards your left foot with both hands.

    As mentioned in the first paragraph, repeating these warm-up activities and stretches after your workout is extremely beneficial. This "cool down" period at the end will help your body gradually recover from a vigorous workout. Do not just stop and sit down! A good cool down should last around five minutes with some jumping jacks or jump ropes, followed by some light jogging and stretching. Of great importance, a cool down will decrease soreness, lower the heart rate, return the blood flow to a normal state, and prevent your muscles from tightening.

Outline of Drills

I. BASIC BALL HANDLING
  A. Wake Up Drills
  1. Side to side slap
  2. Rainbow – arch motion
  3. Banana – hard
  4. Banana – fast
  5. Banana – behind legs
  6. Vice – chest level
  7. Vice – above the head
  8. Ball smack – throw above head, pop at face level

  B. Fingertips
  1. Popcorn – chest level
  2. Popcorn – above the head
  3. Basic tip drill – fast fingers
  4. Above the head to feet and back up
  5. Arms extended – above the head
  6. Arms extended – below the waist
  7. Arms extended – above the head to waist and back up
  8. Behind head
  9. Behind back
  10. Behind legs
  11. Arms extended (lying down) – above the head to waist and back up

  C. Ball Around Body – Basic
  1. Head (reverse)
  2. Waist (reverse)
  3. Chest (reverse)
  4. Knees (reverse)
  5. Ankles (reverse)
  6. Snowman – head, waist, and knees (reverse)
  7. Right leg (reverse)
  8. Left leg (reverse)
  9. Pyramid – right leg, waist, left leg, waist (reverse)
  10. Quick feet back – both legs, right leg back, both legs, left leg back (reverse)
  11. Quick feet up – both legs, right leg up, both legs, left leg up (reverse)
  12. Both legs spread apart (reverse)
  13. Both legs spread far apart (reverse)
  14. Figure 8 (reverse)

Outline of Drills

D. **Ball Rolls**
1. Right leg (reverse)
2. Left leg (reverse)
3. Both legs together (reverse)
4. Both legs spread apart (reverse)
5. Figure 8 (reverse)
6. Down on left knee – around right leg (reverse)
7. Down on right knee – around left leg (reverse)
8. Sitting Indian style around body (reverse)

II. BASIC DRIBBLING
A. **Stationary Dribbling**
1. Both hands in front – side to side
2. Right hand in front – side to side
3. Left hand in front – side to side
4. High front dribbling – side to side with both hands
5. High front dribbling – side to side with right hand
6. High front dribbling – side to side with left hand
7. High to low, low to high with both hands
8. High to low, low to high with right hand
9. High to low, low to high with left hand
10. Along right side with right hand
11. Along left side with left hand
12. Between legs high – right foot in front
13. Between legs high – left foot in front
14. Between legs low – right foot in front
15. Between legs low – left foot in front
16. Crossover dribble – right to left
17. Crossover dribble – left to right
18. Crossover dribble – continuous

B. **Dribbling Around Body – Basic**
1. Right leg (reverse)
2. Left leg (reverse)
3. Right leg with right hand (reverse)
4. Right leg with left hand (reverse)
5. Left leg with left hand (reverse)
6. Left leg with right hand (reverse)
7. Both legs together (reverse)
8. Both legs together with right hand (reverse)
9. Both legs together with left hand (reverse)
10. Both legs spread apart (reverse)
11. Both legs spread far apart (reverse)
12. Figure 8 (reverse)

C. Sitting Dribbling
1. Alternating dribble with both hands – on top of ball
2. Alternating dribble with both hands – side to side
3. Dribble with right hand – side to side
4. Dribble with left hand – side to side
5. Side to side over right leg with right hand
6. Side to side over right leg with left hand
7. Side to side over left leg with left hand
8. Side to side over left leg with right hand
9. Side to side over legs with both hands – 4 dribbles
10. Side to side over legs with right hand – 4 dribbles
11. Side to side over legs with left hand – 4 dribbles
12. Alternating dribble with hands under legs
13. Alternating dribble under lifted legs – on top of ball
14. Alternating dribble under lifted legs – side to side
15. Dribble under lifted – back and forth with continuous low dribbles

D. Lying On Side
1. On left side with right hand – front
2. On right side with left hand – front
3. On left side with right hand – behind
4. On right side with left hand – behind
5. On left side with right hand, between legs
6. On right side with left hand, between legs
7. Continuous – on left side, front and behind with right hand
8. Continuous – on right side, front and behind with left hand

III. INTERMEDIATE BALL HANDLING
A. Ball Around Body – Intermediate
1. Figure 8 two-step – right leg planted (reverse)
2. Figure 8 two-step – left leg planted (reverse)
3. Standing on right leg – around left leg (reverse)
4. Standing on left leg – around right leg (reverse)
5. Standing – around alternating legs (reverse)
6. Standing – figure 8 (reverse)
7. Sitting Indian style around body (reverse)
8. Sitting – around lifted legs (reverse)
9. Sitting – figure 8 around lifted legs (reverse)

B. Down On One Knee
1. Down on left knee – around right leg (reverse)
2. Down on right knee – around left leg (reverse)
3. Down on left knee – around right leg with right hand – flip
4. Down on left knee – around right leg with left hand – flip
5. Down on right knee – around left leg with right hand – flip
6. Down on right knee – around left leg with left hand – flip
7. Down on left knee – figure 8 (reverse)
8. Down on right knee – figure 8 (reverse)

Outline of Drills 19

  C. **Cradle Drills**
  1. Front to back
  2. Side to side
  3. Front to back with clap
  4. Side to side with clap
  5. Side to side – alternating feet back and forth
  6. Down on right knee – front to back
  7. Down on left knee – front to back
  8. Down on right knee – side to side
  9. Down on left knee – side to side
  10. Sitting – front to back
  11. Sitting – side to side

  D. **Spider Tap**
  1. ½ spider tap – right side
  2. ½ spider tap – left side
  3. Full spider tap
  4. Full spider tap – walking
  5. Down on right knee – ½ spider tap – left side
  6. Down on left knee – ½ spider tap – right side
  7. Down on right knee – ½ spider tap – right side
  8. Down on left knee – ½ spider tap – left side
  9. Down on right knee – full spider tap
  10. Down on left knee – full spider tap
  11. Sitting – ½ spider tap – right side
  12. Sitting – ½ spider tap – left side
  13. Sitting – full spider tap

  E. **Scissors – Pass Through Drill**
  1. Shuffling feet – in place (reverse)
  2. Walking (reverse)
  3. Walking backwards (reverse)
  4. Running (reverse)
  5. Running backwards (reverse)

IV. **INTERMEDIATE DRIBBLING**
  A. **Dribbling Around Body – Intermediate**
  1. Figure 8 with right hand (reverse)
  2. Figure 8 with left hand (reverse)
  3. Figure 8 while walking (reverse)
  4. Right leg standing with right hand – whip dribbles (reverse)
  5. Left leg standing with left hand – whip dribbles (reverse)
  6. Figure 8 standing – whip dribbles (reverse)
  7. Down on both knees – around body with both hands (reverse)
  8. Down on both knees – around body with right hand (reverse)
  9. Down on both knees – around body with left hand (reverse)
  10. Sitting Indian style – around body with both hands (reverse)
  11. Sitting Indian style – around body with right hand (reverse)
  12. Sitting Indian style – around body with left hand (reverse)

Outline of Drills

    13. Sitting – around lifted legs with both hands (reverse)
    14. Sitting – around right leg with both hands (reverse)
    15. Sitting – around left leg with both hands (reverse)
    16. Sitting – figure 8 (reverse)

B. Down On One Knee
    1. Down on left knee – around right leg with both hands (reverse)
    2. Down on left knee – around right leg with right hand (reverse)
    3. Down on right knee – around left leg with both hands (reverse)
    4. Down on right knee – around left leg with left hand (reverse)
    5. Down on left knee – beneath right leg – alternate dribbles
    6. Down on right knee – beneath left leg – alternate dribbles
    7. Down on left knee – figure 8 with right leg out (reverse)
    8. Down on right knee – figure 8 with left leg out (reverse)

C. Behind Body
    1. Behind back standing – side to side with legs together
    2. Behind back standing – side to side with legs spread apart
    3. Behind back with knees bent – side to side with legs together
    4. Behind back with knees bent – side to side with legs spread apart
    5. Behind legs – back and forth with continuous low dribbles
    6. Behind ankles – side to side
    7. Standing on right leg – behind right leg – side to side
    8. Standing on left leg – behind left leg – side to side
    9. Behind the back dribble – stationary
    10. Behind the back dribble – walking
    11. Behind the back dribble – walking backwards
    12. Down on right knee – side to side over right leg with right hand
    13. Down on left knee – side to side over left leg with left hand
    14. Down on right knee – behind the back dribble
    15. Down on left knee – behind the back dribble
    16. Behind back sitting Indian style – side to side
    17. Sitting Indian style – behind the back dribble

D. Spider Dribble
    1. ½ spider dribble – right side
    2. ½ spider dribble – left side
    3. Full spider dribble
    4. Full spider dribble - walking
    5. Down on right knee – ½ spider dribble – left side
    6. Down on left knee – ½ spider dribble – right side
    7. Down on right knee – ½ spider dribble – right side
    8. Down on left knee – ½ spider dribble – left side
    9. Down on right knee – full spider dribble
    10. Down on left knee – full spider dribble
    11. Sitting – ½ spider dribble – right side
    12. Sitting – ½ spider dribble – left side
    13. Sitting – full spider dribble

Outline of Drills

E. **Scissors – Dribble Through Drill**
 1. Between legs with right hand – right foot in front
 2. Between legs with left hand – left foot in front
 3. Between legs with right hand – left foot in front
 4. Between legs with left hand – right foot in front
 5. Shuffling feet – in place with both hands (reverse)
 6. Walking with both hands (reverse)
 7. Walking backwards with both hands (reverse)
 8. Walking with right hand (reverse)
 9. Walking with left hand (reverse)
 10. Walking with both hands – low dribbles (reverse)
 11. Walking backwards with both hands – low dribbles (reverse)

F. **Moving Dribbling Drills**
 1. Control dribble
 2. Speed dribble
 3. Hesitation dribble
 4. Retreat (backward) dribble
 5. Crossover dribble
 6. Half-cross dribble
 7. Double-cross dribble
 8. Spin dribble
 9. Between the legs dribble
 10. Behind the back dribble

G. **Wall Dribbling**
 1. Right hand
 2. Left hand
 3. Alternating with both hands
 4. Backwards with right hand
 5. Backwards with left hand
 6. Backwards alternating with both hands
 7. Backwards with right hand down at side
 8. Backwards with left hand down at side
 9. Backwards alternating with both hands down
 10. Right hand walking (reverse directions)
 11. Left hand walking (reverse directions)
 12. Alternating with both hands walking (reverse directions)

V. ADVANCED BALL HANDLING
A. **Flip Drills**
 1. Flip-flop with right hand
 2. Flip-flop with left hand
 3. Flip-flop with right hand and clap
 4. Flip-flop with left hand and clap
 5. Flop-flop with both hands back and forth
 6. Hand roll – right hand to left hand
 7. Hand roll – left hand to right hand
 8. Hand roll – continuous

Outline of Drills

    9. Flip ball behind back over opposite shoulder – each side
   10. Flip ball behind back over opposite shoulder – continuous
   11. Flip ball behind back over same shoulder – each side
   12. Flip ball behind back over same shoulder – continuous
   13. Ball in right hand, under left arm, flip behind head over right shoulder
   14. Ball in left hand, under right arm, flip behind head over left shoulder
   15. Ball in right hand, through legs, flip over left shoulder
   16. Ball in left hand, through legs, flip over right shoulder
   17. Ball through legs, flip over shoulder – continuous
   18. Ball behind back, switch hands – continuous
   19. Flip ball back and forth behind head
   20. Flip ball off chest from side to side – continuous

B. Coordination Drills
    1. Throw ball over head, catch behind back
    2. Ball behind back, throw over head, catch in front
    3. Throw ball over head, catch, then back to front – continuous
    4. Throw ball over head, catch behind back with right hand
    5. Throw ball over head, catch behind back with left hand
    6. Throw ball over head, catch between legs in back with both hands
    7. Throw ball over head, catch between legs in back with right hand
    8. Throw ball over head, catch between legs in back with left hand
    9. Throw ball above head, catch between legs in front with right hand
   10. Throw ball above head, catch between legs in front with left hand
   11. Throw ball up, bounce in front, catch behind back
   12. Throw ball up, bounce behind back, catch in front
   13. Throw ball up, bounce behind back, catch behind back
   14. Sitting Indian style – throw ball over head, catch behind back
   15. Sitting Indian style – ball behind back, throw over head, catch in front
   16. Sitting Indian style – throw ball over head, catch, then back to front – continuous
   17. Sitting – crab throw over head, catch, then back over – continuous
   18. Ball around waist lying down – arched back (reverse)
   19. Teeter-totter - continuous

C. Quickness Drills
    1. Ball behind knees, front clap, catch behind feet
    2. Ball at waist, drop, slap pockets (front or back), catch
    3. Ball behind head, front clap, catch behind back
    4. Ball behind head, two front claps, catch behind back
    5. Ball in front (face level), back clap, catch in front (waist level)
    6. Ball behind head, drop down back, catch behind legs
    7. Hamster wheel with both hands (reverse)
    8. Hamster wheel with right hand (reverse)
    9. Hamster wheel with left hand (reverse)

Outline of Drills 23

D. **One Hand Cradles**
1. Right hand and right leg
2. Left hand and left leg
3. Right hand and left leg
4. Left hand and right leg
5. Right hand and left side of body
6. Left hand and right side of body
7. Down on left knee – right hand and right leg
8. Down on right knee – left hand and left leg
9. Down on right knee – right hand and left leg
10. Down on left knee – left hand and right leg
11. Sitting – right hand and right leg
12. Sitting – left hand and left leg
13. Sitting – right hand and left leg
14. Sitting – left hand and right leg

E. **Ricochet**
1. Front to back
2. Back to front
3. Continuous – back and forth
4. Continuous with knees bent – back and forth
5. Continuous – back and forth with right hand only
6. Continuous – back and forth with left hand only
7. Cannon – front to back – fast and hard
8. Behind head to front
9. Front to behind head
10. Front to back, throw over head, catch in front – continuous
11. Back to front, throw over head, catch behind back – continuous
12. Front to back – trap between legs
13. Back to front – trap between legs

F. **Miscellaneous Drills And Tricks**
1. Tip drill with each set of fingers
2. Roll along arms – behind neck
3. Ball circles (around the arms)
4. Roll ball down body and kick back up – both sides
5. Bounce ball, kick over head, catch behind back
6. Feet together, drop ball, catch on top of feet
7. Ball between feet, lift up to waist in front
8. Ball between feet, lift up to waist in back
9. Bounce ball, bend over, rest ball on neck
10. Hourglass pass (reverse)
11. Figure 8 with drop (reverse)
12. Figure 8 with partner or off wall (reverse)
13. Behind the back pass with partner or off wall (reverse)

Outline of Drills

VI. ADVANCED DRIBBLING
  A. **Speed Dribbling – Low Dribbling**
   1. Right hand
   2. Left hand
   3. Alternating dribble with both hands – on top of ball
   4. Alternating dribble with both hands – side to side
   5. Right hand – each finger
   6. Left hand – each finger
   7. Alternating dribble with each set of fingers
   8. Right fist
   9. Left fist
   10. Alternating dribble with both fists – on top of ball
   11. Alternating dribble with both fists – side to side
   12. Alternating dribble with right fist and left hand
   13. Alternating dribble with left fist and right hand
   14. Alternating dribble with palms
   15. Alternating dribble with sides of hands – chops
   16. Alternating dribble with back of hands
   17. Alternating dribble with both elbows
   18. Down on right knee – alternating dribble under left leg
   19. Down on left knee – alternating dribble under right leg
   20. Alternating dribble behind heels
   21. Alternating dribble between legs (reverse)
   22. Alternating dribble under lifted legs

  B. **Crab Dribbling**
   1. Right hand
   2. Left hand
   3. Alternating dribble with both hands
   4. Right hand walking
   5. Left hand walking
   6. Both hands walking

  C. **Dribble Lying Down On Back**
   1. Right hand on right side
   2. Left hand on left side
   3. Right hand on right side – each finger
   4. Left hand on left side – each finger
   5. Right hand on left side
   6. Left hand on right side
   7. Arm extended behind head with right hand
   8. Arm extended behind head with left hand
   9. Arms extended behind head with both hands
   10. Semi-circle dribble – right side, around head, left side (reverse)
   11. Underneath butt – alternating dribble
   12. Underneath butt – side to side
   13. Circle dribble – right side, around head, left side, underneath (reverse)
   14. Between legs with right hand
   15. Between legs with left hand

Outline of Drills

16. Between legs with both hands – alternating dribble
17. Sit-ups – each side

D. Dribble Lying Down On Stomach
1. Right hand on right side
2. Left hand on left side
3. Right hand on right side – each finger
4. Left hand on left side – each finger
5. Arm extended above head with right hand
6. Arm extended above head with left hand
7. Arms extended above head with both hands
8. Semi-circle dribble – right side, around head, left side (reverse)
9. Between legs with right hand
10. Between legs with left hand

E. Leg Dribbling
1. Right foot – continuous
2. Left foot – continuous
3. Off bottom of right foot
4. Off bottom of left foot
5. Off right knee with right hand
6. Off right knee with left hand
7. Off left knee with left hand
8. Off left knee with right hand
9. Both knees continuous with one dribble

F. Miscellaneous Advanced Dribbling Drills
1. Dribble off ground with right hand
2. Dribble off ground with left hand
3. Dribble off ground with right fist
4. Dribble off ground with left fist
5. Crossover slap with right hand
6. Crossover slap with left hand
7. Crossover slap – continuous
8. Dribble off butt
9. Dribble behind head over left shoulder with right hand
10. Dribble behind head over right shoulder with left hand
11. Wraparound dribble – right hand and left side
12. Wraparound dribble – left hand and right side
13. Box dribble – 4 dribbles outside of legs (reverse)
14. Box dribble – continuous low (reverse)
15. Hourglass dribble – 4 dribbles inside of legs (reverse)
16. Hourglass dribble – continuous low (reverse)
17. Butterfly dribble – 4 dribbles (reverse)
18. Combination dribble (reverse)

Outline of Drills

VII. TWO-BALL WORKOUT
A. Two-Ball Dribbling – Stationary
1. Dribble – same time/same height
2. Dribble – alternating bounces
3. Dribble right hand high, left hand low
4. Dribble left hand high, right hand low
5. Dribble off ground – both balls at same time
6. Dribble with arms crossed
7. Dribble with crossing arms every other dribble
8. Each finger – both hands at same time
9. Side to side dribbles in front – same direction
10. Side to side dribbles in front – opposite directions
11. Along each side with each hand – same direction
12. Along each side with each hand – opposite directions
13. Whip dribbles – alternating bounces
14. Whip dribbles – both balls at same time
15. Over/under dribble – standing
16. Over/under dribble – sitting
17. Roundabout dribble – standing (reverse)
18. Roundabout dribble – sitting (reverse)
19. Cone dribble – standing (reverse)
20. Cone dribble – sitting (reverse)
21. Sit-ups with one ball dribbling on each side

B. Two-Ball Dribbling – Around Body
1. Right leg (reverse)
2. Left leg (reverse)
3. Dribble one ball out in front, other around right leg (reverse)
4. Dribble one ball out in front, other around left leg (reverse)
5. Figure 8 (reverse)
6. Both legs together (reverse)
7. Both legs spread apart (reverse)
8. Two-ball dribbles – one in front, one behind the back (reverse)
9. Two-ball dribbles – one in front, one between the legs (reverse)
10. Down on left knee – around right leg (reverse)
11. Down on right knee – around left leg (reverse)
12. Down on both knees around body (reverse)
13. Sitting Indian style around body (reverse)

C. Two-Ball Dribbling – Moving
1. Dribble – same time/same height
2. Dribble – alternating bounces
3. Figure 8 – walking (reverse)
4. Two-ball dribbles – one in front, one behind the back (reverse)
5. Two-ball dribbles – one in front, one between the legs (reverse)
6. Over/under dribble – walking
7. Roundabout dribble – walking (reverse)
8. Cone dribble – walking (reverse)
9. Dribble ball off stationary ball placed on floor

Outline of Drills

D. **Ball Handling With Two Balls**
1. Balance balls on top of each other with both hands
2. Balance balls on top of each other with right hand
3. Balance balls on top of each other with left hand
4. Hold one ball with both hands, bounce other one on top
5. Leapfrog – up and under
6. Two-ball quick switch
7. Toss both balls high in the air, catch in same hand at same time
8. Throw balls over head, catch in same hand behind back
9. Lying down – toss both balls up, catch in same hand at same time
10. Two-ball behind the back passes with partner or off wall (reverse)

VIII. SPINNING
A. **One Ball**
1. Each finger on both hands
2. Each finger on each hand – continuous
3. Alternate hands with each set of fingers
4. Each knuckle on both hands
5. Flip spinning ball from one hand to the other hand – each finger
6. Flip spinning ball high up in the air
7. Hit off back of hand
8. Hit off fist(s)
9. Hit off elbow
10. Hit off head
11. Hit off knee(s)
12. Kick off foot
13. Spin after bouncing ball on floor
14. Spin ball on floor, pick up spinning
15. Throw spinning ball over head, catch behind back with both hands
16. Throw spinning ball over head, catch behind back with same hand
17. Spin between legs – switch hands (reverse)
18. Spin behind back – switch hands (reverse)
19. Spin between legs, flip ball up, catch spinning in front

B. **Two Balls**
1. Spin one ball in right hand – dribble other ball with left hand
2. Spin one ball in left hand – dribble other ball with right hand
3. Spin one ball in each hand at same time
4. Throw spinning balls over head, catch in same hand behind back
5. Spin one ball on top of a stationary ball

I. Basic Ball Handling

A. Wake Up Drills

After you have done your warm-up and stretching, loosening up your hands, fingers, wrists, arms, and shoulders can make the rest of the ball handling drills a little smoother. These few drills are a great way to get you started in Basic Ball Handling or for any basketball workout. Each exercise will have an associated goal for you to complete, such as a number of repetitions or performing the drill for a specific amount of time.

1. **side to side slap** – To begin, place the ball in your right hand and then slap the ball hard with the left hand at chest level. Next, put the ball in your left hand and then slap the ball again, this time with the right hand. Continue to move and slap the ball from side to side, quickly alternating hands with each slap. Twenty slaps (ten with each hand) should be a good start to strengthen and "wake up" your hands, fingers, and wrists.

2. **rainbow – arch motion** -- The previous drill was completed at chest level, but this slap will be done over your head. This drill is termed "rainbow" because the ball is moved quickly from one side to the other in an arched fashion like a rainbow. Begin with the ball in your right hand and extend your arm straight out to the right side. The left arm will be lifted straight up in the air. Next, quickly bring the ball over your head and smack (slap) the ball with your left hand (both arms extended directly over your head). Transfer the ball to your left hand and continue the left arm down to your side until it touches the left leg (keep the right arm extended over your head). Once the ball touches the leg, quickly take it back up over your head, smack it with the right hand, and then continue the ball down to your right side to finish one complete cycle. Start with five complete cycles and eventually work up to ten. To maintain the arch motion, it is important to keep both arms extended throughout the drill. This exercise moves quite fast and it will help to loosen up your arms and shoulders.

I. Basic Ball Handling

3. banana – hard -- The arm and ball movements in the next two drills are executed just the opposite of the rainbow. Start with the ball in your right hand and your arm extended straight out to the side. In the last drill you went over your head with the ball, but now you will go the other way. To begin, quickly bring the ball down low (just below the waist) and smack the ball hard with your left hand (both arms remain extended). With the ball now in the left hand, continue on until the left arm is high above your left shoulder. Next, swing the ball back the opposite way and smack it hard again with your right hand (just below the waist) and continue on until the right arm is high above your right shoulder.

To help you better understand this drill, you will be moving the ball almost in a "U" shape, just like a banana. This is different from the rainbow drill where the ball traveled like an inverted "U". Concentrate on smacking the ball hard each time to get those hands and fingers awake and loosened up. It is important to keep your arms straight throughout the exercise to maintain the "U" shape. For this drill, ten complete "bananas" is a good starting goal.

4. banana – fast -- This banana drill should be easy because it is done almost exactly the same as the last one. The only exception is this drill is done at a much faster speed (quickness, not strength). Instead of smacking the ball really hard, simply exchange the ball as fast as you can with your other hand so you are moving the ball at a much quicker pace. The more you do this drill, the faster and more efficient you will become. Be sure you bring your arms high above your shoulder each time to maintain the banana shape. This exercise is great for getting your hands and arms ready for some of the more difficult drills you will be performing later. Ten fast "bananas" should be completed.

5. banana – behind legs -- This exercise should be a good challenge because all of the arm and ball movements are done behind you. With your feet together and the knees bent, hold the ball behind your legs and then start executing a banana from side to side. Try to swing your arms up as high as you can. It will probably be best to start this drill out slowly until you have mastered it and can increase the ball speed. Try to keep your head up to get a good feel for where the ball is since you are unable to see it. Transfer the ball between hands just behind the knees, not down near the ankles. A total of ten "bananas" should be completed.

I. Basic Ball Handling 31

6. **vise – chest level** -- Just like the vise you would see in a hardware store, this drill has the same concept. With the ball at chest level and your elbows out, put your hands on the sides of the ball and squeeze (push) it together as hard as you possibly can for ten seconds. This is the same position you would use after pulling down a rebound. This is also a great way to strengthen the hands, wrists, and arms.

7. **vise – above the head** -- This drill is not much different from the previous one. Position the ball about a foot directly over the top of your head and squeeze it as hard as you can with both hands like a vise. As you can tell, more emphasis is put on working your shoulders with this exercise. After ten seconds you will start to feel those shoulders and arms getting a good workout.

8. **ball smack – throw above head, pop at face level** -- This is the last exercise to complete this section and it will not be too difficult because the movements are similar to grabbing a rebound. Simply throw the ball about two or three feet above your head and then pop (smack) it hard with both hands simultaneously when it comes down to face level. Once you have executed this two-handed smack, quickly toss the ball back up to complete another one. Five of these ball smacks are a good beginning, but eventually work up to ten.

I. Basic Ball Handling

B. Fingertips

This section focuses on improving fingertip control, which is essential to successfully completing the rest of *Just A Basketball*. These eleven fingertip drills are excellent for strengthening your hands and fingers. Strong hands and fingers make it easier to take care of the basketball and prevent turnovers during game conditions. In addition, fingertip control allows you to develop a feel for the ball to improve your ability to dribble, pass, and shoot. By the end of these exercises your fingers should be sore, but the more you do these drills, the quicker and stronger your hands and fingers will become. Please read each of the exercises carefully in order to understand all the steps involved and find out what the suggested goal is for each one.

1. **popcorn – chest level** -- Start with the ball resting on either hand and then simply squeeze your fingertips together so the ball "pops" straight up out of your hand a few inches. Catch the ball with the other hand and repeat the squeeze again. Continue to alternate the ball back and forth from one hand to the other at chest level. Squeeze your fingertips together more quickly each time you do this drill and you will see why it is called "popcorn." Try to complete the drill for at least fifteen seconds.

2. **popcorn – above the head** -- This exercise is similar to the last drill except you will extend your arms above your head so that the ball is "popping" up high. You can begin by looking at the ball "popping" over your head, but eventually this drill should be done while looking straight ahead. Remember from the last drill that the ball only "pops"

out of your hand a few inches each time. Complete this drill for at least fifteen seconds. If you get brave, attempt a one hand popcorn above your head. Instead of alternating the ball back and forth from hand to hand, use just one hand to squeeze the ball. Try the one hand popcorn with the right hand and then give the left one a shot. This one hand popcorn is obviously more difficult because you have to move your fingertips so quickly. Now that you have learned the popcorn drills, you are ready to move on to the various tip drills.

3. **basic tip drill – fast fingers** -- This exercise is the basis for the rest of the drills in this section so it is crucial to get this one correct. The ball is going to be "tipped" back and forth between the fingertips on each hand. It will almost seem as though you are throwing the ball, but it is the fingers that are tipping the ball back and forth to keep it moving. The elbows should be slightly bent and your hands need to be positioned a little farther than the width of the ball to allow your fingers  to tip the ball very quickly. The ball only touches each hand briefly before being tipped to the other side. Tip the ball as fast as you can, always keeping it under control and out of the palms of your hands. Do the drill out in front of you at chest level for at least fifteen seconds.

I. Basic Ball Handling 33

4. **above the head to feet and back up** -- This drill will determine if you have the tip method down pat. Start with the ball a few inches over your head (elbows bent) and

begin tipping the ball, taking it gradually down to your waist and then continuing the tip drill all the way to your feet. Once you get down to the feet, start tipping the ball back up to where you started (above the head). Tip the ball down and back up five times and continue to increase your tipping speed each time.

5. **arms extended – above the head** -- This exercise is similar to the "popcorn – above the head" drill (#2), but the ball is now tipped instead of squeezed. Extend your arms straight over your head and tip the ball back and forth while looking straight ahead. Unlike the last drill, there should be no bend in your elbows. Remember to tip the ball instead of catching and throwing it. Fifteen seconds is a good goal for you to begin with because extending your arms above the head for fifteen seconds while tipping a ball is not easy. This exercise may be challenging, but it will become easier after a few times.

6. **arms extended – below the waist** -- Here is a drill that will test your tipping abilities. Stand up straight and extend both arms down below your waist and tip the ball. What makes this drill so difficult is that your arms are kept extended the whole time; there should be <u>no bend</u> at all in them. Keep in mind that you are tipping the ball with only the fingertips and not your hands and palms. To do this drill effectively, you must tip the ball very quickly or it will drop to the floor. Once again, fifteen seconds should be accomplished.

7. **arms extended – above the head to waist and back up** -- You are going to combine the last two drills to create this one. Start with the arms extended above your head (just like drill #5) and begin tipping the ball. While still tipping the ball and keeping your arms extended, progressively bring the ball down below your waist (drill #6) and then tip it back up over your head. It is very important to keep your arms fully extended to make the most of this drill. If you want a real challenge, move your arms up and down slowly and you will certainly feel them becoming stronger. Remember: the more slowly you move your arms, the more rapidly the ball must be tipped to keep it from falling to the floor. Five times down and back up should be completed.

I. Basic Ball Handling

8. behind head -- It is now time to do some tip drills behind your body. This drill and the next two are good examples of being able to handle the ball without seeing it. Position the ball behind your head with both hands (near the neck area) and start tipping the ball. Keep your back straight and the head facing forward to help your body feel comfortable. You must tip the ball very quickly or it will drop to the floor. Go for at least fifteen seconds on this one.

9. behind back -- To begin, reach behind your back with both hands (at waist level) and begin tipping the ball. Again, keep your back straight and your head looking forward. Make sure that the ball does not lean or hit against your back because that will keep you from doing the drill correctly. Also, it is important that you are tipping on the side of the ball and not beneath it. Fifteen seconds should be your goal once again.

10. behind legs -- For this exercise, place your feet together and slightly bend your knees so you can reach down and tip the ball behind the legs (just below the knee area). This drill will stretch the back of your legs, especially the lower you tip the ball behind them. Tip the ball behind your legs for fifteen seconds.

11. arms extended (lying down) – above the head to waist and back up -- This is the last drill for this section. By now you should have the "tip" concept down to a science. You will now get a little tricky and do a drill with your body flat on the floor. While lying down, extend your arms (above your head) and place the ball down on the floor. Begin tipping the ball near the floor and continue moving the ball straight over your upper body and then down to the waist area. Your arms should be fully extended the entire time, with absolutely <u>no bend</u> at all in them. Once you have brought the ball to the waist, reverse the process and tip the ball back over your upper body and down to the starting point above your head to complete one cycle. During the drill your head should not move or lift off the floor. Try to execute five complete cycles, which will be a real test.

I. Basic Ball Handling

C. Ball Around Body – Basic

It is now time to get into the meat of Basic Ball Handling. This section contains some common drills and is an excellent foundation for you to build your coordination, quickness, fingertip control, and strength. It is important to master these ball handling drills to further develop your workouts. As you are passing the ball from hand to hand in these exercises, be sure to use your fingertips exclusively to keep the ball out of the palms of your hands. This will allow you to move the ball quickly around your body. Also, the ball should never touch the floor at any time. Most of the drills are explained in detail, but only in one direction. Every exercise in this section is also reversed, which means that there are actually <u>two parts for each drill</u>. For example, if you take the ball around your waist clockwise, then once you finish that set of rotations, perform it again counterclockwise. For this section, at least ten rotations for each drill (twenty with the reversal) should be completed. As you become proficient with these drills, see how many rotations you can complete in thirty seconds.

1. **head (reverse)** -- For this first drill, you will simply pass the ball from hand to hand as you rotate it around your head. Since the ball has to travel part of the time behind your head, you will not always be able to see it. Be sure not to tilt your head forward, and concentrate on looking straight ahead the whole time. As with all the drills in this section, start the exercise slowly and work towards increasing speeds, but remember to always keep good control of the ball.

2. **waist (reverse)** -- This time the ball is going to rotate around your waist, the spot where you would wear a belt. Some important reminders are to keep your feet close together, stand up straight, look directly ahead, and <u>do not</u> sway your hips as you are rotating the ball. After a few successful tries, you will be amazed how fast you can move the ball around your waist.

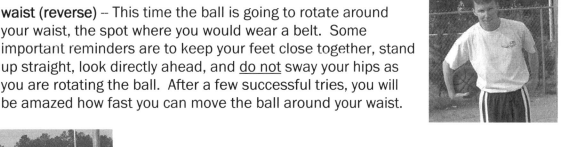

3. **chest (reverse)** -- This exercise is very similar to going around your waist, except now rotate the ball as high as you can around your chest. The ball should go around your chest just below the armpits and high on your back when the ball is traveling behind you. This position can be awkward; therefore, the ball does not move as fast in this exercise.

4. **knees (reverse)** -- With your feet together and the knees slightly bent, reach down and rotate the ball around your knees. This area should be another spot where you can move the ball rapidly around your body. Outstanding fingertip control is essential for you to move the ball quickly in this drill.

I. Basic Ball Handling

5. **ankles (reverse)** -- Start the exercise by bending over with your feet still together and your knees slightly bent; then rotate the ball around the ankles (or as low as you can get the ball to your feet). You should concentrate on keeping your upper body still. Try not to bounce up and down as you are moving the ball. This is an excellent drill for stretching the back of the legs.

6. **snowman – head, waist, and knees (reverse)** -- This continuous motion drill brings together a few of the exercises you have just learned. Start by taking the ball around your head clockwise for one full rotation. Next, bring the ball down and take it clockwise around your waist for a rotation and then finally move the ball down to your knees for one complete clockwise rotation. When you have finished the rotation around the knees, bring the ball back up to your waist for a rotation and then continue the ball up to your head. Once the ball is back near the head area, repeat the entire process. As you can tell from the description, the ball will always move in a clockwise fashion. On the other hand, when you reverse it, the ball will go in a counterclockwise fashion. Begin slowly until you feel comfortable enough to move at a faster pace. As you can see, the drill is done in three segments: up top, in the middle, and down below; like the shape of a snowman. Taking the ball around your head, waist, and knees and then back up equals one complete "snowman". For this exercise, finish five snowmen both clockwise and counterclockwise. After a few times you will be able to move the ball quickly up and down your body using this snowman pattern.

7. **right leg (reverse)** -- Begin this exercise by placing your right leg forward and then rotating the ball around the leg just below your right knee (the upper calf area). The left leg is not used at all during this drill. Try to keep your head up and use only your fingertips to help you move the ball exceptionally fast.

8. **left leg (reverse)** -- Exactly like going around the right leg in the last exercise, except now your left leg is used. Simply place your left leg straight out in front of you and then rotate the ball quickly around it. Work on controlling the ball smoothly to prevent any mistakes.

9. **pyramid – right leg, waist, left leg, waist (reverse)** -- Like the snowman, this exercise combines some of the previous drills. As you will find out, this drill involves a lot of up and down movements, and the ball sequence creates a pyramid-like shape. Start with your legs a little more than shoulder width apart and your knees bent. Begin by rotating the ball once around the right leg. Once you have completed that rotation, bring the ball up and take it around your waist; then move the ball back down and rotate it around your left leg. The last

I. Basic Ball Handling   37

step is to reverse directions and rotate the ball around the waist again and then back down around the right leg to start the rotations over. The steps just described equal one complete pyramid. Rotate the ball in a clockwise motion for five pyramids and then counterclockwise for five more.

10. **quick feet back – both legs, right leg back, both legs, left leg back (reverse)** -- This drill and the next one are outstanding for increasing your quickness, ball control, and rhythm. Start with your feet together and take the ball around your legs (knee area) in a clockwise fashion. Just before you finish one complete rotation, move the right foot straight back. Now take the ball once around your left leg. When that rotation is complete, bring both feet together again for another rotation. Next, move the left foot straight back and take the ball around your right leg. Finally both feet will come together and the whole process starts
again. The sequence of the rotations is both legs, right leg back, both legs again, and finally the left leg back. These four rotations equal one complete cycle. For this drill, try to finish five continuous cycles. In the reverse mode the steps are executed the same except the ball travels in a counterclockwise direction. This drill sounds complicated, but it is quite simple once you get a feel for what is happening. It takes time, but you will succeed with practice.

11. **quick feet up – both legs, right leg up, both legs, left leg up (reverse)** -- Begin with your feet together and take the ball around both legs clockwise. Just before you finish one complete rotation, move the right foot straight up. Now take the ball once around your right leg. When that rotation is complete, bring both feet together again for another rotation. Next, move the left foot straight up and take the ball around your left leg. Last, both feet come together again and the whole process starts over. The sequence for this drill is both legs, right leg up, both legs again, and then the left leg up. Strive to complete five continuous cycles, first clockwise and then counterclockwise.

12. **both legs – spread apart (reverse)** -- Start with your legs at shoulder width apart. Next, bend your knees and move the ball around the outside of your legs (near the knee area). The ball <u>never</u> goes through your legs; it always stays around the outside. Try to keep your head looking forward throughout the drill. Your back needs to remain relatively straight instead of being hunched over.

I. Basic Ball Handling

13. **both legs – spread far apart (reverse)** -- This could be a real challenging drill for some players, but it is not as difficult as it may seem. Begin with your legs spread <u>very</u> far apart and your knees bent. Once again, the ball will only go around the outside of the legs (near the knee area). Since your arms and legs are so far apart, it is almost impossible to "hand" the ball from one hand to another. Instead, the ball is passed from hand to hand, both in front and behind your legs. In fact, the ball will be thrown from one leg to another in front, then brought behind you, and thrown from one leg to another again. Just as in the last drill, try to keep your head looking forward, although you might have to look at the ball when you are passing it behind you because it is difficult the first few times.

14. **figure 8 (reverse)** -- You will find that many of the exercises in this book refer to this figure 8 drill. You will be on your way to great things in ball handling if you can successfully complete this drill. More difficult figure 8 drills are introduced in Intermediate Ball Handling. Begin with your legs a little more than shoulder width apart and the knees bent. Hold the ball in front of the right knee with your right hand. Next, take the ball between your legs to hand it off to your left hand behind the left leg. With the ball now in the left hand, take the ball from behind your left leg around to the front near the left knee. Next, take the ball through the legs (the opposite direction from the previous one) and hand it back to your right hand behind the right leg. Once the ball is in the right hand, bring it around the outside of the right leg and back to the

front where you will start the whole process again. As you can tell, the entire drill is done in a figure 8 pattern. You will need to move the ball slowly in the beginning so you can become familiar with all the ball movements. For an added challenge, try walking slowly using the figure 8 ball movements to develop ball control and agility.

I. Basic Ball Handling 39

D. Ball Rolls

The ball rolls were put into Basic Ball Handling because the ball is never actually dribbled. Since Basic Dribbling is the next part, these ball rolls are an excellent warm-up for some of the upcoming dribbling drills. Ball rolls are quite simple, but they will help develop your fingertip control and allow you to get a better feel for the ball. You may not want to always use these exercises in your ball handling workouts, although it is a good idea to learn them. Five repetitions in each direction without the ball ever touching your feet should be completed for each drill. Both hands will be used in every drill to roll the ball. The more times you practice, the faster the ball will zoom around your legs!

1. **right leg (reverse)** -- Lay the ball on the floor in front of your right foot and tap it around the outside of the leg with your right hand so it rolls behind the right foot. Now tap it back up through your legs with the left hand to where you started. Basically, what you are doing is tapping (rolling) the ball in circles around the right leg. Remember that the ball <u>never</u> comes off the floor and it is only tapped around your right leg. This exercise was just described in a clockwise direction; do not forget to also tap the ball counterclockwise.

2. **left leg (reverse)** -- Once again, lay the ball on the floor, this time in front of your left foot and tap it around the outside of the leg with your left hand. Next, roll the ball behind the left foot and then between the legs with the right hand to the front so you can begin another rotation. Continue tapping the ball around the left leg in these counterclockwise circles before reversing directions.

3. **both legs together (reverse)** -- Begin the drill by putting both legs together and bending your knees slightly. Tap the ball around both feet so it rolls behind the legs and then back up to the front. To give yourself better ball control, concentrate on using only the fingertips and not the palms of your hands.

4. **both legs spread apart (reverse)** -- Position yourself so both legs are a little more than shoulder width apart and the knees are bent. Begin tapping the ball so it rolls around the outside of your right leg, then behind your body, around the outside of the left leg, and finally back to the front where you started. Since the legs are spread apart, the ball does more rolling and you will perform less tapping than in the previous drill. The ball is <u>never</u> to roll between the legs, only around the outside of the legs.

I. Basic Ball Handling

5. **figure 8 (reverse)** – In section C, you learned the figure 8 around the legs, with the ball being passed off from hand to hand. This time the ball will move in the same manner (figure 8 style), but the method will be slightly different because the ball is going to roll on the floor around your legs instead of being handed off. Remember to have the knees bent and your back relatively straight, not hunched over. Try to tap the ball as fast as you can while still maintaining control.

6. **down on left knee – around right leg (reverse)** -- To begin, get down on the left knee and put your right leg out. Simply tap the ball around your right leg (foot) with both hands. Try to keep the ball as close to your right foot as you can, but make sure the ball never actually touches the foot. Since the ball does not have a long way to travel, this exercise can be completed very quickly.

7. **down on right knee – around left leg (reverse)** -- This time stick your left leg out and get down on the right knee. Tap the ball swiftly around your left leg (foot) with both hands. Be sure to use quick soft taps to roll the ball instead of hard taps, which could cause you to lose control.

8. **sitting Indian style around body (reverse)** -- While sitting Indian style (legs crossed), tap the ball so it rolls around your body. Since you cannot see the ball when it is traveling behind you, you will have to roll it all the way from one side of your back to the other. Work on keeping the ball close to your body so it does not roll away and cause you to get up and chase after it. These rotations will take a little longer than the previous drills because the ball has farther to travel.

Conclusion of Part I

– Congratulations! You have just completed the first part of *Just A Basketball*. As mentioned in the introduction, progression is a key element throughout the book. For you to become successful, you must first learn and develop the basic fundamentals before progressing to the intermediate and advanced levels. Basic Ball Handling introduced drills to help you establish the necessary fundamentals to become a good ball handler. If you have mastered Basic Ball Handling, then you are well on your way to success! Continue to practice all these ball handling drills, because the skills you have just learned will help achieve your goal of becoming a complete basketball player. Good luck in the next part of your workout, Basic Dribbling.

II. Basic Dribbling

A. Stationary Dribbling

It is now time to begin the first dribbling portion of *Just A Basketball*. Dribbling is entirely an individual skill and can easily be improved with practice. In game situations, dribbling allows you to move the ball around the court, to get out of defensive trouble, and to advance the ball towards the basket. No matter what position you play, dribbling is an essential part of basketball and a skill that often goes unnoticed. Being able to dribble the ball proficiently makes a player stand out, particularly at the elementary school age. The dribbling drills in this section may be the drills that you will find the most beneficial. It is important to know a few basic techniques in dribbling before beginning the exercises.

- Slightly cup the hand and then comfortably spread your fingers. Your dribbling hand should always be loose and relaxed, not tight and uncomfortable.

- Keep the ball out of the palms of your hands by using the pads of your fingers (fingertip area) to dribble the ball because this will help with ball control and quickness. Keeping the ball under control helps prevent turnovers during game situations.

- Make your wrist very flexible when dribbling but only use short bends in the wrist. This also will help with quickness and a better handling of the basketball. It is not necessary to slap or pound the ball while dribbling; be relaxed and let the ball do the work. The wrist action is similar to movements you would use while working a yo-yo or playing the drums, thus the need to develop a smooth rhythm. Learn to dribble on all five sides of the basketball (top, left, right, front, and back). Dribbling only on top of the ball limits your ability to change directions and maneuver around the court.

- Do not get into the habit of looking at the ball while dribbling; the ball will come up each time. If you have to, close your eyes or blindfold yourself to avoid looking at the ball. Dribbling with your head up will give you court awareness and the ability to see your teammates, opponents, and the entire floor for opportunities. If you cannot dribble without watching the ball during these stationary drills, then you will have great difficulty when performing the Moving Dribbling Drills (section F) in Intermediate Dribbling.

II. Basic Dribbling

As a warm-up, try a few waist high dribbles with each hand using the techniques just mentioned before attempting the drills. For all the drills in this section, be sure to use each hand with confidence, the importance of this cannot be over emphasized. Developing your weak hand will make you become a strong offensive threat and a much better basketball player. The goal for each exercise is to keep dribbling for at least a full fifteen seconds, unless told otherwise in the drill description. To become a great ball handler, practice your dribbling to the point where it becomes instinctive. Repetition is the key for you to become an outstanding and confident dribbler.

1. **both hands in front – side to side** -- In this drill and the next two, the ball is going to be dribbled waist high. The knees must be slightly bent and your feet should be shoulder width apart and stationary the entire time. Simply dribble the ball from one side to the other in front of you, with the ball always bouncing in the same spot. Basically, you will be alternating hands as the ball is traveling in a "V" pattern back and forth in front of you. When the ball is on your right side you will use the right hand and, of course, when the ball is on your left side you will use the left hand. The ball will continually move without any pauses. Start out dribbling the ball slowly and move up to faster speeds once you have full control of the basketball. These side to side dribbles develop your ability to use both hands, and they are a good introduction to the crossover dribbles at the end of this section.

2. **right hand in front – side to side** -- This exercise is the same as the previous drill, except you will use your right hand <u>exclusively</u>. Dribble the ball back and forth using the V dribbling pattern you just learned. When the ball is on the left side you will almost have to backhand the ball with the right hand to bring it back to the middle. Try to hit that same spot each time.

3. **left hand in front – side to side** -- Once again, everything is identical to the first drill but <u>only</u> the left hand will be used. Use the V pattern from drill #1 to dribble the ball back and forth in front of you. When the ball is on your right side, you will have to move the left hand over quickly to push the ball back to the middle. These one hand side to side dribbles you just completed provide the basic techniques for the half-cross dribble you will learn in section F of Intermediate Dribbling.

II. Basic Dribbling 43

4. **high front dribbling – side to side with both hands** -- Hopefully you have quickly mastered the last three exercises and are ready to do the high dribbling drills to increase your ball control. Before you had been dribbling the ball up to your waist; now you should dribble the ball as high as chest level while alternating hands (using the V pattern). Use both hands for this drill and do not let the ball bounce very far away from your body.

5. **high front dribbling – side to side with right hand** -- For this exercise, get that right hand up really high to dribble the basketball using the V pattern. Be sure to dribble the ball at chest level from side to side at a speed where you have full control of the ball. Also, do not be tempted to use that left hand when the ball comes over to the left side.

6. **high front dribbling – side to side with left hand** -- Just like the last drill but switch over to the left hand and get the ball dribbling up high. A good idea might be to put the right arm behind your back so you will not cheat and sneak it in there.

7. **high to low, low to high with both hands** -- Start by dribbling the ball high with alternating hands (using the V pattern) as you did in the earlier exercise (#4). After a few dribbles, gradually start to decrease the height of the bounces, going down to the waist, knees, and eventually the ankles to complete very low dribbles. Once you have made it down to the ankles, begin to bounce the ball higher, steadily back up to where you started. Two times down and back up are a good beginning goal.

8. **high to low, low to high with right hand** -- Just as in exercise #5, dribble the ball back and forth at chest level using the V pattern with the right hand only. Gradually decrease the size of the bounces until you get to a low dribble and then slowly work your way back up to the high dribble again. You will notice that the lower you dribble using this one hand V pattern, the faster your hand must move to maintain the dribbles. Your goal is to dribble down and back two times.

II. Basic Dribbling

9. **high to low, low to high with left hand** -- All the procedures in this drill are the same as the last one except you will be using the left hand. Bounce the ball back and forth going from high to really low and then back up to where you started. Again, two times down and back is your goal; but if your left hand is the weak hand, try to complete three or four.

10. **along right side with right hand** -- This drill and the next are wonderful for increasing the dribbling skills of your strong hand and also developing the weak hand. With your feet shoulder width apart, move your left foot slightly forward and bend the knees a little. Now dribble the ball knee to waist high along your right side so the ball always bounces a few inches from the outside of the right foot. The ball should go back and forth along the right side in the V pattern using push and pull movements. The ball is pushed forward and then pulled back to maintain the V pattern. Quick hand movements are important to do this drill correctly.

11. **along left side with left hand** -- For this exercise, put your right foot out in front of the left and slightly bend the knees. The ball will be dribbled knee to waist high along your left side with the left hand. Dribble the ball using the push and pull V pattern mentioned in the last drill. Keep your left hand quickly moving back and forth so the ball always bounces just to the outside of your left foot.

12. **between legs high - right foot in front** -- This is your first drill where the dribbled ball will go behind you and you will lose sight of it for a brief second. This exercise and the next three are just a few of the many drills in this book in which the ball travels between your legs; it is important to learn to do this effectively. Begin with your feet shoulder width apart and then place the right foot forward about a foot and a half. Make sure you are standing completely upright and balanced with a very slight bend in the knees. Start the ball from the left side of the front of your body (in the left hand) and dribble the ball so it hits the floor directly underneath your butt. The ball should bounce up to meet your right hand, which is behind your right leg. Next, quickly dribble the ball back through your legs with the right hand bouncing it between the legs again and returning to your left hand in front. Concentrate on dribbling the ball hard on the floor so it bounces up high (at least to the waist). After a few times you will be able to do the drill without looking at the ball.

II. Basic Dribbling 45

13. **between legs high – left foot in front** -- Again, put your feet shoulder width apart but now place the left foot out in front a foot and a half. Begin the ball in front of your body on the right side (in the right hand) and dribble the ball so it hits the floor directly beneath you and bounces up to your left hand, which is behind the left leg. Now dribble the ball back through the legs and up to your right hand to repeat the process. Continue dribbling the ball back and forth between your legs using this high dribble technique. Be sure that you are standing straight and the ball bounces up high (at least to the waist).

14. **between legs low – right foot in front** -- This drill is a good introduction to the between the legs moving dribble in Intermediate Dribbling (section F). Begin with your feet shoulder width apart and place the right foot ahead of the left as you did in drill #12. This time, bend your knees and squat down, just enough to be able to touch your ankles. The ball will be dribbled using the same steps as the last two "between the legs" drills, except the ball will be dribbled much lower, so low that the ball should never bounce higher than your knees. Also, try not to bounce your body up and down by keeping your legs firmly planted. Speed is not crucial for these between the leg dribbles; work on technique and developing a smooth dribbling rhythm.

15. **between legs low – left foot in front** -- Repeat the same process as in the prior drill except this time put the left foot out in front. Dribble the ball very low between your legs (not any higher than the knees) and keep your head up. The ball should always be dribbled in the same spot between your legs.

16. **crossover dribble – right to left** -- The crossover dribble is very different from a basic side to side dribble because it is quicker, lower, and closer to your body. This

exercise and the next one are a great introduction to the moving crossover dribble you will perform in section F of Intermediate Dribbling. Developing a good, quick crossover dribble will make you a much better offensive player because it is an excellent change of pace dribble to blow by your opponent and keep him/her off balance. To begin, place your feet shoulder width apart and bend the knees. Dribble the ball once with your right hand (just in front of the right foot) and when it bounces up, slide the hand from on top of the ball to the outside. Do not bring your right hand under the ball because this will cause you to "carry" or "palm" the ball. Next, quickly dribble (push) the ball across the front of your body with a quick snap of the wrist. You must cross the ball close to your body and very low to the floor as it travels over to the left side. This will help you keep the ball away from your opponent and make it almost impossible to steal. Do not forget to bring the left hand down low to receive the ball because each dribble should bounce no higher than the top of your knees. To maintain good balance, you will need to quickly shift your weight from right to left as you perform the crossover dribble. <u>Your feet will remain stationary throughout the entire drill</u>. When you have received the ball with your left hand, dribble one time and then place the ball back in your right hand to start another crossover dribble. As you will learn from the moving crossover, this concluding dribble with the left hand will allow you to complete the crossover with the opposite hand and explode down the court. Each crossover dribble set will consist of three dribbles: the initial dribble with the right hand, the crossover dribble from the right hand to the left hand, and the last dribble with the left hand. Complete at least ten crossover dribble sets. Once you feel comfortable with this crossover dribble, focus on not looking at the ball to help simulate game conditions.

17. **crossover dribble – left to right** -- For this exercise, remain in the same stance as in the last drill and place the ball in your left hand. Dribble the ball once with your left hand (just in front of the left foot) and then move the hand from the top to the

outside of the ball. Next, quickly dribble (push) the ball across the front of your body with a quick snap of your wrist. As in the previous drill, do not forget to cross the ball close to your body and also to shift your weight from left to right as the ball crosses over. Remember that you must keep the ball low to the floor, which requires the right hand also to be low as it receives the crossover dribble. Once you have the ball in your right hand, dribble one time and then put the ball back in your left hand to start again. Each crossover dribble set will have three dribbles: the first dribble with the left hand, the crossover dribble from the left hand to the right hand, and the last dribble with the right hand. Perform a minimum of ten crossover dribble sets with your head up.

18. **crossover dribble – continuous** -- This drill combines the last two exercises to form a continuous crossover dribble using both hands. Remain in the same stance and place the ball in your right hand. For a good beginning, dribble the ball once just in front of the right foot, and then complete a quick crossover dribble from the right to left hand (drill #16). When you receive the ball with your left hand, dribble it once just in front of the left foot and then perform a crossover dribble from the left to right hand (drill #17). Repeat these hand and ball movements until you are able to develop a smooth dribbling rhythm. Once you become skilled with these dribbles, execute continuous crossovers back and forth without the dribbles on each side. It is important to make each crossover dribble quick, low, close to your body, and with the head up. Since your feet are stationary during the entire drill, shift your weight from one side to the other with each crossover dribble (a rocking motion). Remember that each crossover dribble should bounce no higher than the top of your knees. Complete a total of twenty consecutive crossover dribbles (ten with each hand).

II. Basic Dribbling 47

B. Dribbling Around Body – Basic

This section is the foundation for Basic Dribbling, therefore, it is important for you to utilize these drills to the fullest. Most of the exercises are similar so some of them may be easy for you. As you learned in the last section, let the ball do all the work by using the fingertips as a guide. In order to keep the ball moving forward (or backward), dribble more on the side of the ball instead of the top to push the ball in the direction you want it to go. A few of the drills may be new, so you can look at the ball while you are learning the drill; but after some quality practice you should be able to do these drills with your head up. For all the drills in this section, dribble the ball low enough to keep it under control. The better you become, the closer the ball should be dribbled to the floor. All the exercises should be completed clockwise and also counterclockwise. This means every drill has a reversal mode associated with it; <u>be sure to always change directions</u>. Complete at least five rotations for each drill (actually ten with the reversal) unless noted otherwise in the drill description. When you get the ball moving well, see how many rotations you can complete in thirty seconds. The title of the drill sometimes describes what the whole drill is about, so there will not be long descriptions for every exercise.

1. **right leg (reverse)** – With your feet shoulder width apart, place your right leg forward about a foot and a half and dribble the ball around the right leg using both hands. Use your right hand when going around the outside of the leg and your left hand when the ball is bouncing through the middle of the legs. The hardest part of the exercise is going to be when the ball is dribbled behind your foot because the location of the ball makes it a little difficult to reach.

2. **left leg (reverse)** – Just like the last drill, but you will switch and dribble the ball around the left leg with both hands. If you were successful going around the right leg then this exercise should be a breeze. The left hand will be used to go around the outside of the leg and the right hand when the ball is dribbled through the middle of your legs.

3. **right leg with right hand (reverse)** – This drill and the next three are going to be a little tricky. In the last two drills you used both hands to dribble the ball around your legs, but now only one hand is going to be involved the entire drill. Your hand should not hit on top of the ball when you are dribbling in these one hand drills, but near

II. Basic Dribbling

the side in order to guide the ball around your leg. Put your right leg out about a foot and a half, and dribble the ball around the leg with the right hand only, keeping the ball as close to the right foot as possible. It is important to stretch your right arm out so you can reach behind your right leg and keep the ball dribbling. A quick hand is necessary to help keep the ball moving in order not to dribble the ball too many times in one spot.

4. **right leg with left hand (reverse)** -- Your right leg should still be out in front because this time you will use only the left hand to dribble the ball around the right leg. This should be very challenging for you, and the key is to stretch your left arm so you will

be able to dribble the ball around the outside of the right leg. Dribbling five times around the right leg in each direction with the left hand is much harder than you may think.

5. **left leg with left hand (reverse)** -- Switch legs and put the left leg out in front about a foot and a half, and dribble the ball around the left leg with your left hand only. Keep the ball low to the ground so it is not bouncing up to your knee.

6. **left leg with right hand (reverse)** -- Keep the left leg out and reach far over with your right hand to dribble the ball around the left leg. Remember to use low dribbles to help increase your hand quickness. If you need to, start out slowly and then steadily work towards faster speeds. If you can get the ball around five times and then reverse it five times, you are doing very well.

7. **both legs together (reverse)** -- Put both feet together and bend your knees for a good dribbling position. Dribble the ball around both legs (feet), keeping the ball close to your body. You should be able to move the ball quickly in this drill because the ball does not have far to travel to complete a single rotation.

II. Basic Dribbling 49

8. **both legs together with right hand (reverse)** -- Remain in the same position as the last exercise but now dribble around both legs using the right hand only. It will be very important to move your hand quickly so the ball will never stop bouncing. Try to keep the ball dribbled close to your feet to prevent losing control.

9. **both legs together with left hand (reverse)** -- Now switch hands and do the same thing as in the last drill, using the left hand only. Remember to dribble the ball near the side of the ball and not on top. This will allow you to move the ball faster around your legs.

10. **both legs spread apart (reverse)** -- Spread your legs a little more than shoulder width apart and bend your knees assuming a crouched position. Dribble the ball around the outside of your legs, <u>never</u> letting the ball bounce between your legs at any time. You may have a hard time when the ball is behind your legs, but have the other hand ready in order to dribble the ball back around to the front for another rotation.

11. **both legs spread far apart (reverse)** -- This could be a challenging drill for you, and it will take a little practice before you are able to do it properly. Spread your legs out as far apart as you possibly can (and still feel comfortable). The ball will be dribbled around the outside of your legs just as you did in the last exercise. The big difference comes when the ball is dribbled behind you. After you dribble the ball around the outside of your foot (towards the back), knock the ball with your hand so it bounces a few times behind your body to the other side. You will continue dribbling on the other side by taking the ball around to the front and starting the whole process over again. It is important to shift your body quickly to be able to retrieve the ball on the other side after it bounces behind you. The dribbles in front of you are simpler because the ball is much easier for you to reach.

50 II. Basic Dribbling

12. **figure 8 (reverse)** -- Do you remember the figure 8 that you did in Basic Ball Handling (section C, #13)? This basic figure 8 drill is identical as far as the path the ball travels except now the ball is dribbled instead of handed off. This exercise is valuable because it gives you an introduction to some of the more complicated figure 8 drills you will learn in Intermediate Dribbling. Begin with your legs spread and your knees bent in a comfortable squatting position. Start by dribbling the ball with the right hand in front of the right foot and bounce it between your legs keeping the ball dribbling with the left hand. While the left hand is dribbling the ball, take the ball around your left foot to the front and dribble it through your legs to the right hand. With the ball now in your right hand behind your right leg, dribble the ball around the right foot to the front, which will start the figure 8 over again. Once this figure 8 motion is completed for five rotations, you can reverse the direction of the ball and dribble the other way around your legs. When you learn to do this properly, it will probably become one of your favorites, because the ball is moving all around your body quickly and very low to the ground.

II. Basic Dribbling 51

C. Sitting Dribbling

Sitting and dribbling a basketball is a wonderful warm-up before playing, a good cool down when you are finished, or just part of your everyday ball handling routine. The drills are not difficult, but they require good arm movements; quickness and coordination are necessary to complete the drills correctly. For drills #1-#11, sit down with your legs extended and spread open so your knees are a foot to a foot and a half apart. Drills #12-#15 will have separate instructions because they are performed differently. Your goal should be at least ten dribbles for each exercise unless told otherwise.

1. **alternating dribble with both hands – on top of ball** -- For this exercise, simply dribble the ball between your legs, alternating hands on top of the ball. Since your legs are flat on the floor, the ball is merely dribbled out in front of you. Bounce the ball right between your kneecaps so it hits the floor at the same spot each time. The speed of the ball is not really important for this exercise, because you will get into that later in the Advanced Dribbling part.

2. **alternating dribble with both hands – side to side** -- This drill is similar to the one you just completed but the ball will bounce wider. You are going to dribble the ball at an angle, so instead of bouncing straight up, it bounces out towards your kneecaps.

Once again, the ball will hit the floor right in the middle every time. The ball starts from above the kneecap on the right side (with the right hand), then bounced in the middle to the left hand above the left kneecap, and finally sent back the other way (with the left hand).

3. **dribble with right hand – side to side** -- Let's see how fast you can move your right hand for this drill. This time you are going to dribble the ball from side to side but only with the right hand. Bounce the ball back and forth from over one knee to the other. You must move your right hand quickly, especially over to the left side to be able to bring the ball back to the middle.

II. Basic Dribbling

4. **dribble with left hand – side to side** -- Repeat the same steps as in the last exercise but now use the left hand only. Do not let the ball bounce out farther than the outside of your knees to maintain control. Place the right arm behind your back if you feel that it is trying to sneak up and dribble the ball.

5. **side to side over right leg with right hand** -- These next four exercises are a bit more challenging and require you to dribble the ball much higher. For this drill you will dribble the ball from side to side <u>over</u> the right leg with just the right hand. Bounce

the ball once to the right of the leg (outside) and then bring it over and bounce the ball again to the left of the leg (inside). Continue dribbling the ball over the right leg for the required ten dribbles.

6. **side to side over right leg with left hand** -- Now reach over and dribble the ball over your right leg with the left hand. After the outside bounce, you must reach your hand around to the outside of the ball in order to bring it back over the right leg.

7. **side to side over left leg with left hand** -- Let's try the other side and dribble the ball from side to side over your left leg with the left hand. In the last two drills you probably concentrated on technique; this time work on building your speed. Doing ten consecutive dribbles without an error on this drill should not be too difficult for you to accomplish.

8. **side to side over left leg with right hand** -- For this exercise, switch hands but remain with the same leg. Dribble the ball back and forth over the left leg with your right hand. It will be necessary to get some height on the dribbles so you can reach the right hand around to the outside of the ball and bring it back over the left leg.

II. Basic Dribbling   53

9. **side to side over legs with both hands – 4 dribbles** -- You are probably wondering what kind of drills these are with "4 dribbles". Each cycle consists of four dribbles next to the sides of your outstretched legs. Still sitting, start by dribbling once between your legs with the right hand, and then dribble the ball again (with the right hand) to the outside of the left leg. Now meet the ball with the left hand and dribble back between your legs, and finally one more dribble to the outside of the right leg (still with the left hand) which will make up one entire cycle. After the fourth and final dribble, meet the ball with your right hand to start the process again. For review, there are two dribbles with the right hand and then two dribbles with the left hand. These "4 dribbles" happen very quickly and require good coordination on your part. Complete five cycles (twenty dribbles) for this exercise and the next two.

10. **side to side over legs with right hand – 4 dribbles** -- Use only the right hand to complete this "4 dribble" drill. Remember from the last exercise, the ball is dribbled once between the legs, then outside the left leg, back between the legs, and finally to the outside of the right leg to finish one cycle. The ball is dribbled a little higher in these "4 dribble" drills, although speed is something to work towards. Be sure that only the upper body is in motion; try to keep your legs and feet firmly planted on the floor without shifting and swaying during the exercise.

II. Basic Dribbling

11. **side to side over legs with left hand – 4 dribbles** -- This is the last drill of the "4 dribble" series. The left hand is used exclusively moving from one side to the other with the "4 dribble" method. Begin slowly, but eventually the ball should move very quickly back and forth over your legs.

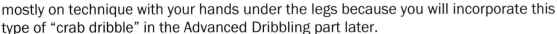

12. **alternating dribble with hands under legs** -- While you are sitting, move your feet towards your body so the knees are now bent. Place your hands on the outside of both legs and reach underneath to dribble the ball, alternating with both hands. Work mostly on technique with your hands under the legs because you will incorporate this type of "crab dribble" in the Advanced Dribbling part later.

13. **alternating dribble under lifted legs – on top of ball** -- Keep your butt on the floor and lift both legs with the knees slightly bent. Dribble directly on top of the ball under your lifted legs, alternating dribbles between each hand. Bounce the ball in the same spot every time, directly under your knees. <u>Do not</u> lie completely on your back; keep your back off the floor. As you can see, body balance is important to do the drill correctly.

14. **alternating dribble under lifted legs – side to side** -- In the last exercise, you dribbled the ball directly on top with the hands under the legs. This time the ball will bounce in the same spot again but your hands are going to be on the outside of both legs. Dribble the ball from one side to the other under your lifted legs by hitting the ball on the side, not on top. Hand and wrist action is the focus of this drill; the arms and shoulders barely have to move. This drill also works on the stomach muscles, so keep your body balanced to make the drill beneficial for you.

15. **dribble under lifted legs – back and forth with continuous low dribbles** -- Although you are in the same position as in the last two exercises, the ball will have more movement in this drill rather than being dribbled in the same spot. The ball is going to be dribbled back and forth in a straight line under your lifted legs, going from one side to the other while performing continuous low dribbles. Be sure to lift your legs high enough to allow the ball to be dribbled beneath them. While using quick hands, try to go back and forth under your legs at least five times.

II. Basic Dribbling 55

D. Lying On Side

Lying on your side to dribble the basketball is an excellent method to improve your ball handling skills. These eight drills can be done while you are watching TV or just lying down waiting for the next game to be played at the local playground. As you will see, emphasis is placed on dribbling the ball low to the ground with a steady rhythm. Please give these exercises a try because you will find them to be valuable. This section begins to introduce a little trickery, which is a good beginning for some of the more difficult drills in Intermediate and Advanced Dribbling. For exercises #1-#6, dribble the ball for at least fifteen seconds, and for exercises #7 and #8, read the drill description for the suggested goal.

1. **on left side with right hand – front** -- To start, simply lie down on your left side with the legs extended and the left hand holding your head (just as you would lie on the floor to watch television). Now dribble the ball with the right hand in front of you, a few inches out from your waist area. Be sure that only the fingertips are being used to bounce the ball and that you are dribbling the ball on top instead of on the side. One way to prevent this problem is to make sure your elbow stays up at all times (do not get lazy).

2. **on right side with left hand – front** -- Rotate your body around so that you are now lying on the right side and the right hand is holding up your head. Dribble the ball in front of your body with the left hand, a few inches out from your waist area. The ball should bounce just high enough for you to get a comfortable rhythm going. Do not forget to keep your left elbow raised so you are dribbling on top of the ball.

3. **on left side with right hand – behind** -- The positioning for this one is the same as drill #1, but now you will dribble the ball just behind your butt with the right hand. Bounce the ball just behind your butt in the same spot every time. You will most likely have to glance back a few times to make sure you are doing it correctly; but once you get the ball bouncing in the same spot, you will be able to dribble this way for a long time.

4. **on right side with left hand – behind** -- Roll over to the other side again so you are lying on your right side with the right hand on your head. Dribble the ball with the left hand behind your butt as you did in the last drill. Do not let the ball start to drift up near the back area or down towards your knees. Fifteen seconds should be no problem once you have developed a nice rhythm.

5. **on left side with right hand, between legs** – This exercise is similar to the last two, but slightly different. Lie on the left side with your left leg extended out and your right leg lifted up and also extended (the legs should look like a pair of scissors). Now reach through the legs and dribble the ball with your right hand just to the right of the left leg (behind). Note that the ball is always dribbled in the same spot. You may have to come up on your left elbow in order to reach through your legs with the right hand. Keeping the right leg up high will help considerably to strengthen your leg. You can also try the opposite, reaching through the legs from behind and dribbling the ball in front. In either case, the ball must be dribbled low to the floor because of your leg and arm positioning.

6. **on right side with left hand, between legs** – Roll over to the right side with your right leg extended out and the left leg lifted up and extended (like a pair of scissors). Reach through the legs with your left hand and dribble the ball just to the left of the right leg (behind). Remember to dribble the ball in the same spot every time. Try to maintain only a slight bend in the left leg and keep your body relatively straight, because it will be tempting to try to curve yourself to help reach through your legs to dribble the ball. As in the last exercise, remain in the same position but now attempt the drill by reaching between the legs from behind and dribbling the ball in front.

7. **continuous – on left side, front and behind with right hand** – Start this drill by lying on your left side with the legs extended. Before, you had placed the left hand on your head, but this time put the left arm down on the floor so that it supports your upper body. In the first six drills of this section, the ball was always dribbled low, but now you will incorporate a high bounce <u>over</u> the legs. Start the drill by bouncing the ball for five seconds with the right hand just in front of your waist (exercise #1), and then quickly take the ball over your legs (with one high dribble) and bounce the ball for five

II. Basic Dribbling

seconds behind you, just a few inches from your butt (exercise #3). Once you are finished dribbling behind you, perform another high dribble over your legs to bring the ball back to the front. Continue these five second dribbles in front and in back while adding the high dribble over the legs to maintain continuity. Be sure that you do not "palm" the ball when performing this high dribble. Your goal is to dribble the ball for five seconds on each side three times, for a total of thirty seconds. This is not an easy exercise but do not give up on it!

8. **continuous – on right side, front and behind with left hand** -- Switch over to the right side and put your right arm on the floor to hold up your upper body. As in the last exercise, a high bounce over your legs will be used to keep the drill continuous. Begin by bouncing the ball for five seconds with the left hand just in front of your waist (exercise #2); then take the ball over your legs with a high dribble and bounce the ball for five seconds behind you a few inches from your butt (exercise #4). When you have completed the dribbles behind you, bring the ball over your legs to the front by executing another high dribble. Continue to dribble the ball using the steps just mentioned for a total of thirty seconds (five seconds on each side three times). Remember that the ball has to be dribbled high to get over your legs, keeping your hand on top of the ball.

Conclusion of Part II

– You have now completed the two "basic" parts of this book. Hopefully, Basic Dribbling gave you a review of some familiar drills, but also introduced you to new ones. Acquiring the necessary techniques and fundamentals for dribbling will be crucial in your development as a basketball player. Learning to dribble the ball with both hands, using fingertip control, keeping your head up, and being a confident dribbler will greatly increase your overall skill level. It is now time to progress towards some of the more creative and challenging drills by jumping into Intermediate Ball Handling. Let's go!

III. Intermediate Ball Handling

A. Ball Around Body – Intermediate

The majority of players will find this section to be a good test of their ball handling abilities. These drills are a step up from the Ball Around Body section you learned in Basic Ball Handling. Some very creative standing and sitting drills are included. Maintaining good body balance is necessary to successfully completing the drills. For increased quickness, keep the ball out of the palms of your hands to allow you to use only the fingertips. Just like the Ball Around Body section in Part I, the exercises are explained for one direction only, which means that there are two parts for each drill. Complete at least ten rotations for each drill (twenty with the reversal). Challenge yourself to see how many rotations you can achieve in thirty seconds.

1. **figure 8 two-step – right leg planted (reverse)** -- This drill and the next are similar to the basic figure 8, but with a little twist. Start with the legs a little more than shoulder width apart and place your left heel even with your right toes. Pass the ball around your legs as in the basic figure 8, except just after the ball goes around the left leg (and starts to go through your legs to the other side), simply step the left foot back. Now your left toe should be even with the right heel. When the ball comes

    back and around your left leg again, step forward so the left heel is even with your toes again. Continue stepping backward and forward with the left foot while the ball travels in the figure 8 pattern. The right leg will remain planted the whole time. The footwork is done the same way in the reverse mode; it is only the direction of the ball that changes the drill.

2. **figure 8 two-step – left leg planted (reverse)** -- As you guessed, this drill is identical to the prior one except your left leg will stay planted. Begin with your right heel even with your left toes. Pass the ball around your legs like the basic figure 8, but after the ball goes around the right leg (and starts to go between both legs to the other side), step back so your right toe is now even with the left heel. Every time the ball goes around your right leg in the figure 8, you will either step up or step back. The left leg remains planted during the drill, and it is only the right leg that moves up and back. This drill incorporates the basic figure 8 you learned with some nifty footwork.

III. Intermediate Ball Handling   59

3. **standing on right leg – around left leg (reverse)** – Start with both feet together and then lift your left leg up so the left knee is waist level and the leg is slightly bent. The right leg will remain still the entire time. Rotate the ball around the lifted left leg (near the knee area) without jumping around. The only things that should be moving are your arms and the ball (the left leg can move just slightly). This is an excellent drill for balance and coordination.

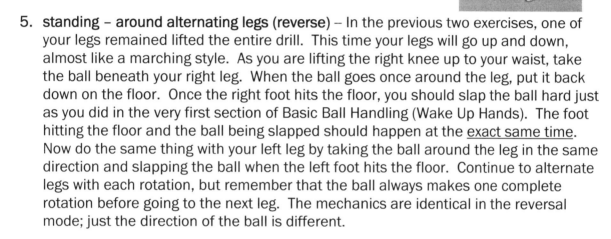

4. **standing on left leg – around right leg (reverse)** – Once again, start out with both feet together and then lift your right leg up so the right knee is waist level and the leg is slightly bent. The left leg is used to keep your body steady. Now rotate the ball around your right leg, preferably close to the knee area.

5. **standing – around alternating legs (reverse)** – In the previous two exercises, one of your legs remained lifted the entire drill. This time your legs will go up and down, almost like a marching style. As you are lifting the right knee up to your waist, take the ball beneath your right leg. When the ball goes once around the leg, put it back down on the floor. Once the right foot hits the floor, you should slap the ball hard just as you did in the very first section of Basic Ball Handling (Wake Up Hands). The foot hitting the floor and the ball being slapped should happen at the <u>exact same time</u>. Now do the same thing with your left leg by taking the ball around the leg in the same direction and slapping the ball when the left foot hits the floor. Continue to alternate legs with each rotation, but remember that the ball always makes one complete rotation before going to the next leg. The mechanics are identical in the reversal mode; just the direction of the ball is different.

6. **standing – figure 8 (reverse)** – Be careful not to confuse this drill with the last one. First, bring the right knee up so that it is even with your waist. Now with your right hand take the ball beneath the right leg and pass it off to your left hand. Once the ball is put in the left hand, set your right leg back down on the floor. Next, lift your left knee up to the waist and take the ball around and beneath your left leg and pass it back off to your right hand where everything starts again. Continue moving the ball in this figure 8 fashion while working hard to improve your ball speed and balance.

You will find it beneficial to understand all the leg and ball movements before trying this drill at full speed. It is important to lift your knees up to waist level each time; do not get lazy in this phase of the drill. As you will see, the leg and ball movements will force your body to bounce up and down. The ball will travel just the opposite when it is reversed, but all the leg movements will be the same. Once you have learned the exercise, see how fast you can move the ball using this standing figure 8 method.

III. Intermediate Ball Handling

7. **sitting Indian style around body (reverse)** -- This exercise will require a little more arm strength than most of the drills in this section. Begin by sitting in an Indian style position (legs crossed) and then rotate the ball around your body just above the waist. Be sure to look straight ahead and keep your back upright without slouching. Try to move the ball with your upper body remaining still instead of bobbing back and forth.

8. **sitting – around lifted legs (reverse)** -- Since you have already loosened and strengthened your arms and legs, you can do a drill to work the stomach muscles. Sit on the floor with your legs together and extended forward. Next, bend the knees a little, lean back, and lift your legs high enough for the ball to come under (probably a foot to a foot and a half off the floor). Now move the ball around your lifted legs near the knee area, while keeping the arms straight and your body as still as possible. If your legs get tired from being off the ground, rest a little while and return to the drill later. Eventually your stomach and legs will be strong enough to handle ten rotations in each direction without any problem.

9. **sitting – figure 8 around lifted legs (reverse)** -- This is another good exercise to build up your leg muscles and also the arms. Begin by sitting on the floor with your legs spread about a foot apart. With the knees bent, lean back slightly and lift a leg about a foot off the floor. Start rotating the ball around your legs using the figure 8 method. Regardless of the direction the ball is traveling, you will lift your leg each time the ball is passed under it and place it down on the floor when the ball is passed over it. As you are passing the ball beneath and around the legs, try not to rock back and forth. For this drill, do five complete figure 8 rotations in each direction.

III. Intermediate Ball Handling 61

B. Down On One Knee

Let's now try something a little different and get down on one knee for these next eight drills. The drills in this section are more challenging and may require additional patience and practice. For every exercise, perform five complete rotations in each direction unless told otherwise. Ten rotations should be your goal once you have completely mastered these exercises.

1. **down on left knee – around right leg (reverse)** -- Simply get down on your left knee and put the right leg out so your toes are pointed straight ahead. Now rotate the ball with both hands around your right leg (near the knee area). You should be able to move the ball in each direction very quickly. Do not forget to reverse the ball.

2. **down on right knee – around left leg (reverse)** -- The leg positioning in this drill is the opposite of the last exercise. Switch over so your left leg is out and you are down on the right knee. Next, rotate the ball quickly with both hands around your left leg. Be sure that the ball is moving around the knee area and not near the upper thigh or down by the ankle.

3. **down on left knee – around right leg with right hand – flip** -- This time you will only be using the right hand instead of both hands to rotate the ball around your right leg. While down on your left knee, bring the ball under the right leg (from the outside) with your right hand and flip the ball up. Once you have flipped the ball, catch it with your right hand over the right leg and start all over again. It is best to flip the ball up in order to catch it directly over your right leg. The flip does not have to be really high, just high enough to allow your right hand to come back and catch the ball. Speed is not as important for this drill and the next three exercises; technique and coordination are the main objectives. If you are having trouble using the right hand exclusively, put your left hand behind your back to keep it away. Notice that the ball moves clockwise the entire time. There is not a reverse mode for this one because the next drill takes care of that. Complete at least five rotations (flips) around the right leg.

4. **down on left knee – around right leg with left hand – flip** -- This drill is considered the reversal of the last one. You will remain down on the left knee, but now take the ball under your right leg (towards the outside) with the left hand and flip it up so that you catch it over your right leg with the left hand. Once you catch the ball, take it back under the right leg and repeat the same steps. As you can tell, the ball moves in a counterclockwise direction and is always handled with just your left hand. Again, complete at least five rotations (flips) around the right leg.

III. Intermediate Ball Handling

5. **down on right knee – around left leg with right hand – flip** -- If you mastered the last two drills, then the next two should be no problem. Switch over so you are down on your right knee and take the ball under the left leg (towards the outside) with the right hand and flip it up so you catch it with your right hand directly over the left leg. Place the left hand behind your back if you are tempted to use it. Complete at least five of these clockwise rotations (flips) around the left leg.

6. **down on right knee – around left leg with left hand – flip** -- Stay down on the right knee, but now bring the ball under your left leg (from the outside) with the left hand and flip it up. Catch the ball over the left leg with your left hand in order to start another rotation. Once more, complete at least five of these counterclockwise rotations (flips) around the left leg. These last four drills (#3-#6) are excellent for working on your hand quickness before getting into some of the more challenging ball handling and dribbling drills later.

7. **down on left knee – figure 8 (reverse)** -- This drill and the next are probably two of the toughest in Intermediate Ball Handling. You should be down on your left knee with the right leg out. Start with the ball in your left hand and take it around the outside of the left leg (which is kneeling on the floor), and pass the ball off between your legs to the right hand. This hand off from behind the left leg is not as easy as you may think. Now take the ball in your right hand all the way around the outside of the right leg and pass it back to your left hand (between the legs) to begin the drill over again. The ball travels more slowly in this type of figure 8 because your leg positioning makes it a little more difficult to maneuver the ball. Be sure that you are able to do this exercise properly before attempting to reverse the ball.

8. **down on right knee – figure 8 (reverse)** -- You should now have the basic fundamentals of the previous drill to make this figure 8 easier. To begin, get down on your right knee and stick the left leg out. Start with the ball in your right hand and take it around the outside of the right leg (which is kneeling on the floor) and pass the ball to your left hand in between your legs (this is the tough part of the drill!). With the ball now in your left hand, bring it all the way around the outside of the left leg and pass it back to your right hand (between the legs) to start a new rotation. Do not forget to reverse the ball. You should really feel good about yourself after correctly learning to do these last two exercises because they are rather challenging.

III. Intermediate Ball Handling

C. Cradle Drills

This section is referred to as "cradle drills" because your hands are cupped and the fingertips are used as though you were cradling a baby. Soft and quick hands are a must for these exercises. Your hands will be constantly moving back and forth around the legs, and the ball is touched with your hands either beneath you or on the sides. These exercises are a wonderful introduction for improving your hand speed, which will be incorporated in Advanced Ball Handling with the Quickness Drills (section C) and the One Hand Cradles (section D). Ten repetitions are the standard for all fifteen drills in this section. Each time you change the position of your hands, either from front to back or from side to side, is considered one repetition.

1. front to back -- Sometimes known as the "seesaw," this drill is often considered the most common of intermediate/advanced ball handling drills. You will need to use only the fingertips to increase your quickness because having the ball in your palms will slow you down. Start in the basic basketball stance by spreading your legs a little more than shoulder width apart and bending the knees so you are evenly balanced. Place your hands in front of your legs and then center the ball directly between the knees. Next, drop the ball and then quickly move both hands from the front to the back to catch the ball before it hits the floor. Reverse the process by releasing the ball again and bringing your hands back around to the front to catch the ball. Your hands will always be moving from front to back and then back to front, going around the outside of the legs.

Initially you may find it easier to flip the ball a little towards the direction that the hands are going. That is okay at first; but as you improve, the ball should be dropped straight down each time. For a challenge, add your best speed to the drill to make the ball barely move. Ten repetitions should be the very minimum but go for twenty-five once you get the ball moving.

2. side to side -- This drill is often called the "pretzel" in case you have heard this term used previously. This is another common drill that you have most likely seen before. Bend your knees again so you are balanced and the legs are spread about shoulder width apart. Start by holding the ball with the left hand behind the left leg and the right hand in front of the right leg. Center the ball with both hands

between your knees with only the fingertips. Next, drop the ball and then quickly alternate hands to catch the ball before it hits the floor (the left hand is now in front of the left leg and the right hand is behind the right leg). Continue alternating your hands quickly back and forth, catching the ball to prevent its touching the floor. All the ball action is done between the legs. Try to keep the ball centered between your knees. In drill #1, both hands were either in the front or in the back. As you alternate hands in this side to side cradle, one hand will always be in front of the legs and the other hand will always be behind the legs. Your hands will eventually be moving so fast that the ball will barely be moving! Although ten repetitions are the goal, aim for twenty-five because being able to do this drill correctly and quickly will make it easier for the rest of the cradle drills.

3. **front to back with clap** -- The front to back cradle (drill #1) was perhaps not too complicated for you; now let's try for something a little harder. Use all the same hand and ball movements as before, but now clap your hands in front each time you let go of the ball to switch hand positions. You will find that it is difficult to clap your hands and then catch the ball behind your legs. Your hands will have to move much faster in this drill compared to the regular front to back cradle. Adding a clap helps to increase your hand speed and to improve your coordination. If you need to, let the ball bounce one time as you are clapping and switching your hands. This will assist you at first, but do not use the bounce after you get all the motions coordinated. Complete the required ten repetitions without letting the ball hit the floor.

4. **side to side with clap** -- Let's go back to the side to side cradle (drill #2) and add a clap every time you change hand positions. If necessary, use the one bounce technique you learned in the last drill to help you understand all the hand movements. This is another terrific drill for developing your hand quickness. If you can do ten repetitions without the ball touching the floor, then you should be able to handle the rest of the drills in this section.

5. **side to side – alternating feet back and forth** -- Only your hands were moving in the previous side to side cradle drills, but now you will add your feet to the equation. This drill requires a great deal of hand quickness and agility. With your feet a little more than shoulder width apart, place the left foot ahead of the right. Center the ball between your knees by having the right hand in front of the right leg and the left hand behind the left leg. At the same time you switch hands, alternate your feet so that the right foot is now up front. Continue to alternate your feet up and back as quickly as your hands are moving. Even try to do all the repetitions without looking at the ball!

III. Intermediate Ball Handling 65

6. **down on right knee – front to back** -- To begin, place the right knee on the floor and start the ball under you with both hands in the front. Flip the ball up a few inches and then quickly move your hands around the legs to catch the ball with both hands behind you. Once you have caught the ball, flip it again and move your hands back around to the front. Obviously, the ball cannot be flipped very high. There is little room for error; using the fingertips effectively will help you to catch the ball and to maneuver your hands back and forth around your legs. You will have to reach the right hand far around the right thigh to help catch the ball behind you. At first, let the ball bounce once as you switch your hands back and forth. This will give you time to learn the proper techniques to help you complete the required ten repetitions.

7. **down on left knee – front to back** -- Switch over to the left knee and place your right leg out. Repeat the same movements as in the last drill and concentrate on not trapping the ball against your body. If necessary, let the ball bounce once so you are comfortable doing the drill. You must reach the left hand far around the left thigh to help catch the ball behind you. This is definitely not an easy exercise and may be frustrating for you in the beginning, but be confident in your ball handling ability.

8. **down on right knee – side to side** -- Now put the right knee back on the floor and complete a side to side cradle as you performed in drill #2. Begin holding the ball between your legs with the right hand in front and the left hand behind the left leg. You will find that the ball has to be moved a little more toward the back so the hands can alternate back and forth evenly. Again, try not to let the ball trap against or even touch either leg. Use the one bounce technique at first to introduce yourself to the drill, and then complete the standard ten repetitions without the bounce.

9. **down on left knee – side to side** -- Switch back to the left knee again and complete the side to side cradle. To start, hold the ball with the left hand in front and the right hand behind the right leg. Alternate your hands back and forth around the legs, especially working the left hand quickly to the back. Try the one bounce method for starters and work your way up to doing the drill so the ball never hits the floor.

III. Intermediate Ball Handling

10. **sitting – front to back** -- Begin the drill by sitting on the floor with your legs extended forward and the knees bent. With your hands over the legs in front, hold the ball between your knees. Now drop the ball and move your hands around the outside of the legs to catch the ball when it comes down. Both hands are now under the legs; flip the ball up a few inches. As the ball is rising, bring your hands back around the outside of the legs to catch the ball on top where you started. Continue to quickly shift your hands back and forth from above to below, without letting the ball get too high or hitting the floor.

11. **sitting – side to side** -- Remain in the same sitting position and start the ball centered between the knees again. This time begin with one hand on top of the legs and the other hand beneath. Use the techniques of the side to side cradle (drill #2), alternating the hands back and forth around your legs after flipping the ball up a few inches. Remember to use only the fingertips for better ball control and quickness. The ball should only be in the fingertips briefly before you flip the ball up again and switch the position of your hands. Finish the ten repetitions never allowing the ball to hit the floor or touch your legs.

III. Intermediate Ball Handling   67

D. Spider Tap

The spider tap is a drill that has many simultaneous arm movements much like a spider. The spider tap is similar to the tip drills you completed in section B of Basic Ball Handling. Like the tip drills, the spider tap uses only the fingertips and the ball is tapped just briefly before being touched by the other hand. All of the exercises are similar; it is the position of the body that distinguishes them (standing, down on one knee, or sitting). The spider tap is also an excellent introduction to the spider dribble that you will learn in Intermediate Dribbling. The ball should never touch the ground at anytime during these spider tap exercises. Once you understand the drills, each one of them should be done for at least fifteen seconds.

1. **½ spider tap – right side** -- These first two exercises may seem elementary for you, but they will help you with the full spider tap. The instructions sound complicated but the drill is rather easy. While standing with your feet a little more than shoulder width apart, bend your knees and center the ball directly between them with the left hand. Drop the ball out of the left hand and catch it with the right hand, which is positioned behind your right leg. Now drop the ball from the right hand and catch it with the left hand in front again. Drop the ball again from the left hand and catch the ball with the right hand, but now in front of the right leg. The left hand <u>will always</u> remain in front and the right hand will continually alternate from the front of the right leg to behind the right leg. The ball is only dropped about two inches each time and should never hit the floor. Be sure only to use your fingertips and "tip" (drop) the ball quickly from hand to hand. Eventually you will be able to move the right arm quickly around your right leg.

2. **½ spider tap – left side** – Now switch over and complete a ½ spider tap on the left side. Bend your legs down and center the ball directly between the knees with the right hand. Drop the ball out of the right hand and catch it with the left hand, which is behind your left leg. Now drop the ball from the left hand and catch it with the right hand in front again. Finally, drop the ball out of the right hand and catch it with the left hand, but now in front of the left leg. The right hand <u>will always</u> stay in front and the left hand will continually alternate from the front of the left leg to behind the left leg. Remember, the ball is held only momentarily each time before being shifted to the other hand.

III. Intermediate Ball Handling

3. **full spider tap** -- Let's put together drills #1 and #2 to complete a full standing spider tap. Before, one hand would remain in front the entire exercise, but now you are going to alternate each hand from the front to the back with both hands constantly moving at the same time. Your sequence of hand movements (taps) will be right hand in front of right leg, left hand behind left leg, right hand behind right leg, and left hand in front of left leg. Continue this sequence of taps while steadily increasing your ball speed. The ball will probably be dropped a little farther because each hand will be working in tandem from front to back and then back to front. Try to keep the ball moving around the knee area and not down towards your feet.

4. **full spider tap – walking** -- To really test your spider tapping ability, you are going to perform a spider tap while walking forward. As in the last drill, alternate each hand from the front to the back with both hands constantly moving to tap the ball. Start with a full spider tap and then slowly begin moving your feet forward. You will not be able to walk fast because your body is in a crouched position. This drill works best when you can perform the full spider tap near the knee area so you do not have to bend far. If you get daring, attempt the spider tap while walking backward. Whether moving forward or backward, try to keep your head up the entire time. Fifteen seconds might seem like a long time, but don't give up!

5. **down on right knee – ½ spider tap – left side** -- Place the right knee down on the floor and start the ball in the right hand between your left foot and the right knee. Drop the ball out of the right hand and catch it with the left hand, which is behind the left leg. Now drop the ball and catch it in the right hand in the middle again. Next, bring the left hand back around to the front to catch the ball when it is dropped out of the right hand. The left hand continues to alternate from behind to the front of the left leg while the right hand remains in front between the left foot and the right knee. You can complete a surprising number of taps in just fifteen seconds.

6. **down on left knee – ½ spider tap – right side** -- Switch over and get down on the left knee. This drill is just like the previous one but the right hand continues to alternate from behind the right leg to the front of the right leg. The left hand remains in front as a "guide" to keep the ball centered between the right foot and the left knee.

III. Intermediate Ball Handling 69

7. **down on right knee – ½ spider tap – right side** -- Before, when you were down on the right knee you worked exclusively on the left side with the left hand doing the majority of the drill. Now you will be on the right knee again and working the right hand around the right leg using the ½ spider tap method. This should be a real challenge alternating the right hand back and forth, because you have to reach far back to get behind the right leg (thigh). Due to the awkward positioning and lack of space, the ball has to be kept close to the floor and maneuvered using fingertip control. The left hand remains centered between the left foot and the right knee throughout the exercise.

8. **down on left knee – ½ spider tap – left side** -- Switch over again to the left knee and use the ½ spider tap method working the left hand around the left leg. The left hand needs to move very quickly since the ball is barely dropped and kept close to the floor. Also, keep the ball farther back which will help when you have to reach behind the left leg (thigh) to tap the ball. The right hand will stay in front to keep the ball centered between the right foot and the left knee.

9. **down on right knee – full spider tap** -- Now that you can work both hands around each leg, you should be able to complete a full spider tap while down on your right knee. Simply alternate each hand from the front of each leg to behind each leg so both hands will be moving simultaneously, as in drill #3. The sequence of taps will be right hand in front of right leg, left hand behind left leg, right hand behind right leg, and left hand in front of left leg. The challenge comes when you have to reach behind the right leg to tap the ball because you will need to move the right hand very quickly to get behind the leg.

10. **down on left knee – full spider tap** -- If you had no problems with the full spider tap on the right knee, then this exercise will be no problem for you. Alternate your hands from the front of each leg to behind each leg so both hands are continuously moving. The sequence of taps is identical to the last drill. One key point is to try to tap the ball in the same place every time; this way you will not have to adjust your hands as much to do the tapping.

11. **sitting – ½ spider tap – right side** -- While sitting with your legs out, bend your knees and center (hold) the ball between them with the left hand. Drop the ball out of the left hand and catch it with the right hand that is under the right leg. Next, toss the ball back up to your left hand and then bring the right hand to the top to catch the ball once it leaves the left hand. Then drop the ball from the right hand to the left hand and start the sequence all over again. The left hand remains on top and the right hand will continually alternate from on top of the right leg to under the right leg. Technique should be your first priority and eventually work toward faster speeds. Remember that the ball is tapped just briefly before being touched by the other hand.

III. Intermediate Ball Handling

12. **sitting – ½ spider tap – left side** -- Keep your knees bent and center (hold) the ball between the knees again, but now with the right hand. Drop the ball from the right hand and catch it with the left hand, which you have reached under the left leg. Toss the ball back up to your right hand and then bring the left hand over the left leg to catch the ball again once it leaves the right hand. To complete the sequence, drop the ball from the left hand to the right hand. The right hand will always stay on top and the left hand will continually alternate from above the left leg to under it. Do not spread your legs too wide because that will cause you to reach farther and is not beneficial for ball control, especially when you complete the full spider tap in the next drill.

13. **sitting – full spider tap** -- Between sitting, down on one knee, and standing, the full spider tap sitting down is probably the most comfortable for your body. Also, you may find this one to be the most successful. You are going to combine the last two sitting exercises to complete this. Simply alternate each hand from on top of each leg to under each leg to tap the ball. The sequence of taps is right hand over right leg, left hand under left leg, right hand under right leg, and left hand over left leg. Continue this sequence while trying to move your hands so quickly that the ball barely moves. If you are having problems, toss the ball up a few inches to give more time for your hands to get around the legs. Again, the ball never hits the ground at any time during the drill.

III. Intermediate Ball Handling

E. Scissors – Pass Through Drill

You are probably wondering what these "scissor" drills are really about. For these exercises, the ball is passed (not dribbled) through your legs as the legs are constantly in motion. Your legs will eventually be moving back and forth very quickly, similar to a pair of scissors cutting. As you will discover, coordination between the hands is necessary to properly execute the drills. The section starts with the shuffling (in place) scissors, then adds more movements by doing the walking scissors, and finally closes with the running scissors. For a great workout, go thirty seconds for each exercise.

> **Note:** For every drill, all the leg movements are identical in the reversal mode; it is just the direction of the ball going through your legs that changes. For example, if the first pass is supposed to go between the legs from behind your right leg to in front of the left leg, change in the reversal mode so the first pass moves from in front of the right leg to behind the left leg. Likewise, if the second pass is supposed to go between the legs from behind your left leg to in front of the right leg, change in the reversal mode so the second pass moves from in front of the left leg to behind the right leg.

1. **shuffling feet – in place (reverse)** -- This combines two earlier drills. These are the figure 8 from Basic Ball Handling (section C) and the side to side cradle in section C of Intermediate Ball Handling in which you were alternating your feet back and forth (in place). Start with your feet shoulder width apart and position the right foot about six inches in front of the left. Now begin the basic figure 8 between your legs, but after the ball is passed through the legs, shuffle your feet. The right foot should now be in the back and the left foot should be up front. Continue shuffling your feet back and forth each time the ball is passed through your legs. Do not hunch your body; instead, bend your knees to stay balanced. To better understand the movements, begin the drill slowly and work your way up to faster speeds to get those feet scissoring. Use short shuffles up and back compared to longer steps that will keep you off balance and slow your ball speed down. Remember that the ball is passed from hand to hand between your legs and it is not to touch the floor at any time. For all the scissor drills, it is important to pass the ball in a straight line through your legs instead of making wide circles. This will allow you to move the ball swiftly. Your feet movements are the same in the reversal mode; it is just the direction of the ball that changes.

III. Intermediate Ball Handling

2. **walking (reverse)** -- You remained in place during the first drill; now let's start moving using the scissors method. This exercise is similar to the one you just completed, but now you will be moving forward. You must stay low and take longer strides in this drill, passing the ball under the legs (thigh area) and staying completely balanced. There is not much circular motion with the ball in this exercise. Instead, the ball is passed directly through your legs from one hand to the other. It is a good idea to

start walking very slowly to work on synchronizing the ball and leg movements. There is no need to go fast because you will be doing that soon in the running portion. Remember that reverse means to change the direction of the ball and not the direction you are walking. Keeping your head up is important so you can see where you are going!

3. **walking backwards (reverse)** -- This exercise is not much different from the walking forward scissors you just finished. All you have to do is simply walk backwards while passing the ball directly through your legs from one hand to the other. There is no need to move fast because you should be concentrating on coordinating the ball and leg movements and taking long steps straight back and not toward the sides. Also, remember to look back before you begin so you have an idea of how much distance is behind you.

4. **running (reverse)** -- These next two scissor drills are a great conclusion to this section. These exercises combine hand quickness, technique, coordination, and agility into one while you are moving quickly. The running scissors has the same ball and leg movements as the walking scissors, only the drill is sped up considerably. The ball must be passed off quickly between hands as you are running down the court. Like the walking scissors, stay low and pass the ball directly through your legs (under the thighs) from one hand to the other. By now you should not have to look down; keep your head up to increase your speed and to see where you are going. Remember that your legs can only go forward as fast as the ball is traveling between them.

5. **running backwards (reverse)** -- You can show off your ball handling abilities when you execute this scissors drill running backwards. Pass the ball quickly through your legs but do not let it hit the ground during the exercise. This drill is more like a fast walk backwards in which you are using mainly your toes and not the back of your heels. Be sure to check the area behind you for hazards and to see how much distance you have in which to work.

Conclusion of Part III
-- If you have already developed the basic fundamentals of ball handling, then you probably found this part to be extremely valuable. Intermediate Ball Handling involved a great deal of balance, coordination, and quick hands because most of the drills were quite challenging. For improved ball handling performance, continue to practice the exercises in these sections on a regular basis. The next part, Intermediate Dribbling, will have some similar drills but with a dribbling approach.

IV. Intermediate Dribbling

A. Dribbling Around Body – Intermediate

These around the body dribbling drills are unique because they are performed while standing, down on both knees, and sitting. Being able to dribble the ball equally well with both hands is stressed in this section. Much practice may be required to successfully complete all these drills. Like the Dribbling Around Body section in Basic Dribbling, all of the exercises should be completed clockwise and also counterclockwise. This means every drill has a reversal mode associated with it; <u>be sure to always change directions</u>. Complete at least five rotations for each drill (actually ten with the reversal) unless noted otherwise in the description.

1. **figure 8 with right hand (reverse)** – Just when you thought the figure 8 drill from Basic Dribbling was conquered, a tougher one comes along. For this drill, all the steps are the same as in the last exercise, but now you will use your right hand exclusively to complete the figure 8 (the left hand will never be used). The difficult part comes when the ball is going around the left leg because you are going to have an extended reach to keep the ball dribbling.

2. **figure 8 with left hand (reverse)** – Keep yourself in the same position and switch over to have your left hand do the entire figure 8 dribbling. Dribble the ball close to your foot when it is going around the right leg because you have to reach so far. Start dribbling the ball slowly to help you maintain complete control. This could be a real challenge if your weak hand is the left one. If so, this drill is excellent for strengthening the weak hand and a great confidence builder once you master it.

3. **figure 8 while walking (reverse)** – For this exercise, the ball is going to have all the same movements as the regular figure 8 but with an added twist. Once the ball is dribbled around either leg and begins to go through the middle to the other hand, step forward with the leg that the ball just went around. Long strides are not necessary; just a step at a time. Get the ball moving quickly around your legs and

IV. Intermediate Dribbling

you will be walking fast enough. It is strongly suggested that you start this drill slowly and gradually increase speed. Aim for thirty seconds.

4. **right leg standing with right hand – whip dribbles (reverse)** – In Basic Dribbling, you went around your right leg with many low bouncing dribbles; now you will do just the opposite, using one high dribble. This is another drill in which the right hand is used entirely. Start with your feet a little more than shoulder width apart and make sure that your knees are bent. To move the ball clockwise (forward), cradle the ball in your right hand and whip it around the right side of your body and bounce it through your legs catching it in front with the right hand. You must bring the right hand quickly from the back to the front to catch the ball. The ball should bounce directly between your legs in the same spot each time to help the drill run smoothly. As previously

stated, each rotation around the leg will have only one bounce associated with it. When you are going counterclockwise (backward), bounce the ball with the right hand once between your legs toward the back. Next, quickly bring the right hand behind you to catch the ball and then cradle it back to the front to start over again.

5. **left leg standing with left hand – whip dribbles (reverse)** – Stay in the same position as in the last drill, with your feet a little more than shoulder width apart and the knees bent. For the counterclockwise (forward) direction, cradle the ball in your left hand and whip it around the left side of your body and throw it through your legs so it bounces once and you catch it back in front with the left hand. Remember that each rotation around the leg only has one dribble and that it always bounces directly between your legs. Keep in mind that only the left hand is used in the drill. When you take it clockwise (backward), bounce the ball once between your legs with the left hand so it goes behind you. Next, catch the ball with your left hand behind your back and then cradle it to the front and start a new rotation. You will discover the clockwise rotations in this drill are more difficult and cannot be completed as rapidly.

6. **figure 8 standing – whip dribbles (reverse)** – This drill combines what you just learned in the two previous exercises to create a figure 8 pattern. Remain standing with your feet spread and your knees bent. This time when you dribble through the legs, the ball will go diagonally so you catch it with your other hand. When you grab the ball, take it around your leg and bounce it back through your legs again (diagonally) and catch it with the same hand with which you started the drill. A complete figure 8 consists of two diagonal whip dribbles. It will probably help to start out slowly and take this drill step by step. Do not forget to reverse the direction of the ball.

IV. Intermediate Dribbling 75

7. **down on both knees – around body with both hands (reverse)** – Just as the title says, get down on both knees and dribble the ball around your entire body using both hands. The hardest part of the drill will be when the ball is bouncing behind your back near your feet. When the ball is behind you, turn your torso in order to be able to reach back and dribble (push) the ball to the other side to keep the ball bouncing until you can reach it again with the other hand.

8. **down on both knees – around body with right hand (reverse)** – Remain on both knees and dribble the ball around your whole body using the right hand only. You will really have to stretch so you can keep the ball going while it is behind you. To keep the ball continuously moving, dribble it a little bit on the side and not directly on top. In this exercise you should use short dribbles, not high ones because that will help you get the ball bouncing much faster. The counterclockwise rotations will be a real challenge!

9. **down on both knees – around body with left hand (reverse)** – Stay on both knees, but now dribble the ball around your body with the left hand only. If this is your weak hand, you may have to dribble the ball a little higher at first until you can do it successfully. It is crucial really to stretch your left arm in order to get good angles to help you dribble the ball. If you are able to do this drill or the previous one without turning your head around to see where the ball is, then you are becoming an excellent ball handler. For this drill, you will find the clockwise rotations to be more challenging.

10. **sitting Indian style – around body with both hands (reverse)** – Begin by sitting Indian style (legs crossed) and then dribble the ball around your entire body using both hands. This time, when the ball is bouncing behind your back, you will not be able to turn around easily to see it. You will need to push the ball toward the other side to keep the ball moving. It is important to keep the ball bouncing when it comes around to the other side to maintain a continuous dribble. Concentrate on not looking at the ball during this drill. It will be difficult to dribble the ball very high because of the sitting position; there is no choice but to keep a low dribble. Be sure to keep the ball close to your body and under control.

76 IV. Intermediate Dribbling

11. **sitting Indian style – around body with right hand (reverse)** -- Remain sitting Indian style, but now dribble the ball around your body using only the right hand. You will have no choice but to move your right hand quickly from one side to the other to keep the ball bouncing. As in the last exercise, you must push the ball a little when going around your back so the ball will continue to the other side.

12. **sitting Indian style – around body with left hand (reverse)** -- Stay seated in the Indian style position and dribble the ball around your body with just the left hand. If you have problems with keeping your right hand out of the way, place the right arm behind your back. You must move the left arm quickly so the ball never stops bouncing. This exercise may be a little more difficult if you are not left handed since the success of the drill is determined by the accuracy of the dribbles around your body. Hopefully you will be able to keep the ball within an arm's length unless you enjoy getting up to chase the ball!

13. **sitting – around lifted legs with both hands (reverse)** -- This exercise will give your stomach a good workout and is one of the most difficult drills in this section. Begin in a seated position with your legs together and extended forward (the knees should be bent slightly). The drill will be done similarly to the exercises when you were sitting Indian style except now lift both legs and dribble the ball with both hands around your body (butt). You will need to lift your legs high enough for the ball to be dribbled under them, probably a foot to a foot and a half off the floor. It will be very challenging because the stomach muscles will be tested and your legs are probably not used to remaining in this position for such a long time period. The hardest part is to keep the ball bouncing behind your back as it travels to the other side to maintain a continuous dribble.

IV. Intermediate Dribbling 77

14. **sitting – around right leg with both hands (reverse)** – For the next three drills the ball will be dribbled only around the legs instead of around your entire body. Begin by lifting your right leg about a foot off the floor and dribble the ball under it from one hand to the other. Once the ball reaches the other hand, place your leg down on the floor; then bring the ball over the leg and bounce it back to the hand with which you started the drill. As you can tell, there are two dribbles to be executed with each rotation. The right leg is lifted when the ball is dribbled under it and then it is placed on the floor when the ball is brought over. Your leg will continually move up and down in a circular fashion as the ball is dribbled (rotated) around it. Try to complete ten rotations around your leg in each direction instead of only five.

15. **sitting – around left leg with both hands (reverse)** – For this drill you are going to dribble (rotate) the ball around your left leg using the same type of ball, hand, and leg movements that you performed in the last exercise. If you had no problems with that exercise, then you can try to increase your ball speed in this one. Keeping the ball close to your left leg will help your control and speed. Again, aim for ten rotations in each direction.

16. **Sitting – figure 8 (reverse)** – By combining the last two exercises with the sitting figure 8 in section A of Intermediate Ball Handling (drill #9), you can complete a sitting figure 8 while dribbling. Instead of dribbling the ball around one leg, you will move the ball in a figure 8 fashion around both legs. Whether the ball is going over or under the legs, it will be dribbled between your legs each time as it changes hands. <u>This means there are only two dribbles with each figure 8 rotation</u> (one dribble in each direction). Your legs will alternate moving up and down as the ball moves around them in the figure 8 pattern. Try to keep the ball as close to the legs as you can; this will greatly increase your speed. Five complete figure 8 rotations around your legs in each direction should give your arms and legs a good workout.

78 IV. Intermediate Dribbling

B. Down On One Knee

It is time to add more variety to Intermediate Dribbling by getting down on one knee for the next eight drills. Some of these exercises are tough and involve many hand movements, particularly the last two. You will find these to be great drills for developing the weak hand. Complete five rotations in each direction for every drill (ten with the reversal), unless told otherwise in the description.

1. **down on left knee – around right leg with both hands (reverse)** – Place the left knee down on the floor and dribble the ball around your right leg with both hands. Use the right hand when going around the outside of the right leg and your left hand when coming through the middle to the inside of the leg. Since your body is closer to the floor, the ball must be dribbled lower to get beneath the right leg.

2. **down on left knee – around right leg with right hand (reverse)** – In the last drill you utilized both hands; now only one hand is to be used the entire drill. Remain down on the left knee and dribble the ball around the right leg with the right hand only, keeping the ball as close as you can to the right foot. The right hand must move very quickly when you bring it over the top of the right leg to keep the ball dribbling.

3. **down on right knee – around left leg with both hands (reverse)** – This drill is going to be just like exercise #1, except switch your legs so you are down on the right knee. Dribble the ball around the left leg using both hands. The left hand will be used to dribble around the outside of the left leg and the right hand when the ball comes along the inside.

4. **down on right knee – around left leg with left hand (reverse)** – Stay down on the right knee with the left leg still out and dribble the ball around the left leg with your left hand only. You must move the left hand quickly over your left leg so there are no pauses and each rotation is done smoothly. Always try to keep the ball dribbling near your left foot to avoid having to reach out continually for the ball.

IV. Intermediate Dribbling 79

5. **down on left knee – beneath right leg – alternate dribbles** -- Get down on the left knee again and be certain that your back is straight. Dribble the ball from side to side beneath the right leg, alternating dribbles between your hands. The ball should bounce back and forth in the same spot every time, directly below the right thigh.

Your goal for this exercise and the next is to dribble the ball continuously for a full fifteen seconds. A similar drill with added dribbling speed will be introduced to you in section A of Advanced Dribbling.

6. **down on right knee – beneath left leg – alternate dribbles** -- For this exercise, switch legs and place the right knee on the floor with your back straight. This time, dribble the ball from side to side beneath the left leg (thigh), alternating dribbles between your hands. The ball has to be dribbled back and forth very low in order not to hit the bottom of the left leg.

7. **down on left knee – figure 8 with right leg out (reverse)** – These next two exercises are a little complicated; therefore, it will take a few more attempts to completely learn the drills. Start the drill down on your left knee with the ball in front of the right foot. Dribble the ball with the right hand to the outside of the right foot and then through the middle of your legs to the left hand. Next, take the ball to the outside of your left knee and keep dribbling the ball all the way around the left foot (which is a considerable distance behind you) and bounce the ball back up through the middle of your legs to your right hand to start another rotation. It is important to reach back with the left hand to get the ball dribbled around your left foot. Because the reversal mode is difficult, it also needs to have a detailed description. Begin with the ball again in front of your right foot and dribble with the left hand through the legs to your right hand. Dribble the ball all the way around the left leg by reaching far back with the right hand. When you get to the outside of the left leg, bounce the ball up to the left hand and take it back through the legs to your right hand. Dribble up to the front of the right foot and start the whole process again. Please read all the steps slowly to help you understand the drill better. This is a wonderful exercise once you figure out all the movements, it just takes a little practice.

80 IV. Intermediate Dribbling

8. **down on right knee – figure 8 with left leg out (reverse)** -- This exercise should be a little easier now that you have executed the last drill. Start the exercise down on your right knee with the ball in front of the left foot. Dribble the ball with the left hand to the outside of the left foot and then through the middle of your legs to the right hand. Take the ball to the outside of your right knee with the right hand and keep dribbling all the way around the right foot. Now dribble the ball back up between your legs to the left hand to start the exercise again. Be sure to twist around in order to get the ball around the right foot. In the reversal mode, start the ball again in front of the left foot and dribble to the inside of the left leg with the right hand and then bounce the ball through the legs to your left hand. Dribble all the way around the right leg, by reaching far back with the left hand. When you get the ball to the outside of the right leg, bounce the ball up to the right hand and take it back between the legs to your left hand. Last, dribble the ball up to the front of the left foot to begin another rotation. Congratulations, you did it!

IV. Intermediate Dribbling   81

C. Behind Body

Dribbling a basketball behind your body is great for increasing your ball handling skills and giving creativity to your workouts. You have already done some exercises in which you were not able to see the basketball, but this entire section is about dribbling behind your body and learning to handle the ball completely by feel. Developing a good dribbling rhythm and keeping the ball under control are two important points that are stressed in this section. Start out slowly in order to understand what each drill is all about and then gradually increase your dribbling speed. All the drills should include at least ten dribbles, unless told otherwise. Do not cheat yourself; learn to do all of these exercises.

1. **behind back standing – side to side with legs together** – Start the exercise by standing straight with your legs (feet) together. Dribble the ball from side to side behind your back so it always bounces just a few inches away from your heels. The ball is dribbled using the V pattern you learned in Basic Dribbling. Since you are standing straight, the ball has to be dribbled hard enough to bounce up to your hand at waist level each time. Once you achieve a good rhythm of dribbling from side to side, the drill will become less awkward. Be sure to look straight ahead because this will require you to get a good feel for the ball as it is bouncing behind your back.

2. **behind back standing – side to side with legs spread apart** – Simply remain standing straight and spread your legs out so they are a little more than shoulder width apart. Next, dribble the ball waist high behind your back from side to side (V pattern) and look directly ahead to keep from glancing back at the ball. The ball does not come around to the front, it stays behind your body the entire drill. It is important to reach far enough behind you to avoid arching your back. Do not get in the habit of trying to "find" the ball with your hand; once you discover the proper amount of bounce, the ball will come up to "meet" your hand each time. Try to dribble the ball so it bounces at the same spot every time; this will help you develop a good dribbling rhythm. You may find it necessary to use a bouncing/rocking motion as you are moving the ball from side to side. This drill provides good preparation for the moving behind the back dribble in section F.

IV. Intermediate Dribbling

3. **behind back with knees bent – side to side with legs together** -- Almost identical to exercise #1, except this time bend your knees far enough down in a comfortable

squatting position. Since your feet are together with the knees bent, balance is very important to perform the drill successfully. Dribble the ball behind your back from side to side using the V pattern and be sure that you keep the ball under control (not bouncing far away from your body). The ball should bounce no higher than the back of your knees.

4. **behind back with knees bent – side to side with legs spread apart** -- This is very similar to exercise #2, except now your knees will be bent. Make sure your feet are at least shoulder width apart and firmly planted. Once again, a good dribbling rhythm and a bouncing/rocking motion from side to side will make the drill easier. Learn this drill while knowing where the ball is every dribble. Remember that the ball should always hit the floor at the same spot and this time it will be dribbled under your butt since you are in a squatting position. Try to dribble from side to side as low and as fast as you can.

5. **behind legs – back and forth with continuous low dribbles** -- Begin this exercise with the knees still bent and your feet spread apart. The ball is going to be dribbled back and forth in a straight line behind your legs, going from one side to the other. Dribble the ball low four or five times behind your right leg; then smack it over so it bounces to the left hand and you dribble the ball low four or five more times behind the left leg before sending it back to the right side to start again. Remember that the ball is dribbled low to the ground, not up to your knees. This drill moves more quickly than you may think. Try to go back and forth from one side to the other at least five times.

6. **behind ankles – side to side** -- Put your feet together and bend the knees slightly, being able to reach down to your feet. Dribble the ball from side to side behind your ankles just a few inches away from the heels. Ideally, the ball should not bounce higher than mid-calf. You will learn a speed dribble using this body position in Advanced Dribbling (section A).

IV. Intermediate Dribbling   83

7. **standing on right leg – behind right leg – side to side** – – Start with both feet together; then lift the left knee up to your waist. Dribble the ball waist high from side to side behind your right leg (foot) using the V pattern. As you can tell, balance is crucial to complete the drill. Once you lift the left knee, try to stay completely balanced until you finish all ten dribbles.

8. **standing on left leg – behind left leg – side to side** – This time lift the right knee up to your waist and dribble the ball behind the left leg (foot). Using the V pattern, strive to bounce the ball (waist high) in the same spot each time. After doing this exercise successfully a few times, work on increasing the speed of your dribbles.

9. **behind the back dribble – stationary** – The behind the back dribble is an exceptional move for deceiving your opponent on the court. In a game situation, the behind the back dribble protects the ball from your defender while you change directions. It is important to learn the basic fundamentals of the behind the back dribble because it can be utilized in many ways, both on the court and with ball handling routines. Start by standing with your knees slightly bent and your feet a little more than shoulder width apart. Dribble the ball once with the right hand just to the outside of your right foot. As the ball comes up, place your right hand on the front of the ball and pull it behind your back so the ball bounces behind the left foot and up to your left hand. It is important to extend your right hand and follow through to help push the ball over to the left side. Once you receive the ball in your left hand, repeat the same steps on the left side, dribble once with the left hand and then pull the ball behind your back

so it bounces behind the right foot and up to your right hand. If you have trouble doing this stationary exercise continuously, just do one side at a time before attempting the whole drill together (ten consecutive behind the back dribbles).

IV. Intermediate Dribbling

10. **behind the back dribble – walking** -- In the previous drill you remained stationary, but now you are going to add some movement to the exercise. With the ball in your right hand, dribble once on your right side and then execute a behind the back dribble. As you bring the ball behind your back to the left side, step forward with the left foot to prevent your hitting the ball against it. Dribble once on the left side with the left hand, and as you bring the ball behind your back to the right side, step forward with the right foot. Continue to do these movements on each side and you will be dribbling the ball behind your back while walking. Of course the faster you walk, the quicker the behind the back dribbles must be. Complete at least ten successful behind the back dribbles. You will really get this behind the back drill going when you perform this move while running in the Moving Dribbling Drills section (F).

11. **behind the back dribble – walking backwards** -- The only difference between this drill and the last one is the direction you are walking; all the ball movements are identical. Dribble the ball once on your right side and then perform a behind the back dribble to the left side. When you receive the ball with the left hand, dribble once on the left side and then execute a behind the back dribble to the right side. Start out slowly moving backwards and then gradually increase to a normal walking speed. Once you achieve a comfortable speed, complete the goal of ten behind the back dribbles.

12. **down on right knee – side to side over right leg with right hand** -- If you did the back stretches before starting your drills, then you should be prepared for this exercise and the next one which will give your shoulders and back a great workout. Begin the drill down on the right knee and twist your body around to the right. Now dribble the ball with the right hand behind you, going from one side of the right leg to the other. The ball will be dribbled over the calf area of the right leg. As you can tell, the ball must bounce high enough to allow you to move your hand to dribble the ball over the leg. Once you become proficient, you should be able to complete the dribbles without twisting your back and looking at the ball.

13. **down on left knee – side to side over left leg with left hand** -- Switch over so you are down on the left knee and twist your body around to the left. Dribble the ball with the left hand over your left leg (in the calf area). The lower the ball is dribbled, the quicker your hand movements have to be. If you can do the drill without twisting your back, then you are extremely flexible!

IV. Intermediate Dribbling 85

14. **down on right knee – behind the back dribble** -- For the next two exercises, the ball will come all the way around your back instead of only being dribbled side to side behind you. These drills will develop your behind the back dribble and are similar to exercise #9. Once you have mastered these drills, you can complete them quickly. Place the right knee on the floor again and hold the ball in your right hand. Begin by doing a simple dribble near your right knee. Once the ball bounces up to your right hand, perform a behind the back dribble over to the left side as you have previously learned. When the ball reaches your left hand, repeat the same steps on the left side   by bouncing the ball once with the left hand and then executing a behind the back dribble to the right side. Because of your body position, you have to really pull the ball around your back to make it come to the other side. Do not look for the ball as it comes around your back each time; learn to do these dribbles completely by feel. Aim for ten behind the back dribbles, five with each hand.

15. **down on left knee – behind the back dribble** -- Switch back and get down on the left knee with the ball in your right hand. As in the last exercise, dribble once with the right hand and then complete a behind the back dribble to your left side. Once the ball reaches the left hand, dribble it one time near the left knee and then perform a behind the back dribble from the left side back to the right. Continue this pattern and complete ten behind the back dribbles, five with each hand.

16. **behind back sitting Indian style – side to side** -- Sit in the Indian style position (legs crossed) and lean your body forward. Reach both arms behind your back and dribble the ball from side to side using alternating dribbles. The ball should bounce in the same spot every time, just a few inches from your butt. Notice that the further you lean forward the easier it is to dribble the ball. This drill is done completely by feel since you are not able to see the ball behind you.

17. **sitting Indian style – behind the back dribble** -- What a test this drill will be for your behind the back dribbling! The ball will have the same movements as exercises #14 and #15. Everything is identical except that you will be sitting Indian style instead of down on one knee. Your hands have to be quicker when pulling the ball behind your back since the ball is not dribbled very high. It may be necessary to lean slightly forward to help get the ball around your back each time. Complete five behind the back dribbles with each hand while remaining in this sitting position. This exercise will provide you with a good shoulder workout.

IV. Intermediate Dribbling

D. Spider Dribble

The spider tap you learned in Intermediate Ball Handling (part III, section D) was a prelude to this spider dribble. In fact, all of the drill titles are exactly the same in the two sections. The ball never touched the ground during the spider tap, but it will be dribbled constantly in this section. All of the hand moves are the same as the tap, but the spider dribble involves a little more coordination between your hands because of the dribbling aspect. The exercises involve standing, being down on a knee, and sitting, all of which use ½ spiders and full spiders. If you do not remember, ½ spiders are completed around one leg exclusively, while the full spider incorporates both legs. Since all of the drills in this section are quite similar with the hand movements, detailed descriptions will only be given for the standing spiders (#1-#3). Once you understand each drill, execute all twelve spider dribbles for at least fifteen seconds. Work hard on not looking at the ball and developing quick hands. Some of the best ball handlers have trouble with the spider dribble, but you can do it!

1. **½ spider dribble – right side** – The ½ spiders are a great beginning for the full spiders you will soon be performing. Start in a good basketball stance, with your feet spread a little more than shoulder width apart and the knees bent. The left hand <u>will always</u> remain in front and the right hand will continually alternate from the front to behind the right leg. Your sequence of dribbles will be left hand, right hand in front of right leg, left hand, and right hand behind right leg. Continue this series of dribbles (between your feet) as many times as you can for the full fifteen seconds. Your right hand needs to move incredibly fast around the right leg to keep up with all the low dribbles.

2. **½ spider dribble – left side** – Now shift over to the left leg and complete a ½ spider. In this exercise, the right hand <u>will always</u> remain in front and the left hand will continually alternate from the front to behind the left leg. The order of dribbles this time is right hand, left hand in front of left leg, right hand, and left hand behind left leg. Continue alternating your left hand around the left leg as quickly as you can because this is the hand that makes the drill work. The key is to use only the fingertips instead of the whole hand to increase your speed. Also, keep the ball dribbled in the same spot (between your feet) the entire drill because having the ball wander will only slow you down.

IV. Intermediate Dribbling 87

3. **full spider dribble** -- Combining exercises #1 and #2 will give you a full standing spider. In the ½ standing spider dribbles, one hand would always remain in the front, but now you are going to do a dribble alternating both hands between the front and the back of your legs. This time the sequence of dribbles will be right hand in front of right leg, left hand behind left leg, right hand behind right leg, and left hand in front of left leg. Continue this series of dribbles using only your fingertips and keeping the ball under control. Start with knee high dribbles and work towards dribbles about ankle high. As you continue to progress in this exercise, try doing the whole drill without ever looking at the ball. Make sure you understand all the hand movements before you begin so you will not become confused and end up frustrated. Like the ½ spider dribbles, the ball needs to be dribbled directly beneath you (between the feet) and not toward the direction of your next dribble. If you are in a rhythm, do not stop at fifteen seconds, keep on going!

4. **full spider dribble – walking** -- Get your feet moving for this exercise and execute the full spider dribble while walking forward. As in the last drill, alternate each hand from front to back with both hands constantly moving to dribble the ball. Since your body is in a crouched position, take small steps forward instead of long strides. Completing the moving spider dribble for fifteen seconds with your head up will be a great accomplishment. Also try this full spider dribble while walking backwards.

5. **down on right knee – ½ spider dribble – left side** -- Place your right knee on the floor in order to do a ½ spider dribble around the left leg. Keep the right hand up front while the left hand continues to alternate from the front to behind the left leg. All of the dribbles should bounce a few inches to the right of the left foot. Focus on quickly working the left hand back and forth around the left leg.

6. **down on left knee – ½ spider dribble – right side** -- Switch over so you are down on your left knee and complete a ½ spider dribble around the right leg. This drill is just like the previous one but the right hand continues to alternate from the front to behind the right leg and the left hand remains in front. Each dribble should bounce a few inches to the left of the right foot.

7. **down on right knee – ½ spider dribble – right side** -- When you were down on your right knee in drill #4, you worked solely with the left side and the left hand did most of the work in the exercise. You will be on the right knee again, but now work the right hand around the right leg (thigh) using the ½ spider dribble technique. The left hand will remain in front. It is a challenge alternating the right hand back and forth

IV. Intermediate Dribbling

because of the extended reach to dribble behind the right leg. Let the ball barely touch your fingertips when you reach behind the right leg to do the dribble. Every dribble should bounce a few inches to the left of the right knee.

8. **down on left knee – ½ spider dribble – left side** – Switch over so you are on your left knee again but use the ½ spider dribble method working the left hand around the left leg (thigh). Keep the ball dribbled farther back which will help when you have to reach behind the left leg. Each dribble needs to bounce a few inches to the right of the left knee.

9. **down on right knee – full spider dribble** – The full spider dribbles down on one knee are the most difficult drills in this section. By combining the ½ spider drills in #4 and #6, you will be able to complete a full spider dribble while down on your right knee. Alternate your hands from the front of each leg to behind each leg so your hands are continuously moving as you did in the standing full spider dribble (drill #3). One key point is to consistently maintain the location of all your dribbles, which should always be directly beneath you.

10. **down on left knee – full spider dribble** – If you had no problems with the full spider dribble down on the right knee, then this will be easy for you because the hand movements are comparable. This drill combines the two down on left knee ½ spider dribbles (drills #5 and #7) to form a full spider. Simply alternate each hand from the front of each leg to behind each leg so both hands will be moving simultaneously. For best results, try to dribble the ball in the same place every time to avoid having to adjust your hands continually.

11. **sitting – ½ spider dribble – right side** – You may find the sitting spiders to be the most successful because you can see the ball better (the ball is right in front of you the whole time). This ½ spider drill is comfortable for your body, compared to the other spider exercises, since you are sitting with your legs out and the knees bent upward. Try to be consistent and bounce the ball directly between your bended knees because centering every dribble will help when you progress to the full sitting spider. The left hand always remains on top (in front) and the right hand will alternate back and forth around your right leg from the top to beneath. You must use the fingertips exclusively on <u>every</u> dribble because this will help you develop a quick right hand to increase the speed of the drill. Also keep your legs steady throughout the exercise and do not spread them too wide.

IV. Intermediate Dribbling

12. **sitting – ½ spider dribble – left side** -- Trade sides so you will now keep the right hand on top (in front) and the left hand will rotate back and forth around your left leg. If necessary, start out slowly and then work towards faster dribbling speeds because technique should be your first priority. You can certainly begin with higher dribbles, but eventually work toward quick low dribbles. The left hand needs to move very quickly each time you change hand positions from top to beneath and vice versa.

13. **sitting – full spider dribble** -- In this exercise you will clearly see why all the drills in this section are "spider" dribbles. Both hands will be moving very quickly and simultaneously, much like a spider. As in all the other full spiders, simply alternate each hand from in front of each leg (top) to behind each leg (beneath). If necessary, refer to drill #3 in this section to get the hand/dribble sequence. Try to move your hands back and forth around the legs without actually touching the legs. This is not an easy task, especially with your hands moving so rapidly. Furthermore, keep the ball dribbled in the middle (directly between your legs) as you did with the ½ sitting spiders. You will be amazed at the number of dribbles you can do in fifteen seconds using this full spider method.

IV. Intermediate Dribbling

E. Scissors – Dribble Through Drill

Undoubtedly this section will be a formidable task for you. Do you remember the between the legs dribbles in section A of Basic Dribbling and the Scissors – Pass Through Drills in section E of Intermediate Ball Handling? All of those drills formed the basis for this section. Here is a chance to show off your dribbling skills, especially in the later drills in the section. The first five drills, which are all completed in place, need to be performed for at least fifteen seconds. All of the walking exercises (#6-#11) should be completed for thirty seconds, or two court lengths if you are on a basketball court. This section combines hand quickness, technique, and coordination, but it will take time and patience to perfect all of the drills. Most of the exercises entail longer explanations because they have very specific actions that need to be described.

Note: With the exception of the first four drills, all the leg movements are identical in the reversal mode; it is just the direction of the ball going through your legs that changes. For example, if the first dribble is supposed to go between the legs from behind your right leg to in front of the left leg, change in the reversal mode so the first dribble moves from in front of the right leg to behind the left leg. Likewise, if the second dribble is supposed to go between the legs from behind your left leg to in front of the right leg, change in the reversal mode so the second dribble moves from in front of the left leg to behind the right leg.

1. **between legs with right hand – right foot in front** -- The first four between the legs exercises are similar to some of the Basic Dribbling drills (part II) and are a good introduction to the rest of this section. It is vital for you to learn these four stationary drills even though they may seem very elementary for some of you. Every dribble in this exercise is performed by <u>only</u> the right hand; keep the left hand out of the way. Begin with your feet shoulder width apart and then place the right foot forward about a foot. Make sure you are standing upright with a slight bend in your knees. Start the ball from the left side of the front of your body with the right hand and dribble the ball between your legs so it hits the floor directly under your butt. The ball should bounce up to meet your right hand, which you have just quickly swung around the right leg behind you. Next, dribble the ball back through your legs so it bounces between the legs again and meets your right hand, which you have rotated back around the right leg to the front where you began. Continue dribbling the ball knee to waist high back and forth between your legs and eventually complete the drill without looking at the ball.

IV. Intermediate Dribbling 91

2. **between legs with left hand – left foot in front** – Again, bend the knees slightly and put your feet shoulder width apart, but now place the left foot forward about a foot. In this drill, all the dribbles will be done with <u>only</u> the left hand. Begin the ball from the right side of the front of your body with the left hand. Dribble the ball through your legs so it hits the floor directly beneath you and bounces up to your left hand, which you have quickly rotated around the left leg. Next, dribble the ball back through your legs so it bounces up to your left hand, which you have swung back around the left leg. Continue this dribbling process using fingertip control with the left hand. It is important to perform knee to waist high dribbles to give you enough time to move the left hand back and forth around the left leg.

3. **between legs with right hand – left foot in front** – The next two stationary drills are necessary in order to do the one hand walking dribbling exercises later in this section (drills #8 and #9). You will find there is a difference between these drills and the first two; these are much tougher! The knees will need to be bent a little further down to make your body more flexible because of the positioning of your right hand during the drill. Place the left foot out and start the ball up front on your right side with the right hand which is used exclusively in this drill. Now dribble the ball diagonally through your legs from in front of the right leg to behind the left leg. As the ball is traveling between your legs, bring your right hand around the left leg in order to dribble the ball back through your legs. Continue moving your right hand back and forth around the left leg to dribble the ball, which involves some serious flexibility on your part. When your right hand is behind the left leg, you will use somewhat of a backhand technique because of the angle of your right arm. If you are having problems with this exercise, one suggestion is to execute the dribbles in sets of two. For example, dribble the ball through your legs to the back, dribble it back through to the front, and then catch the ball so you can start another two dribble set. Keep doing these two dribble sets until you are able to dribble the ball continuously without any pauses.

4. **between legs with left hand – right foot in front** – As in the last drill, it may be best to begin this exercise with two dribble sets. Place the right foot out and start the ball up front on your left side with the left hand. The left hand will be utilized the whole time; keep your right hand out of the way. Begin the ball on the left side and dribble it diagonally through your legs from in front of the left leg to behind the right leg. Bring your left hand around the right leg in order to dribble the ball back through your legs. Continue rotating your left hand back and forth quickly around the right leg. You will need to use the backhand method that was mentioned in the last drill when your left

hand is behind the right leg. Try not to let the ball hit any part of your legs because it will only slow you down when you perform this type of dribble during the walking drills. As pointed out before, start out with two dribble sets to get a feel for the exercise. As you progress, see how many consecutive left hand dribbles you can achieve.

5. **shuffling feet – in place with both hands (reverse)** -- It is time to start the main portion of this section and to show you all about the "scissors" dribble. The ball is dribbled through the legs at the same time your legs are moving (shuffling). For this exercise, your legs will need to be shuffled up and back very quickly, like a pair of scissors cutting. Begin with one foot out in front of the other and do the basic between the legs dribble (part II, section A). After the ball goes through the legs, shuffle your feet in place by switching their positions. Continue dribbling the ball back and forth in a straight line between your legs while constantly shuffling your feet up and back. Your feet will exchange positions each time the ball is dribbled through

the legs. You need to bend straight down to stay balanced instead of hunching your back. Use short shuffles up and back compared to long strides, which will slow you down and keep you off balance. Since your body is low, each dribble also has to be low to make it through your legs. Start out slowly and work your way up to faster speeds to move your feet like a pair of scissors.

6. **walking with both hands (reverse)** -- You have probably seen the walking scissors drill performed by other players because it is a very common exercise. You are going to put the last drill into a walking mode, still staying balanced with a slight bend in your knees. Begin walking in a normal fashion while dribbling the ball back and forth between your legs from one hand to the other. A between the legs dribble must be performed with each step you take. It is a good idea to start the drill out slowly, taking one or two steps and then starting up again so you can coordinate the ball and leg movements. It is permissible to look at the ball in the beginning, but try to keep your head up as though you are in a game situation. When you become proficient with this walking scissors, try performing the drill while skipping. You will find that skipping while using this dribbling method will require some agility on your part.

IV. Intermediate Dribbling 93

7. **walking backwards with both hands (reverse)** – This drill is not much different from the walking forward scissors in the last exercise. Simply dribble the ball back and forth between your legs while walking backwards. The between the leg dribbles will go directly from one side to the other; take your steps <u>straight back</u> and not off towards the side. Keep in mind that your legs can only move backwards as fast as the ball is traveling between them. Look behind you before you begin to have an idea how much room you have and if anything is in your path.

8. **walking with right hand (reverse)** – Combine the two earlier right hand dribble drills in this section (#1 and #3) to incorporate them into a walking dribble using the scissors format. First, step forward with your right foot and dribble the ball between your legs from behind the right leg up to the left side. As the ball is passing in front of the left leg, quickly bring the right hand over to the left side and step forward with the left leg at the same time. Next, dribble the ball back through your legs to the right side with the right hand by using the backhand technique you learned in drill #3 of this section. Just after the ball passes by your right leg, bring the right hand back around to the front and step forward with the right leg. Once the ball is back over on your right side, take the ball behind the right leg again and repeat the process. These two procedures just mentioned happen quickly and only describe two steps forward. It is   imperative to move the right hand rapidly back and forth across your body to keep up with your walking pace. To get a feel for all the hand and leg movements, start out with only two dribbles and two steps (as just explained). When you complete the two dribble set, stop the ball and try another set. Keep doing these two dribble sets until you can continuously walk forward down the court while dribbling between your legs with only the right hand. Please keep in mind that this is a difficult dribble sequence to execute.

9. **walking with left hand (reverse)** – This walking dribble drill with only the left hand also requires some synchronizing of the ball, hand, and legs. To begin, step forward with the left foot and dribble the ball between your legs from behind the left leg up to the right side (as in drill #2). As the ball is passing in front of the right leg, quickly move the left hand over to the right side and step forward with the right leg at the same time. Next, bounce the ball back through your legs to the left side with the left hand by using the backhand technique you learned in drill #4. When the ball is back on your left side, take the ball behind the left leg again to start everything over. Use two dribbles sets as explained in the last exercise if you are struggling with all the hand and leg movements. These two dribble sets will help you acquire the basics before moving any further and possibly becoming frustrated. As you learn to walk forward continuously while dribbling between your legs, try doing the entire drill without looking down at the ball and your feet. These moving between the legs dribbles with one hand will take some time and patience on your part because clearly they are difficult drills.

94 IV. Intermediate Dribbling

10. **walking with both hands – low dribbles (reverse)** -- Exercise #6 was a walking drill with only one dribble going between your legs each time. In this exercise you will dribble the ball about four times between the legs with each step you take and the bounces will be considerably lower. While you were standing almost completely upright in the last four exercises, this drill forces you to bend down low because of the short dribbles you will be executing. Of course, this is a slower moving drill as far as moving forward, because the ball is dribbled more times back and forth between the legs. You can consider yourself a "master of the scissors" if you can complete this entire drill without looking at the ball.

11. **walking backwards with both hands – low dribbles (reverse)** -- Combine exercises #7 and #10 in order to perform low dribbles while moving backwards. Dribble the ball about four times between your legs with each step you take backwards, and remember that both hands are involved in this exercise. Keep dribbling the ball back and forth (very low) between the legs, taking a step straight back once the ball passes through your legs each time.

IV. Intermediate Dribbling

F. Moving Dribbling Drills

Without a doubt, you will find these practical moving dribbling drills useful for game situations. This is the first section in which all the drills include movement instead of the usual stationary position. This section also contains some common moves such as the crossover dribble, the spin dribble, and the between the legs dribble. Practice these dribbling drills to the point at which you can make them automatically. Most of your moves are dictated by the action of your opponent. Every situation is different; know when to use the proper dribble. Quick dribbling maneuvers are great for shaking your defender and driving to the basket. The closer your move is to the defender, the less time they have to react. Also, vary your moves to keep opponents guessing. Using the same dribble repeatedly gives defenders an advantage because they can anticipate your actions. Do not be predictable!

Learn to perform correctly all these moving dribbles with each hand. In fact, use your weak hand as much as possible to develop your overall dribbling abilities. Dribbling with your head up and developing a quick change of direction while dribbling are two concepts that are highlighted. Do not forget: low dribbles for quick moves and waist high dribbles for speed. The control and speed dribbles should be mastered before you move on to the more difficult moving dribbles. To simulate game conditions, use stationary objects such as cones or chairs as imaginary defenders. If necessary, you may also use specific spots on the court (like lines) as pretend defenders to complete the moves. Read the descriptions carefully to find the suggested goal for each moving dribble.

Note: A section on moving dribbling drills cannot be discussed without mentioning the "**triple threat position.**" From this stance three actions can be accomplished: you can

dribble (drive), shoot, or pass. This position keeps defenders guessing because they do not know what you are going to do. A balanced stance with your feet a little more than shoulder width apart is required. The knees are slightly bent and your head is up to see what is happening around you. Keep the ball at waist level with a hand on each side with the intention of performing one of the three actions. Of course you will need to face the basket and, if necessary, use jab steps to gain space. These quick steps are made with the non-pivot foot as a way to "back off" your opponent to allow you extra room to dribble, shoot, or pass. The triple threat position is a fundamental part of basketball and a maneuver that every player should learn to perform.

1. **control dribble** -- This is considered the basic dribble and the most common one used in basketball. Each bounce is done under "control," thus the name. To execute the dribble, it is important to use the basic dribbling techniques you learned in part II: a relaxed hand, fingertip control, a flexible wrist, and the head up to help you see the whole court. Keep your knees bent to maintain good balance for low dribbling and to allow you to make quick moves. Dribble the ball low (knee to waist high) and close to

IV. Intermediate Dribbling

the body (near the back foot) for better control. As a means of protection, dribble the ball with the hand that is away from your opponent. Shield the ball with the opposite arm to prevent its being stolen. During games, use this dribble when you have a purpose, not for the sake of just bouncing the ball. Also, do not pick up your dribble unnecessarily. This gives the defense a major advantage because they can quickly apply pressure and double-team. To feel comfortable, start walking to develop a good feel for the dribble; then gradually increase to a jogging speed. Your goal is to dribble down the court and back at least two times while focusing on the fundamentals of the control dribble. The best practice is to dribble in a zig-zag pattern around stationary objects (a good introduction to the crossover dribble). When employing this zig-zag pattern, dribble with the hand in the direction you are moving.

2. **speed dribble** -- This is a great dribble for the fast break and getting the ball quickly down the court. The most important aspect of this dribble is to bounce the ball out in front of your body. You can do this by shifting your hand towards the back of the ball to keep it out in front. You will notice the faster you are dribbling the further the ball must be pushed ahead. Because your body is in more of an upright position, you must perform waist high dribbles. As in all moving dribbling drills, keep your head up to locate teammates and evade defenders. It is crucial to keep the ball under control so you can quickly stop when necessary. Your goal is to dribble down the court as fast as you can with the right hand and then back with the left hand (also work both hands by alternating hands with every other dribble). As a way to monitor your progress and speed, have somebody time your dribbling up and down the court, and try to improve your speed each time (especially with your weak hand).

3. **hesitation dribble** – The hesitation dribble is a great change of pace dribble and one that is very deceptive. This dribble is difficult to defend and it keeps your opponents off balance because they cannot react fast enough. As you can tell from the title, the dribble involves a hesitation (pause) when you make a slow to fast movement to drive by or around your opponent. This slow to fast action must be quick and explosive. To begin the move, perform a control or speed dribble. Just when you slow down, lift your shoulders, give a good head fake, and then quickly "blow" by your opponent using a speed dribble. Like the goal for the speed dribble, move the ball down the court with the right hand and then back with the left. Perform the hesitation dribble at least two times with each trip down the court. Of course you will use waist high dribbles for the speed portion of this dribble. It is important to learn to use this dribble effectively with both right and left hands.

IV. Intermediate Dribbling 97

4. **retreat (backward) dribble** -- Dribbling does not always involve moving forward, thus the need for the retreat dribble. This is a great dribble to use against zone defenses and when you are being pressed or double-teamed. It allows you to get out of situations when you are unable to pass or dribble forward. Obviously this dribble is not as fast as the other moving dribbles because your body is going in reverse. To retreat, shuffle backward by performing step-slide movements (much like defensive slides). This is accomplished by stepping with the back foot and then sliding (dragging) the other one. Keep your head up to see the entire court and also maintain good balance allowing you to be ready to make a move or change directions quickly. When executing the dribble, use the hand farthest from your defender. Protect the ball by staying low and shielding it with your opposite arm. Dribble backward to half court with the right hand; switch hands and dribble the rest of the way with the left hand (total of one court length).

5. **crossover dribble** -- It is safe to say that the crossover dribble is one of the most effective maneuvers in basketball. This is a good move to drive past your defender because you can change directions so quickly. This quick and deceptive dribble is difficult to defend (even when you are being closely guarded). More room and agility are required for this dribble compared to the previous stationary crossover drills in Basic Dribbling (section A). Begin by dribbling the ball with your right hand and then slide the hand from on top of the ball to the outside. Attempt to keep your right hand from coming under the ball to prevent "carrying" the ball. Next, quickly dribble (push) the ball across the front of your body. You must cross the ball close to your body and very low to the floor as it travels over to the left side. This will help you keep the ball away from your opponent and make it almost impossible to steal. Do not forget to bring the left hand down low to receive the ball because each dribble should bounce no higher than a foot off the floor. To maintain good balance, you will need to plant the right foot and then quickly shift your weight from right to left as you perform the crossover dribble. As the ball is coming across your body, make a hard step with the left foot and explode down the court with your left hand. Once you have developed a good crossover move, pretend you are in a game situation and practice driving past your opponent. Dribble the ball down the court and back in a zig-zag pattern and execute a crossover dribble in front of each cone (or other object). Dribbling in this zig-zag pattern forces you to develop the crossover with each hand. Try to complete at least six crossover dribbles for each court length (total of twelve dribbles).

IV. Intermediate Dribbling

6. **half-cross dribble** -- This is a great complement to the crossover you just learned. The difference between the two dribbles is that the ball does not come all the way across the body and only one hand is used for this move. As you are dribbling the ball with the right hand, begin a crossover dribble by sliding your hand from on top of the ball to the outside. As soon as you release it, quickly move your right hand around the ball to the other side and perform a backhand dribble so it comes back to where you started. This quick hand movement is essential to perform the move correctly. Try to keep the ball as low as you can to prevent its being stolen. To keep your defender off balance, give a good body fake by quickly shifting your weight from left to right, make a hard step with the right foot, and then explode down the court. This dribble should sound familiar because it is exactly like the one-hand V dribbles in Basic Dribbling. The goal for this drill and the next one is to dribble down the court and back while executing the half-cross dribble at least four times for each court length. Dribble in a straight line instead of the zig-zag pattern and make quick moves each time.

7. **double-cross dribble** -- The double-cross is a counterpart to the basic crossover and the half-cross dribbles. Complete a crossover from the right hand to the left and then immediately bring the ball back across your body from the left hand to the right. These consecutive crossover dribbles have to be performed quickly for this move to be effective. Just like the other two crossover dribbles, you must cross the ball close to your body and very low to the floor. You will need to shift your weight quickly from right to left and then from left to right. This body movement is a critical component and must occur under control to keep yourself balanced. Once the second dribble comes back across your body, make a hard step with the right foot and explode down the court.

IV. Intermediate Dribbling 99

8. **spin dribble** -- Like the crossover dribble, the spin dribble is another excellent change of direction move. This dribble provides a good way to get around a defender who is closely guarding you. To start this dribble, plant the foot opposite your dribbling hand and then pivot (swing) your body and quickly bring (pull) the ball around to complete the move. You will need to change dribbling hands once the spin dribble is executed to advance the ball and keep it away from your defender. Throughout the dribble, maintain a low and balanced stance and protect the ball by keeping it close to your body (this also helps for better ball control). In the beginning, try to complete the spin dribble at slower speeds and then move toward faster dribbles. The chief benefit of this move is that the dribble keeps the ball from changing hands in front of your defender. The major disadvantage of the spin dribble is that you briefly lose sight of your teammates and defenders (possible double-team). Because this is mostly a change of direction dribble, your best practice is to use the zig-zag pattern. Try to complete two court lengths and at least six spin dribbles with each trip down the court.

9. **between the legs dribble** – This is the moving portion of the between the legs dribble you performed in section A of Basic Dribbling; of course, this dribble is more difficult. It is a very quick dribble and another effective change of direction dribble. It is

helpful to start slowly to develop the proper footwork. To make this move successfully, your body and the ball must remain low. You have the option of dribbling the ball from front to back or from back to front. For the front to back dribble, step forward with the leg opposite the dribbling hand and push the ball through your legs to the other hand (in back). It is best to use the front to back between the legs dribble when you are closely guarded because you do not expose the ball to your opponent. The back to front dribble starts by stepping forward with the same leg as the dribbling hand. At the same time, quickly bring the ball behind the leg, pushing it between your legs to the other hand (in front). Complete two court lengths and at least six between the leg dribbles with each trip down the court (using the zig-zag pattern).

IV. Intermediate Dribbling

10. **behind the back dribble** – The behind the back dribble is one of the most difficult moving dribbles and must be executed carefully because of the great possibility for error. This is one of the best change of direction dribbles that you can utilize; learn to use this as a weapon when you really need it. This dribble is similar to some of the behind the body dribbles you performed in section C of this Intermediate Dribbling part. If you were able successfully to complete behind the back dribbles while either stationary or walking, you are ready to start running. As you recall from the earlier section, place your right hand on the front of the ball and pull it behind your back so it bounces behind the left foot and up to your left hand. It is essential to extend your right hand and follow through to help push the ball over to the left side. You must push the ball at an angle to help it come around your body to meet the other hand in order to continue dribbling. It is important to dribble the ball close to your body, to

stay balanced, and to keep your head up to see the entire court. The best suggestion is to start off jogging slowly and work your way up to faster speeds. Keep in mind that the ball <u>does not</u> have to go behind your back with every step you take. If you are running fast, there is no way that you could dribble behind your back with every step; establish a rhythm and dribble behind your back every few steps for two court lengths. As a good test, combine this move with the speed dribble and execute behind the back dribbles at full speed. You may also complete this drill using the zig-zag pattern to work on sharp changes of direction. Once you become an expert, perform this behind the back dribble while bouncing the ball all the way over to the same side instead of just to the other side. This will require you to pull the ball around your body where you started the dribble.

IV. Intermediate Dribbling 101

G. Wall Dribbling

Dribbling against a wall will provide variety instead of always bouncing the ball on the floor. These drills will help increase your fingertip control, hand quickness, and also strengthen the wrists and hands. Although it may be tempting, try not to look at the ball; you need to develop a "feel" for where the ball is at all times. One of the chief fundamentals of wall dribbling is the ability to maintain control of the ball at all times (using the fingertips). All of the dribbles in this section should be four inches or less (not bouncing far away from the wall). At least fifteen seconds for each drill should be completed. Almost any hard surface, such as a wall made out of tile, brick, or cinder block will work. Wall dribbling may seem difficult at first, but it is easy to accomplish after a few times. Stick with it!

1. **right hand** -- Dribble the ball against the wall with your right hand at face level. Your right arm should be in an "L" shape as you are dribbling. You will need to place your hand a little under the ball so the ball does not start to drift down the wall. You do not have to stand right up against the wall; about two feet away should be sufficient. The ball should bounce just a few inches off the wall for each dribble.

2. **left hand** -- Dribble the ball against the wall with your left hand at face level (left arm in an "L" shape). Try to keep the ball bouncing in the same spot on the wall each time to develop a smooth dribble rhythm. Do not let the ball drift because it is extremely difficult to regain control once it begins to change positions.

3. **alternating with both hands** -- Still standing about two feet away from the wall, dribble the ball directly in front of your face, alternating hands with each dribble. After completing the first two exercises, you will be able to dribble the ball rapidly by using both hands. Be sure to keep your hands positioned slightly under the ball to prevent it from dropping.

4. **backwards with right hand** -- Begin with your back a few inches from the wall so you are facing outward. Dribble the ball just over your right shoulder against the wall with your right hand. As you can tell, it is important to dribble a little under the ball to keep it going consistently. The ball should always be dribbled at the same spot on the wall instead of moving all over the place. Since this is a difficult exercise, try a few bounces off the wall at first to get the "hang" of it; then do it for the full fifteen seconds. You will not be able to dribble as fast in this position.

IV. Intermediate Dribbling

5. **backwards with left hand** -- Continue standing and facing outward with your back a few inches from the wall. Dribble the ball this time with your left hand just over your left shoulder. Because of your positioning and the location in which the ball is bouncing off the wall, keep your head looking forward.

6. **backwards alternating with both hands** -- In the last two drills, the ball was dribbled off the wall over your shoulder, but now it will be bouncing higher on the wall. Remain with your back to the wall and standing upright. With your hands directly over your head, drop your palms down and dribble the ball against the wall, alternating dribbles between each hand. Remember the importance of hitting the ball low with your fingertips to keep it going so it does not hit you on top of the head. This exercise is more difficult than you may think.

7. **backwards with right hand down at side** -- With your back almost against the wall, place your right hand down to your right side and dribble the ball against the wall (at waist level). You will have to bend your wrist considerably and come almost beneath the ball to keep it from falling. Start with a few practice bounces off the wall before performing continuous dribbles. Once you get the ball moving, you will be able to perform numerous dribbles using this technique. This is not a drill that you will be able to do the first time, but keep practicing!

8. **backwards with left hand down at side** -- Repeat the same procedures as in the last exercise, but now use your left hand only (at waist level). Position your left arm down your left side and dribble the ball against the wall. The left arm should be straight or bent slightly allowing you to bend the wrist and come from beneath to dribble the ball.

9. **backwards alternating with both hands down** -- While you are still facing outward, step out from the wall about two feet. While standing upright, put both hands behind your back (at waist level) and dribble the ball against the wall, alternating hands with each dribble. There is no way that you will be able to see the ball; you will have to do the whole exercise just by feel. This is another tough exercise!

IV. Intermediate Dribbling 103

10. **right hand walking (reverse directions)** -- Begin standing sideways with the right side of your body about two feet away from the wall. Now dribble the ball against the wall at shoulder height with the right hand. Start walking along the wall, then after fifteen seconds, reverse directions and walk backwards for fifteen more seconds, still dribbling with just the right hand. You do not have to walk fast; a steady pace is sufficient.

11. **left hand walking (reverse directions)** -- Now you can turn the other way and have your left side two feet away from the wall. Start walking along the wall, dribbling with the left hand at shoulder height and then reverse directions by walking backwards. Dribble against the wall for at least fifteen seconds in each direction.

12. **alternating with both hands walking (reverse directions)** -- Start by turning your body so you are looking straight at the wall at least a foot away. Dribble the ball against the wall at face level, alternating dribbles with each hand. As you begin dribbling, slowly shuffle along the wall, <u>never</u> crossing your feet at any time (like a defensive slide). Shuffle down the wall for fifteen seconds; then reverse directions and shuffle back the other way for fifteen more seconds.

Conclusion of Part IV -- A wide variety of dribbling drills were included in this part, which can be both beneficial and fun, because many of the drills provided an excellent method for you to demonstrate your dribbling talents. Intermediate Dribbling incorporated many of the fundamentals that you had already learned to enable you to increase your skill level. Previously, all the dribbling drills had been stationary, but this part introduced some moving dribbles that you will find helpful during games. Progression was a term mentioned earlier in the book to describe the different levels (parts) you must achieve to complete *Just A Basketball*. You just finished the second level of dribbling, and now it is time to advance your skills even further and jump into Advanced Ball Handling.

V. Advanced Ball Handling

A. Flip Drills

These flip drills will definitely add creativity to your ball handling workout. They will also be a good start for improving your coordination before getting into the actual coordination exercises in the next section. All of these exercises may involve a considerable amount of determination and patience because you may have difficulty executing the drills right away. This section contains some of the more difficult drills in the book. You will be able to do all the drills while remaining in a stationary position. Complete a minimum of ten flips for each drill, unless otherwise indicated.

1. **flip-flop with right hand** -- Begin with your right hand holding the ball in front of you at waist level. Flip the ball up so it rises above your head. As the ball begins to fall, simply spread your fingers out and turn your hand over with the palm facing down. Now let the ball "flop" on the back of your hand. Instead of grabbing the ball as you usually would, catch the ball on the back of your right hand. This is not as simple as it sounds, but you will be successful after a few tries. Of course, the higher the ball is flipped, the more difficult it will be to catch it on the back of your hand. It is necessary to spread your fingers, pointing them up a bit to give the ball a good "landing pad".

2. **flip-flop with left hand** -- Now you are going to attempt the flip-flop using the left hand. It may be best to start out using a low flip and working your way up to flips above your head. Once the ball hits the back of the left hand, it should almost stop. Try not to let the ball roll around after it makes contact with your hand. Executing ten of these in a row without the ball falling off your hand is a great accomplishment.

V. Advanced Ball Handling

3. **flip-flop with right hand and clap** -- Let's now add some quickness to the flip-flop drill. After you have flipped the ball up with the right hand, clap your hands once before catching the ball on the back of the right hand. Once you are able to do the exercise with one clap, add another clap to improve your quickness even further. In fact, see how many claps you can do during a single flip-flop.

4. **flip-flop with left hand and clap** -- Now complete the flip-flop using the left hand and including a clap (or two). Flip the ball a little higher the first few times so you are able to complete a single clap. Ultimately the ball should not be flipped any higher than the top of your head. The lower you can flip the ball, clap, and still catch the ball on the back of your hand, the quicker your hands will become.

5. **flop-flop with both hands back and forth** -- Instead of using the normal flip to toss the ball up, only use the back of your hands the entire drill (a flop-flop). Toss the ball up on the back of the right hand and then catch it on the back of the left hand. Continue "flopping" the ball back and forth from hand to hand. Use some very high tosses and also practice some low ones. After successfully completing the first four drills in this section, the flop-flop should not be a problem for you.

6. **hand roll – right hand to left hand** -- The hand roll is not an easy drill initially but you can learn to do it effectively after some practice. This drill involves good hand coordination and quick wrist movements. With the ball in your right hand, flip the ball up an inch or two so it moves to the left. You <u>must</u> flip the ball with some spin to give it the momentum to roll from the right hand to the left hand. After you have flipped the ball, quickly turn your right hand over (flat) with the palm now facing down. As you are turning the right hand over, bring the left hand next to it, also with the palm facing down. Let the ball roll over the top of the right hand and then across the left hand, almost like a bridge. After the ball rolls over and then off the left hand, quickly move the hand around the outside of the ball to catch it (with the left palm now facing up). Once you catch the ball in the left hand, place it back in the right hand for another repetition. This whole sequence should take one to two seconds; that is why this drill requires quick wrist movements and excellent hand coordination. Try to successfully complete ten good hand rolls before moving to the next exercise. If you are having difficulties with the hand roll, you may find it easier to break the drill down into sections before putting all the steps together.

V. Advanced Ball Handling

7. **hand roll – left hand to right hand** – If you were able to do the last drill successfully, then you will have no problem with the hand roll from left to right. Begin by flipping the ball up an inch or two with the left hand so it moves (spins) to the right. As soon as you release the ball, quickly turn your left hand over flat so the ball rolls across the back of the hand. At the same time, bring your right hand over with the palm also facing down allowing the ball to roll across both hands. When the ball rolls off the right hand, quickly move the hand around the outside of the ball to catch it after it falls. After catching the ball in your right hand, begin another hand roll by starting the ball back in the left hand again. Attempt to finish ten consecutive hand rolls.

8. **hand roll – continuous** – Let's combine the last two hand rolls to make the ball go from one side to the other and then back across. Flip the ball up with your right hand making it move (spin) to the left. Next, turn the right hand over and bring the left hand across (palm down) to make a bridge for the ball to roll over. Move your left hand quickly around the ball to catch it after it rolls off the left hand. Once you have caught the ball in the left hand, flip (spin) the ball back to the right and build the bridge with both hands again for the ball to roll across. When the ball falls off the right hand, bring the right hand around the outside of the ball to catch it as you did in the last exercise. Perform the continuous hand roll without stopping for a total of twenty rolls (ten each direction). This hand roll is a great drill to display your abilities once you have completely mastered it.

9. **flip ball behind back over opposite shoulder – each side** – These next two drills will demonstrate a bit of trickery. Begin with the ball in your right hand and then bring the ball along your right side so the right hand is underneath it. Now take the ball behind your back and flip it up so the ball comes over your left shoulder. When the ball makes it over the shoulder, catch it with only the left hand and then place the ball back in your right hand to repeat the drill. Try to keep your body as straight as you can but it may be necessary to lean a little. Make sure you flip the ball <u>over</u> your left shoulder and not along the side of the shoulder. Complete the required ten flips with the right hand before switching to the other side. The same procedures also occur on the left side. Take the ball along your left side with the left hand and then behind your back in order to flip the ball over your right shoulder catching it with only the right hand. Try to achieve ten consecutive flips using the left hand.

V. Advanced Ball Handling

10. **flip behind back over opposite shoulder – continuous** -- There was a reason for catching the ball with only one hand (the opposite hand) in the last drill. The one hand catch was done in order to make continuous behind the back flips in this exercise. Begin by flipping the ball behind your back with the right hand over your left shoulder and catch the ball with only the left hand. Once you catch the ball, bring it behind your back with the left hand and flip it over your right shoulder catching the ball with only the right hand, at the point where the drill began. Continue flipping the ball behind your back over opposite shoulders for a total of ten times (five for each shoulder). Do not flip the ball far from your body to avoid an excessive reach. Try to remain stationary the entire time.

11. **flip ball behind back over same shoulder – each side** -- This exercise is similar to the two previous drills, but the ball is now going to be flipped behind your back over the same shoulder instead of the opposite shoulder. Start by holding the ball in your right hand with the fingers pointed forward. Turn your right hand and wrist so the fingers are now pointing inward and your right elbow is pushed out. Take the ball along your right side and just after it passes the right hip, flip it up and over your right shoulder. When the ball comes over the right shoulder, catch it in your left hand and then place the ball back in your right hand to repeat the drill. The flip over your shoulder requires a lot of wrist action to get the ball high enough and at the proper

angle. This is not a drill that you will do correctly the first time; give it a few tries. After you have completed the right side, switch to the other side flipping the ball over the left shoulder with the left hand. For this flip, be sure to catch the ball with only the right hand and then put the ball back in your left hand to complete another flip. Try to do ten consecutive same shoulder flips on each side.

12. **flip ball behind back over same shoulder – continuous** -- For this drill you are going to continue these opposite hand catches to help the drill have a smooth transition from one side to the other. Start on the right side and flip the ball behind your back over the right shoulder with the right hand. When the ball comes over your shoulder, catch it in the left hand and take it to the left side. Next, flip the ball over the left shoulder with the left hand and catching it in the right hand. Continue alternating shoulders and flipping the ball five times on each side for a total of ten flips.

13. **ball in right hand, under left arm, flip behind head over right shoulder** -- This drill has a different twist from the last four flip drills. With the ball in your right hand, take it under the left arm (arm pit area) and wrap it around your left side. Flip the ball so it goes behind the upper part of your back, passes behind the head, and comes over the right shoulder. The ball must travel <u>behind</u> your head and not over the head. When the ball comes over your right shoulder, catch it with the right hand. This flip and catch with the right hand must be quick in order to execute the drill successfully. The left hand never touches the ball because the flip and the catch are done with the right hand only. This is not an easy exercise; give yourself some space to allow for any problems you might encounter the first few times. Completing ten flips in a row without any errors will be a good challenge for you.

14. **ball in left hand, under right arm, flip behind head over left shoulder** -- Now put the ball in your left hand and do just the opposite of the last exercise. Take the ball under the right arm with the left hand and flip (wrap) it around the right side of your

body. The ball should travel behind the upper part of your back, behind the head, and over the left shoulder. Catch the ball in the left hand when it comes over the left shoulder. Once you catch the ball, take it under the right arm again for another flip. Since the ball travels behind the head, it will be important to make a good flip because you will be unable to see the ball until it comes over the left shoulder.

15. **ball in right hand, through legs, flip over left shoulder** -- Begin the drill with your feet spread far apart and the ball in the right hand. Take the ball through your legs to the left side of the buttocks and flip it over your left shoulder. You need to reach really far back between your legs to get a good flip. If you do not, the ball will hit you in the butt or it will come along your left side and not over the shoulder as it should. Catch the ball with <u>both</u> hands when it comes over your left shoulder. Going through the legs ten times in a row to flip the ball will certainly give you a workout. Try it and see!

V. Advanced Ball Handling 109

16. **ball in left hand, through legs, flip over right shoulder** -- Switch the ball over to the left hand to begin this drill. Bring the ball between your legs with the left hand and flip the ball so it comes over your right shoulder. Remember to reach really far back through your legs to flip the ball. You will need to try to keep your body balanced (square the shoulders) so you are not twisted to the right. Also, flip the ball high enough so it will come over the right shoulder to avoid lowering it. Catch the ball with <u>both</u> hands when it comes over your right shoulder.

17. **ball through legs, flip over shoulder – continuous** -- You probably figured that this would be the next drill, a combination of the last two. With the legs spread wide, take the ball through your legs with the right hand and flip it over the left shoulder. When you catch the ball in front (with both hands), bring the ball back through your legs, but this time with the left hand, and flip it over the right shoulder. Catch the ball in front with both hands again to repeat the drill. Continue alternating the flips over each shoulder for a total of ten, five on each side. Be sure that the ball is flipped <u>over</u> the shoulders and not along the sides of your body.

18. **ball behind back, switch hands – continuous** -- This drill will require quickness, putting to use your ability to flip the ball. To start the exercise, hold the ball in your

right hand behind your back at waist level and put the left hand on your left front pocket. Now flip the ball up a few inches behind your back. As soon as you release the ball, switch your hands so the left hand comes behind your back to catch the ball at waist level and the right hand is moved to your right front pocket. Continue alternating your hands from behind the back to the front pockets. Flip the ball only two or three inches high, but remember that the lower the flip, the quicker your hands must be. Flip the ball straight up because the ball is not supposed to hit your back at any time. Your goal of ten flips is to be done quickly but smoothly.

19. **flip ball back and forth behind head** -- Here is another exercise in which the ball is flipped behind your body. This drill is slightly different from the fingertip drill behind your head in Basic Ball Handling (section B, drill #8). In that drill, the ball was tipped behind the neck only. This time, flip the ball from shoulder to shoulder behind your head using just the fingertips. You may bend your head down slightly but try to keep it still (looking straight ahead). Remember that the ball needs to be flipped <u>behind</u> the head, not over the head. Attempt twenty flips instead of ten.

V. Advanced Ball Handling

20. flip ball off chest from side to side – continuous – Start by holding the ball in your right hand out in front of you. The ball should be held about a foot away from your body at waist level. Flip the ball against the right side of your chest just under the shoulder. The ball needs to be flipped at an angle so the carom off your chest takes the ball to the other side to be caught with the left hand. Once you catch the ball in your left hand, flip it off the left side of your chest so it bounces at an angle and lands in your right hand. You are now at the same point at which you began. Continue flipping the ball off your chest so the ball moves from side to side. These flips <u>do not</u> have to be very hard, just powerful enough for the ball to bounce off your chest into the other hand. As you continue to get better with this drill, increase the speed of the ball to see how quickly you can finish the required ten flips.

V. Advanced Ball Handling 111

B. Coordination Drills

These drills will significantly help your coordination, also giving you more creativity in your workouts. Many of the drills involve throwing the ball up in the air, so be sure there is plenty of clearance above you. It is a good idea to visualize each drill after you read it before trying to do it "live." When you completely understand and can do the drills, five repetitions should be completed for each.

1. **throw ball over head, catch behind back** -- This is a great drill to start off the coordination section. With the ball at your waist, toss it over your head with both hands; reach behind your back and catch the ball at waist level. The ball needs to be caught with your hands reaching out from your back to avoid trapping the ball against your body. Once you catch the ball, bring it back around to the front for another repetition. Keep your feet planted the entire drill and hold your back as straight as you can. The first few tosses should go about a foot or two over your head, but as you progress the ball can be tossed much higher. Vary the heights of your tosses to give the drill variety. In fact, clap your hands a few times when the ball is in the air before you catch it behind the back. The more times you clap, the faster your hands must move behind your back to catch the ball. If you throw the ball up extremely high, then you may be forced to move around to catch the ball. This will give you time to position yourself under the descending ball.

2. **ball behind back, throw over head, catch in front** -- This drill should be no problem for you because it is just the opposite of the previous drill. Begin with the ball extended in both hands behind your back (at waist level). Using wrist and hand action, throw (flip) the ball (from behind you) over your head and catch it in front at waist level with both hands. Once you catch the ball, bring it around to the back to start again.

Throw the ball so it clears your head by about a foot, but begin increasing the height of your tosses once you can execute everything successfully. Some important items are to maintain a straight back, remain stationary, and keep your head straight throughout the drill. You do not have to turn your head to the side or look up because the ball <u>will</u> come over. Of course you may hit yourself on the head a few times before you get everything down pat. It is also helpful to bend your knees a little and push up as you are throwing the ball from behind your back to give it a boost.

V. Advanced Ball Handling

3. **throw ball over head, catch, then back to front – continuous** – You are going to combine the last two exercises to create this drill. In the two previous drills, you stopped the ball after one repetition and started the process again. Now the ball will travel continuously over your head from front to back and then back to front. A total of ten continuous flips should be completed (five in each direction). Remember to keep your head straight and your feet planted at all times. Use a lot of wrist action as you are tossing the ball back and forth over your head.

4. **throw ball over head, catch behind back with right hand** – It is time to increase the difficulty of these coordination drills. The next two drills are almost identical to drill #1 of this section but you will need a little more accuracy with your tosses and catches. Now when you toss the ball a foot or two over your head, reach behind your back and catch the ball at waist level with just the right hand. It may take you a few times before you are able to complete the exercise satisfactorily. Be sure not to trap the ball with the right hand against your back; reach your hand out. Use the fingertips to catch the ball, not the palm of your hand. Once the ball is caught, bring it back around to the front and repeat the process.

5. **throw ball over head, catch behind back with left hand** – This drill is like the last one, but when you throw the ball over your head, reach out behind your back to catch the ball with only the left hand. As you can tell, the outcome of the drill is determined by the accuracy of the toss, not the catch itself. An accurate toss makes it much easier to receive the ball because you are unable to see it after it has left your hands. Once you catch the ball, bring it back around to the front with the left hand to finish your repetitions.

6. **throw ball over head, catch between legs in back with both hands** – This drill and the next two will be extremely challenging, but they are really fun to do once you have mastered them. If you can perform these drills consistently, then you are well on your way to ball handling stardom! Begin by holding the ball at waist level in front of you with both hands, and position your feet a little more than shoulder width apart with the knees slightly bent. Next, toss the ball a foot or two over your head. As the ball is traveling in the air, quickly bend down and reach between your legs with both hands to catch the ball behind you. You must reach through the inside of your legs to

V. Advanced Ball Handling 113

catch the ball, not around the outside of the legs. The ball will probably hit your back or butt the first few times, but do not give up. The ball should be caught with the fingertips just as it passes by your butt. You must reach your hands as far back as you can through your legs to catch the ball. The importance of a good toss cannot be overemphasized because you have very little room for error. You may have to do the drill numerous times before you can finally put it all together. For a greater challenge, throw the ball up much higher so you will have to position your body perfectly to catch the ball between your legs.

7. **throw ball over head, catch between legs in back with right hand** -- If you thought it was difficult to catch the ball between your legs with both hands, try catching it with only one. Despite what you may think, it is possible! Throw the ball over your head (with the right hand only) and then reach between your legs to catch the ball behind you with just the right hand. To prevent the left hand from getting in the way, place it on your hip the entire drill. Catching the ball becomes much harder since you do not have the other hand to help if the toss is a little off.

8. **throw ball over head, catch between legs in back with left hand** -- The steps for this exercise are similar to the last drill, but now you are going to reach between your legs to catch the ball behind you with only the left hand. Of course, the ball will be thrown over your head with just the left hand. If necessary, put the right hand on your hip to keep it from getting in the way. Work hard on making an accurate toss and knowing where the ball is going to fall, because it is difficult to catch the ball with just the one hand.

9. **throw ball above head, catch between legs in front with right hand** -- Before, the ball was thrown over your head; now it is going to travel straight up and then drop straight down the front of your body. With your feet a little more than shoulder width apart, toss the ball straight up a foot or two above your head. As the ball starts to descend, bend straight down and reach the right hand behind the right leg and then between your legs to catch the ball in front. The ball should be caught with your right hand just below the knees. Once again, a good toss is crucial to doing the drill properly. The ball needs to be tossed up so it comes straight down the front of your body, because you will not be able to reach very far out with the right hand. Once you can do the exercise perfectly, toss the ball higher to make the drill more challenging for you.

V. Advanced Ball Handling

10. **throw ball above head, catch between legs in front with left hand** – If you had no problem with the last exercise, then this one should be a piece of cake. Throw the ball straight up above your head; and as the ball starts its downward flight, bend straight down and reach behind your left leg and then between your legs with the left hand to catch the ball in front. Remember that the ball must be tossed up so it drops straight down the front of your body.

11. **throw ball up, bounce in front, catch behind back** – These next three drills are very similar, but each one has a different twist. The drills require the ball to be thrown up high, so these exercises should be done outside or in a gym. Begin by throwing the ball high in the air (at least ten feet over your head) and let it bounce right in front of you. Just after the ball bounces above your head, step forward so the ball goes over your head and you can catch the ball behind your back with both hands at waist level. To make the drill challenging for you, vary the heights of the tosses.

12. **throw ball up, bounce behind back, catch in front** – This drill has the exact opposite movements of the previous one. Throw the ball high in the air again, but now let the ball bounce straight down behind your back. As the ball bounces above your head, step backwards so you can catch the ball in front of you with both hands at waist level. Timing the bounce with your step backwards determines the outcome of the drill. For variety, change the heights of the tosses. In fact, try tossing the ball up just a short distance, so it bounces just high enough that it barely clears your head. This low bounce will force you to get your timing down.

13. **throw ball up, bounce behind back, catch behind back** – This exercise will combine the last two drills. Throw the ball high up in the air and let it bounce behind your back. In drill #12 you stepped backward to catch the ball, but now remain stationary and catch the ball <u>behind</u> your back at waist level after it bounces. Be sure to toss the ball as straight as possible to avoid excessive movement in executing the drill correctly.

14. **sitting Indian style – throw ball over head, catch behind back** – This exercise is just like drill #1 in this section except you will be sitting Indian style. Simply toss the ball a foot or two over your head and catch it behind your back. The arms need to be extended outward behind your back since you are in a sitting position. Do not trap the ball against your back; catch the ball out from your body.

V. Advanced Ball Handling   115

15. **sitting Indian style – ball behind back, throw over head, catch in front** -- Now begin with the ball behind your back and throw (flip) it over your head, catching the ball directly in front of you. Do not look to see where the ball is when it comes over your head; let the ball come to you. Since you are sitting, it should be a little more difficult to flip the ball because you are unable to use the lower body. Use your upper body and hand strength to help flip the ball over because the toss is what makes this drill work.

16. **sitting Indian style – throw ball over head, catch, then back to front – continuous** -- Combine the last two drills for this continuous exercise. While sitting, toss the ball over your head and catch it behind your back. Instead of bringing the ball back around, flip the ball back over your head to the front to start another set of flips. Continue to flip the ball back and forth over your head ten consecutive times (five in each direction).

17. **sitting – crab throw over head, catch, then back over – continuous** -- This sitting crab throw is difficult because it requires very accurate tosses every time. Begin seated with your legs out and the knees bent. Reach your hands around and underneath each leg so you have the ball centered between your knees. Now using only your hands and wrists, toss the ball a foot or two over your head. As soon as you release the ball, quickly reach behind your back to catch it with both hands. Be sure to

extend the arms behind your back to catch the ball in order not to trap the ball against your body. Once you catch the ball, flip it back over your head (from behind) using wrist and hand action again. As the ball is traveling back over, quickly reach your hands back underneath the legs to catch the ball in the same position you started. This is where the exercise is difficult because the flip back over must be perfect in order to land directly between the knees where your hands are positioned. Do not look at the ball as it travels back and forth over your head; have confidence in your ability to make accurate tosses. Completing this drill without any errors will be an incredible feat. It will take some practice, but you can do it!

18. **ball around waist lying down – arched back (reverse)** -- Coordination and flexibility are two key ingredients for successful ball handling and this drill requires both. Start by lying flat on your back with the legs straight. Next, arch your back as high as you can so your feet and shoulders are the only body parts touching the ground. Then rotate the ball around your waist five times in each direction. Note that your butt has to be high enough off the ground so the ball can fit underneath. This is also a great exercise to stretch out your body, but do not hurt yourself.

V. Advanced Ball Handling

19. **teeter-totter – continuous** -- The teeter-totter requires much coordination and your whole body to be completely balanced throughout the drill. Position your body flat on the floor with the feet about two inches apart and your arms along each side. Next, place the ball on top of your feet (ankles) and then slowly lift them off the floor. Raising your feet will cause the ball to begin rolling down your legs and then up towards your chest. As the ball comes up the chest to your neck, lift your upper body off the floor allowing the ball to roll back towards your feet. Continue lifting your feet and upper body off the floor in a "teeter-totter" fashion so the ball keeps rolling up and down your body. Keeping the arms to your sides will act as buffers to guide the ball in case it starts to roll off the sides of your body. Start slowly to get all the motions down pat; then slightly increase your teeter-totter speed. Of course the higher you lift your feet and upper body, the faster the ball will travel. Notice that the ball should <u>roll</u> up and down the body and not bounce at any time. Your goal is to finish at least five complete teeter-totters (up and back), which will give your stomach muscles a good workout.

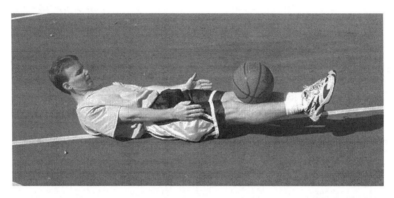

V. Advanced Ball Handling 117

C. Quickness Drills

Developing quickness is an essential part of ball handling and, of course, the game of basketball. The drills in this section have been specifically chosen to increase your quickness and to build more confidence in your ball handling abilities. Perform each drill at least ten times; but if you get discouraged, go to the next exercise and come back to the tough one at another time. Successfully completing some of the earlier drills in Intermediate Ball Handling, such as the Cradle Drills (section C) and the Spider Tap (section D) will make it much easier for these quickness exercises.

1. **ball behind knees, front clap, catch behind feet** -- This drill is an excellent test to see how fast you can move those hands. To begin, put your feet together, slightly bend the knees, and place the ball against the back of your knees with one hand on each side of the ball. Drop the ball, and as soon as you let go of it, clap your hands together in front of the legs. After clapping, bring your hands behind the legs to catch the ball before it hits the floor. Although it may seem too challenging, this drill can be done successfully with very quick hands. If necessary, let the ball bounce once before catching it. This bounce should only be done the first few times to develop technique because the ball is never supposed to touch the floor during the drill. When you can perform this drill without the ball hitting the floor, you have mastered the exercise.

2. **ball at waist, drop, slap pockets (front or back), catch** -- To start, stand up straight and hold the ball with both hands about a foot out from your waist. Drop the ball, quickly slap your front pockets, and then reach down to catch the ball before it hits the floor. Do not flip the ball upwards when releasing it; just let the ball drop out of your hands. For a greater challenge, slap your back pockets before you catch the ball instead of the front pockets.

3. **ball behind head, front clap, catch behind back** -- This drill has been around for many years and remains a popular and wonderful ball handling drill for developing quickness. Begin by standing completely straight with your feet together or just a few inches apart. Place the ball behind your head on the nape of the neck and hold the ball with both hands. Next, let go of the ball so it drops straight down your back.

Immediately after releasing the ball, quickly bring your hands to the front for a single clap and then reach both hands behind your back to catch the ball. The ball should be caught near the waist area behind you. You may also use a partner in this drill, but the procedures are slightly different. Have the partner hold the ball against your neck so you have both arms straight down against your sides. When your partner drops the ball, quickly release your hands for a single clap in front, and then catch the ball behind your back. You will not know when your partner is going to let go of the ball so you must really concentrate. Aim high for this exercise and try to complete ten in a row without any errors.

4. **ball behind head, two front claps, catch behind back** -- Use the same technique for this drill as the previous one, but now clap your hands twice in front before you catch the ball behind your back. Your hands have to move extremely fast for this drill to work properly. If you are having problems doing the two claps, raise the ball up a little higher when you start the drill to give yourself a bit of extra time. You may not have thought that an extra clap would make the drill any harder, but it really does make a difference.

5. **ball in front (face level), back clap, catch in front (waist level)** -- Let's now reverse the process that we used in the last two exercises. Hold the ball up in front of you with both hands about a foot away from your face. Drop

V. Advanced Ball Handling 119

the ball and then clap the hands once behind your back before catching it in front at waist level. It is going to be hard not to flip the ball upward to start the drill, but try to let the ball fall right out of your hands. If you are not able to complete the drill the first few times, hold the ball up a little higher to start the drill. You may want to practice a few back claps without the ball before attempting this drill. You can easily mash your fingers because you are not used to doing a clap behind your body.

6. **ball behind head, drop down back, catch behind legs** -- All of the drills in this section thus far have used mostly hand and arm movements, but this exercise and the next one also involve the legs. Begin with the feet shoulder width apart and your knees bent. Hold the ball out a few inches behind your head with both hands. Next, release the ball so it drops straight down your back. As soon as you let go, bend your knees and catch the ball behind your legs. Try to catch the ball as low as you can, but remember that it is supposed to be caught behind the legs and not behind your back as you have previously done. You may find that the ball will hit your butt as it is dropping down. To help solve this problem, be sure to bend straight down with your legs so the butt is not pushed out. You can increase quickness to this exercise by clapping the hands in front before bending down to catch the ball behind your legs.

7. **hamster wheel with both hands (reverse)** -- You must be wondering what a "hamster wheel" is. It is a drill in which you use only your fingertips and quick wrist movements to turn (spin) the ball in the air, much like a hamster running on its wheel. Hold the ball out in front of you at waist level with both hands. Using only the fingertips (no thumbs), start rotating the ball so it is spinning forward (away from your body). You have to move your fingers rapidly on the under side of the ball by using quick taps to keep it spinning in the air. The ball should be continuously moving; therefore, do not use the thumbs because they will create pauses in the drill. The direction of the turning ball changes in the reversal mode. Now you have to move your fingers so the ball is turning backwards (toward your body). This is a stationary drill so the ball should not cause you to move around the floor. Keep the ball turning for a minimum of fifteen seconds in each direction.

120   V. Advanced Ball Handling

8. **hamster wheel with right hand (reverse)** -- The next two hamster wheels are not easy because the ball is moving very fast and you must have complete control over it the entire time with only one hand. First, hold the ball out with just the right hand. Start rotating the ball with only the fingertips so it is spinning clockwise (from left to right). Your fingers and wrist have to move extremely fast to keep the ball spinning without any pauses for fifteen seconds. It should look as though you are undercutting or slicing the ball, but it is the quickness of the taps with your fingertips that keeps the ball spinning. The ball will rotate  counterclockwise (from right to left) in the reversal mode, and all the techniques are identical as in the clockwise rotations. In either direction, only the right hand is used.

9. **hamster wheel with left hand (reverse)** -- Now switch over and use only your left hand to complete the hamster wheel. Rotate and tap the ball quickly with only your fingertips so it is moving clockwise (from left to right) for at least fifteen seconds. Switch the direction of the ball and complete counterclockwise rotations (from right to left) for another fifteen seconds. If your left hand is considered the weak hand, then it may take you a little longer to coordinate the speed of the ball and the fingertip technique.

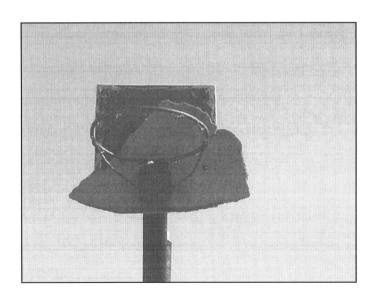

V. Advanced Ball Handling

D. One Hand Cradles

Hopefully you remember how to do all the cradle drills that were in section C of Intermediate Ball Handling. These one hand cradle drills are similar to the regular cradles because the hand is cupped and the fingertips are used as though you were delicately cradling a baby. These one hand cradles require much more hand speed and ball control, because you do not have the other hand to compensate for a bad flip to help regain control of the ball. Complete a minimum of ten repetitions for all fourteen one hand cradle drills. Remember that each time you catch the ball is considered one repetition. All the exercises resemble one another in some way, so the drill descriptions will be very similar.

1. **right hand and right leg** -- Spread your legs a little more than shoulder width apart and bend your knees so you are balanced. Hold the ball with only the right hand centering it between your legs. Flip the ball up a few inches and then quickly move your right hand around the right leg to catch the ball from the back. Your right hand is now behind the right leg. Flip the ball up again and bring the hand back around to catch the ball in front where you started. Once you catch the ball, flip it back up quickly so there are no long pauses in the drill. Continue to move your right hand around your right leg using this one hand cradle technique. During the drill, you will be unable to flip the ball up very high because it will hit your stomach. For that reason, hand quickness is what makes it work. The left hand is never used during the exercise; move it out of the way. Keep the ball in the fingertips the entire drill and out of your palm. Neither the ball nor your right hand ever touches the floor.

2. **left hand and left leg** -- For this exercise, center the ball between your legs with the left hand, using only the fingertips. Flip the ball up a few inches and then quickly move your left hand around the left leg to catch the ball from the back. Reverse the process by flipping the ball up again and bringing the left hand back around to catch the ball in front where you began. All of the ball action is done between the legs. Each flip must come straight up because you do not have the right hand to help catch the ball if the flip is off. Your goal of ten repetitions should be completed in a short period of time because all of the movements happen very quickly.

V. Advanced Ball Handling

3. **right hand and left leg** -- Bring your feet a little closer together and hold the ball in your right hand on the outside of the left leg near the knee area. Flip the ball up a few inches above the knee. After you flip the ball, quickly bring the right hand between your legs so you catch the ball on the outside of the left leg. This between the legs catch is tough and will require a considerable reach to the outside of the leg.

Flip the ball back up again and bring the right hand back around the left leg (through the legs) to catch the ball where you began. The ball always stays to the outside of the left leg, near the knee area. Be sure to flip the ball up only a few inches and not so high that it comes up near your hip.

4. **left hand and right leg** -- Start by moving the ball over to the outside of the right leg with the left hand. Flip the ball up a few inches and quickly bring the left hand between your legs to catch the ball on the outside of the right leg. Flip the ball back up a few inches again, and bring the left hand back through the legs to catch the ball in the same position where you started. Remember that the ball is held just briefly before flipping it back up. Keep the right hand completely out of the way because it will be tempting to touch the ball since all of the action is on your right side.

5. **right hand and left side of body** -- While standing, reach the ball across the front of your body with the right hand and position it near the left hip. To prevent the left arm from interfering with the drill, place your left hand on top of your head. Flip the ball up a few inches and then quickly move your right had around your back to catch the ball by the left hip. Yes, this is a long way for the right hand to travel. Once you catch

the ball, flip it up again and bring the right hand back around your body to catch the ball in the same spot where you started. Obviously players with long arms have an advantage! The ball needs to remain on the left side of your body near the hip area. As you will see, it will be necessary to use some hip action to allow your hand to travel back and forth around your body to catch the ball. Flip the ball up only a few inches, although at first you many need to flip it a little higher to catch the ball successfully each time.

V. Advanced Ball Handling 123

6. **left hand and right side of body** -- This is the exact opposite of the last drill; reach the ball over with the left hand and position it near the right hip. Put the right hand on top of your head to prevent it from getting in the way. Flip the ball up a few inches and then quickly bring your left hand around your back to catch the ball near the right hip. As soon as you grab the ball, flip it back up and bring the left hand around to the front to catch the ball where you began. Try not to hold the ball once you receive it; flip it back up as soon as you catch it each time.

7. **down on left knee – right hand and right leg** -- This exercise is very similar to the first drill in this section. Place your left knee on the floor and hold the ball in front of you in the right hand. Flip the ball up a few inches and then quickly move your right hand around the outside of the right leg and then between your legs to catch the ball before it hits the floor. Flip the ball back up and bring the right hand back around to the front to catch the ball where you started. You will not be able to flip the ball up very high because it will hit you in the chest. For that reason, you will need to move your hands very quickly using only the fingertips. Pretend that the ball is a "hot potato" and you must get rid of it just after it touches your hand.

8. **down on right knee – left hand and left leg** -- Switch over so you are down on the right knee and hold the ball in front of you with your left hand. Next, flip the ball up and then quickly move the left hand around the outside of the left leg and then between your legs to catch the ball before it hits the floor. Hold the ball for just a split second and then flip it up again so you can bring your left hand back around the leg to catch the ball in front. The ball should only touch your fingertips and it is never supposed to hit any other part of your body. As with all cradle drills, a good flip will make it much easier for the drill to work properly.

9. **down on right knee – right hand and left leg** -- In the last two exercises, all of the ball movements were done near the inside of your legs. In these next two drills the ball is cradled on the outside of your legs. Remain down on your right knee and place the ball to the outside of the left leg by reaching over with your right hand. Flip the ball up a few inches and then quickly bring the right hand through your legs to catch the ball (still on the outside). Flip the ball back up and pull the right hand back through your legs to catch the ball at the same position you started. Continue alternating the right hand around the left leg for ten repetitions.

V. Advanced Ball Handling

10. **down on left knee – left hand and right leg** – Switch over to the left knee again and hold the ball to the outside of the right leg with the left hand. To begin, flip the ball up and then quickly move your left hand through your legs to catch the ball (on the outside). Flip the ball back up and bring the left hand back through your legs to catch the ball at the same place you started. Continue alternating the left hand around the right leg as fast as you can. Flip the ball up only a few inches because flipping the ball up near your shoulder defeats the purpose of the drill, which is hand quickness. By now, fingertip control in these one hand cradles should be a habit.

11. **sitting – right hand and right leg** – Sit on the floor with your legs extended forward and the knees bent. Center the ball between your knees with the right hand. Flip the ball up and move your hand around the outside of the right leg to catch it when it comes down. The right hand is now underneath the legs. Flip the ball back up a few inches and bring the right hand back around the right leg to catch the ball where you started. Continue to quickly shift the right hand back and forth around the right leg, using only the fingertips for quickness and better ball control. Do not get in the habit of flipping the ball up high or letting it drop really low. All the ball movements should be done right between the knees.

12. **sitting – left hand and left leg** – Remain seated and start with the ball centered between your knees with the left hand. Flip the ball up and move your left hand around the outside of the left leg to catch the ball. The left hand should now be holding the ball underneath your legs. Next, flip the ball back up a few inches and bring the left hand back around the left leg to catch the ball again. Continue to move your left hand back and forth around the left leg while keeping the ball close to the knee area. Completing ten repetitions will take only a few seconds as long as you can get the ball out of your hand quickly each time.

V. Advanced Ball Handling 125

13. **sitting – right hand and left leg** -- Now let's move the ball to the outside of the left leg. Place the ball in your right hand and reach over the left leg. Begin by flipping the ball up a few inches and then quickly moving your right hand under the left leg to catch the ball as it comes down (on the outside). Toss the ball up and bring the right hand back through your legs to catch the ball on the outside of the left leg where you began. Each toss needs to be perfect so the ball does not hit the left leg or cause you to reach far out to get it.

14. **sitting – left hand and right leg** -- Switch the ball to your left hand and reach across the right knee to begin the drill. Flip the ball up a few inches and bring your left hand under the right leg to catch the ball on the outside of the leg. Flip the ball up and bring the left hand back through your legs to catch the ball again where you started. Keep the ball around the knee area the entire drill. Do not toss the ball as high as eye level or let it drop so low that your left hand hits the floor.

V. Advanced Ball Handling

E. Ricochet

The word ricochet is defined as "the glancing rebound of an object after striking a flat surface at a slanting angle." That definition sounds complicated for a basketball drill, but is it? This entire section includes drills in which the ball is bounced between the legs using many different methods. These "ricochet" drills are excellent for increasing your hand speed and coordination and also developing a feel for where the ball is without always being able to see it. The exercises may be difficult at first, but a little practice will ease any fears you may have. For the first seven drills, complete a minimum of ten repetitions. In the last six drills, a minimum of five repetitions should be completed.

1. **front to back** – Because this is considered the basic ricochet drill, it is imperative to understand all the steps. While standing, your legs should be firmly planted and spread a little more than shoulder width apart. The knees need to be in a locked position. Hold the ball in front of you at waist level with both hands and bounce (throw) the ball between your legs so it hits the ground directly between your feet. Right after the ball is released, quickly reach your hands behind your back in the waist area to catch the ball when it bounces up. Once you catch the ball, bring it back around to the front for another repetition. The entire exercise is done by feel because your head should be facing straight the whole time. At the beginning it would be wise to bounce the ball slowly to get all the movements coordinated.

2. **back to front** – Now that you understand the basic ricochet, let's switch the direction of the ball. Start the ball behind your back with both hands (at waist level) and bounce it between the legs. After you release the ball, quickly move your hands to the front to catch it at waist level. Once you catch the ball, bring it around to the back to start again. Notice the importance of the angle of the bounce as it ricochets up to your hands. Speed at this time is not as crucial as technique. Just as in the last drill, your feet will stay firmly planted the entire time.

V. Advanced Ball Handling 127

3. **continuous – back and forth** -- In the two previous ricochet exercises the ball was brought back around the waist each time to start again. This time you are going to keep the ball continuously moving (ricocheting) back and forth between your legs. Begin in the front and bounce the ball through the legs catching it behind your back (drill #1). Now bounce the ball back through your legs and catch it in front (drill #2). Continue bouncing the ball back and forth, working really hard on your hand speed. Try to increase the speed and forcefulness of the ball each time you do a new set of repetitions.

4. **continuous with knees bent – back and forth** -- You were standing completely upright in the first three ricochet drills with the knees locked, but now a little modification is added to this exercise. All the steps are just like the last drill, but now bend your knees so you are in a squatting position. Since the knees are bent, the bounce does not come up as high, so hand speed plays an important role. The squatting position also requires you to reach farther behind your body to catch the ball.

5. **continuous – back and forth with right hand only** -- Once again you will keep the ball continuously moving back and forth between your legs but now using only the right hand. The knees need to be slightly bent. If necessary, place the left hand on your hip to prevent its getting close to the ball. You will find that it is difficult to start out slowly because you cannot "catch" the ball when switching its direction. Instead of catching the ball, you have to dribble the ball back and forth. Being unable to "catch" the ball really puts a strong emphasis on hand speed.

6. **continuous – back and forth with left hand only** -- All the steps in this exercise are the same as in the last one, but only the left hand will be used. Be sure you stand with the knees slightly bent and bounce the ball continuously back and forth between your legs. For any one-hand ricochet, your hand speed needs to be extremely fast, remembering to use the fingertips for better ball control. Place the right hand on your hip to ensure using only the left hand the entire time.

V. Advanced Ball Handling

7. **"cannon" – front to back – fast and hard –** Remember the first drill of this section that taught you the basic ricochet. Now the same technique is used but the ball is going to travel at extremely high speeds with a fast and powerful bounce, just like a shot out of a cannon. So far the start of all the ricochet bounces have been near waist level. What if you started higher? Begin this   drill by starting the ball near your head, then bringing it quickly and forcefully down the front of your body with both hands so the ball explodes powerfully between your legs. As soon as you release the ball, quickly reach around your waist to catch it behind you. Throw the ball as hard as you can between the legs to demonstrate your fast hands. The ball could injure you in this drill; be careful with the angle of the bounce. The "cannon" only moves in a front to back fashion so once you catch the ball, bring it back around to the front for another repetition.

8. **behind head to front** – Let's now try ricocheting the ball up high in the other direction. With both hands, take the ball over your head as if you were doing a two-handed reverse slam dunk. The ball will travel behind (down) your back and bounce right behind your heels. Just before it hits the floor, thrust your midsection backwards (with the feet still planted) so the ball bounces between the legs to your waist. The timing and movement of your body from forward to backward will help the drill work correctly. Notice how the ball needs to be angled properly down your back in order to bounce up to your waist in the front. Remember to bounce the ball next to your heels because any farther out will not allow it to come up between the legs. This drill will stretch your body, especially your back. The speed of the ball is much slower in this exercise because body movement and technique are emphasized. Complete five ricochets in a row for this drill. If you wish to be brave, you can also attempt this backward slam dunk with only the right or left hand. You may even find this one handed ricochet to be a bit easier.

V. Advanced Ball Handling   129

9. **front to behind head** -- Some drills are not meant to be mastered the very first try; this is one of them. To start, bounce the ball through your legs like the regular ricochet,

but instead of reaching behind your back to catch the ball, reach behind your head. You will need to arch your back (as the ball is traveling between the legs) to make an angle that is possible to catch the ball up near your head. A goal should be to complete five of these ricochets, although not necessarily in a row. Developing your timing and creating a perfect angle on the bounce will make this drill easier for you. This is a tough drill!

10. **front to back, throw over head, catch in front - continuous** -- Let's combine a drill from the ricochet section with one from the coordination section. First, do the basic front to back ricochet just as in drill #1 in this section. When you catch the ball behind your back, throw (flip) it over your head and catch it in front at waist level (section B, drill #2); now you are ready to start the sequence again. To make the drill continuous, the transition between repetitions should be very smooth (with no stops). The ball does not have to travel fast in this exercise; five cycles will not be too hard for you.

11. **back to front, throw over head, catch behind back - continuous** -- Here is another drill combining the ricochet and coordination sections. The ball will travel in the opposite direction from that of the last exercise. Start with the back to front ricochet, just as in drill #2 in this section. When you receive the ball in front, throw (flip) it over your head and catch it behind your back (section B, drill #1). Let the ball and your arms do all the work because your body is in a stationary position the whole time.

12. **front to back - trap between legs** -- The next two drills can probably be considered a ½ ricochet because the ball does not go all the way through your legs. Actually these are more like trick drills, which is a good introduction to the next section. Position your feet so they are a little closer together (about a foot apart) and dribble the ball just like the basic ricochet so it bounces up and you trap it between your knees. Squeeze the ball between your knees for a second or two and then release it. You must move your legs together quickly and forcefully to trap the ball. Timing the closing of your knees with the bounce will determine the success of the drill. Try to trap the ball five times in a row.

13. **back to front - trap between legs** -- Now complete the ½ ricochet from back to front and trap the ball between your legs. You will need to squeeze your legs quickly together and strongly enough to hold the ball; if not the ball will easily slide out. Do not forget that your legs are closer in this exercise because it would be difficult to do five traps in a row if they are spread too far apart.

130 V. Advanced Ball Handling

F. Miscellaneous Drills and Tricks

Basketball, unlike other sports, is a great way to be innovative and show your creativity; this miscellaneous section does that. These exercises will be fun to do, but they can also be very challenging for you. This last section of Advanced Ball Handling is the most difficult to describe, so some of the drills will have longer explanations. Many of the exercises involve balancing the ball in some form or other to improve your coordination and balancing skills. Please read the drill descriptions carefully before beginning them. Each drill will have a goal associated with it.

1. **tip drill with each set of fingers** -- Most of the exercises in this book have been hand or wrist strengthening drills. This tip drill will strengthen your fingers more than any other drill in this book. This exercise bears some resemblance to the tip drills in Basic Ball Handling (part I, section B), except now the ball is "tipped" with only one set of fingers at a time instead of all your fingers at once. Start tipping the ball with only your index fingers, then move on to the middle fingers, the ring fingers, the pinkies, and finally the thumbs. Your goal is to tip the ball back and forth at face level for ten seconds with each set of fingertips (total of fifty seconds). The ball is not to touch anything but those two fingers for the entire ten seconds. You will find that the ball must be tipped very quickly to keep it going.

2. **roll along arms – behind neck** -- Here is another exercise to test your balancing abilities. Extend both arms completely straight out to each side and hold the ball in your right hand (with the palm face up). Toss the ball up a few inches and then quickly turn the right hand over and lift your right arm up slightly. Lifting your right arm creates a slight slope allowing the ball to begin to roll. Let the ball roll down the right arm, behind your neck, and continue down the left arm to your left hand where you will catch it. You will have to bend your head forward so the ball can roll across your neck. Once you can roll the ball all the way from the right hand to the left hand, switch directions to roll it from left to right. Try to complete three successful rolls in each direction.

V. Advanced Ball Handling

3. **ball circles (around the arms)** -- Ball circles are a fun ball handling trick, but they will require you to have patience while trying to develop them. Basically, you will be creating a circle with your arms and have the ball roll around them. Definitely easier said than done! As in the last drill in which the ball rolled along your arms, good balance is also necessary for this exercise to be successful. To get the ball started (from the right arm around to the left arm), spin (twist) the ball counterclockwise with the right hand. Spinning the ball counterclockwise gives the proper rotation for the ball to move around your arms in a clockwise direction. Immediately after you spin the ball, place it on your right hand between the index finger and the thumb. You must also lift your right arm to help the ball travel from your hand down to your shoulder. As the ball is approaching  your right shoulder and chest, lean back a little so the ball rolls across your upper body and eventually down the left arm. It is important to "work" the shoulders to guide the ball, keeping it on the proper path. Try to complete one flawless rotation before you attempt continuous ball circles. You will need to "lock" your hands together for continuous ball circles, much the way a hula-hoop works. The ball rolls on the inside of your arms, not on top of them. When you change directions, begin the drill by spinning the ball clockwise with the left hand so it now starts rolling up the left arm. The success of this drill is determined by your ability to guide and balance the ball with your hands, arms, and shoulders. Do not expect immediate success, but do not give up on it either. Complete at least three ball circles in each direction and then eventually try to complete three continuous circles in both directions.

4. **roll ball down body and kick back up – both sides** -- Here is a soccer-type drill to get your feet involved in ball handling. Begin by placing the ball against the right shoulder and tilt your body back, keeping both feet firmly planted. Release the ball   so it rolls straight down the right side of your body towards the floor. As soon as the ball passes by your right hip, lift the right leg straight outward with your foot pointed upward. This movement by your leg enables the ball to be kicked (lifted) straight up in the air so you can catch it. Make an effort to keep your body and right leg stiff so the ball rolls smoothly down your body without bouncing. Also, lift the right leg very quickly; otherwise the ball will move away from you instead of straight up to be caught. Once you complete five kicks on the right side, place the ball on your left shoulder to start five more kicks on the left. Try to do as many rolls and kicks in a row as you can.

V. Advanced Ball Handling

5. **bounce ball, kick over head, catch behind back** -- This is another exercise that includes a soccer twist. Drop the ball from waist level and let it bounce once. When the ball comes up, kick it over your head (using either foot) and catch it behind your back with both hands. This over the head and catch behind the back action is similar to some of the coordination drills in section B. Once you catch the ball, bring it back around to the front and try again. Complete at least five successful "kicks" and "catches." The ball does not have to be kicked high in the air, just high enough to clear your head. You can even start this exercise without the bounce, much like a football player would do when punting a ball. Obviously this drill works best outside where you have plenty of room. Do not break any of your mom's lights by trying this exercise in the house!

6. **feet together, drop ball, catch on top of feet** -- If you want a difficult exercise, this is it! This is a tricky drill that can aggravate you if you allow it. Begin the drill standing straight with your feet no more than two inches apart. Next, hold the ball at your waist and lean back as far as you can on your heels. Staying balanced, drop the ball

from your waist so it lands (and stays) on top of your feet. The ball will probably bounce off your feet the first few times. Once you have done the drill successfully five times, drop the ball from higher elevations, perhaps as high as your head. This drill seems simple, but you will be amazed how difficult it is to keep the ball from falling off your feet.

7. **ball between feet, lift up to waist in front** -- These next two exercises will improve your jumping skills. Coordination and quick jumps will be required. Begin by placing the ball on the floor with your feet on each side of it. Now make an explosive jump and lift the ball with your feet so it travels up to your waist where you will catch it in the front. Once you have made the catch, position the ball back on the floor to try again. Your goal is to complete five consecutive successful lifts.

V. Advanced Ball Handling 133

8. **ball between feet, lift up to waist in back** -- This exercise is slightly different because now you will lift the ball behind you rather than in front. Place the ball between your feet, but this time position it near the heel area. Now jump and lift the ball behind you by bringing up your feet toward the butt. Kicking your feet in this manner will help raise the ball straight up allowing you to grab it near the back of your waist. Of course you will have to reach behind your back with both hands to catch the ball. As soon as you have control of the ball, place it back on the floor for another lift. Once again, try to complete five consecutive lifts.

9. **bounce ball, bend over, rest ball on neck** -- This drill is very popular with soccer players but it can be used with a basketball as well. To begin, bounce the ball at least to face level. When the ball reaches its peak, bend over, place your head beneath it, and let it land (and rest) on the nape of your neck. You will need to push your shoulders towards the neck to give the ball a small pocket on which to land. Keep your back in a straight line when you bend over; otherwise, the ball will roll off your neck. Once you have the ball situated on your neck, hold the position for five seconds. Try to complete three consecutive "landings." This exercise is easily one of the most difficult drills in this book.

10. **hourglass pass (reverse)** -- Visualize the shape of an hourglass and you will know how the ball travels in this drill. Each complete hourglass is a series of four short and quick passes from hand to hand around the inside of your legs. This exercise is also an introduction to the hourglass dribble you will learn in Advanced Dribbling (part VI, section F). Start with your body in a crouched position with your feet spread about two feet apart. Always keep the ball about four inches off the floor as you pass it from hand to hand inside your legs. The first pass goes from the left toes to the right toes (from the left hand to the right hand). The second pass moves diagonally from the right toes to directly behind the left heel (right hand to left hand). The third pass travels across from behind the left heel to directly behind the right heel (left hand to right hand). The fourth and last pass moves diagonally from behind the right heel up to the left toes where you began (right hand to left hand). The four passes as just described equal one complete hourglass pass. Finish five complete hourglass passes, increasing your speed each time, and then reverse the direction of the ball for five more sets. Once you understand all the ball movements, this drill can be performed in a flash.

V. Advanced Ball Handling

11. **figure 8 with drop (reverse)** -- This drill provides variety to the basic figure 8 you learned in Basic Ball Handling (part I, section C). Although the ball does not travel in the normal figure 8 pattern, this drill title is used because many of the hand movements are similar. Like the regular figure 8, place your body in a crouched position with your feet a little wider than shoulder width apart. Begin the drill with the ball in your right hand (in the front) and then take it between your legs handing it off to the left hand (in the back). Next, bring the ball forward around the left leg, continuing the ball straight across the front of your legs to the right hand and around the right leg. (Before in the basic figure 8, you would put the ball between your legs after going around the left leg; now you will take the ball all the way across to the other side). After taking the ball around the right leg with the right hand, you will meet the ball between your legs with the left hand. Smack the ball hard with the left hand; then simply drop the ball from both hands allowing it to bounce one time. You will need to alternate hand positions quickly after you drop the ball so the right hand is now in front and the left hand is in back. Once you have switched the position of your hands and grabbed the ball, take it around the left leg to the front with the left hand to give the drill another try. With each rotation, the ball hits the floor only once, the time it is dropped. This sounds complicated but follow the drill description step by step, and you will begin to understand all the maneuvers. Complete a total of ten rotations; then reverse directions. The reversal mode is very similar because all the hand movements are virtually the same. Begin with the ball in your left hand and take it between your legs handing it off to your right hand (in the back). Now bring the ball around your right leg to the front and continue the ball straight across the front of your legs and pass it off to the left hand so you can take the ball around the left leg to the back. Next, meet (smack) the ball between your legs with the right hand; then drop the ball out of your hands allowing it to bounce once. Quickly switch hand positions and catch the ball with the left hand now in front and the right hand in back. Finally take the ball around the right leg with the right hand to the front to start the entire process again. All of these actions happen very fast and you will be astonished how quickly you can finish ten rotations.

12. **figure 8 with partner or off wall (reverse)** -- This exercise also has a variation from the regular figure 8 you performed in Basic Ball Handling. Begin by doing a few rotations of the regular figure 8, passing the ball in and around your legs with both hands. You will need to move the ball around your legs so it is always moving forward when it goes around the outside of either leg. This is done so the ball is moving in the direction of your partner or the wall. You should stand six to ten feet away from your partner or the wall. After a few regular figure 8 rotations, pass the ball to your partner as it comes up the outside of your right leg. When you pass to your partner, pass the ball directly between his/her legs so he/she can catch it and begin the figure 8. After finishing the figure 8, he/she will pass the ball back up to you (between your legs) and you can start another rotation. Your body needs to stay in a crouched position the entire time allowing you always to be ready to receive the return pass. If you are using a wall instead of a partner, pass the ball off the wall at an angle in which it will bounce back to you between your legs to keep the drill continuous. The ball <u>does not</u> change directions in the reverse mode; instead, you

V. Advanced Ball Handling 135

pass the ball when it comes up along the outside of the left leg and not the right leg. Complete five passes in each direction, increasing your speed each time.

13. **behind the back pass with partner or off wall (reverse)** -- In Intermediate Dribbling (part IV, section C), you performed a behind the back dribble. In this drill, you will complete a behind the back pass, either with a partner or as an individual exercise. Stand straight with your feet firmly planted and shoulder width apart. You should stand six to ten feet from your partner or the wall. You are going to begin by taking the ball around your back from the right side to the left side with your right hand (quick arm movements). Start the pass by placing your right hand on the front of the ball bringing it behind your back. Continue the ball around your back until reaching the left side where you will let go to complete the behind the back pass.

If you are working with a partner, pass the ball to his/her right side so your partner can mimic you and return the pass to your right side to start again. If you are using a wall, pass the ball off the wall at an angle in which it will bounce up to your right side, keeping the exercise continuous. You may find it easier (or better) to perform the passes while standing sideways to the wall. Once you have found the ideal location on the wall, try to hit that same spot each time. Simply change directions in the reverse mode so you are passing the ball around your back from the left side to the right with the left hand. Complete at least five passes in each direction, eventually working up to ten.

Conclusion of Part V – Initially you probably had difficulty executing some of the drills and tricks in Advanced Ball Handling. It will take time to master all these drills; but practice, practice, and more practice will ultimately help you. Once you learn these exercises, they will become enjoyable because your ability level will be greatly improved allowing you to show off your ball handling skills. All the drills in Advanced Ball Handling involved coordination, quickness, or the combination of the two. Improving these skills will make you a better basketball player and help you in the next part, Advanced Dribbling.

VI. Advanced Dribbling

A. Speed Dribbling – Low Dribbling

The drills you have completed thus far have involved dribbling the ball at only moderate speeds. Now you will put your hands and fingertips in a higher gear for "speed dribbling." Since you will be using many parts of your hand in this section to dribble the ball, pay close attention to each exercise description. For comfort and effectiveness, these speed dribbling exercises need to be completed while sitting, down on one knee, or down on both knees. The ball is dribbled so low to the ground in this section that leaning over for a long period of time while standing would be very uncomfortable. Unless otherwise mentioned, spend at least thirty seconds on each drill because this section is important for successfully completing the rest of Advanced Dribbling. These low dribbling drills are good for developing quick hands and increasing your confidence level. This section will also help you maintain good control of the ball in crucial game situations. You will find that dribbling for thirty seconds is a good strengthening workout for your fingers and wrists. When you complete this section, the ball will be traveling very rapidly. You will be surprised by your rapid improvement in hand speed. For each drill, finding a good dribbling rhythm will dramatically increase your speed dribbling skills.

1. **right hand** -- These first two drills are a good warm-up for most of the drills in this section. In the beginning, the speed of the ball is not as crucial as how well you control the ball. Try to focus on using only your fingertips and a lot of quick wrist movements. Start by dribbling the ball no higher than six inches from the floor. Progressively decrease the height of the ball and begin to increase your dribbling speed. The closer the ball is to the floor, the faster your fingers must move. The only things that should be moving are your right hand and fingers. Your right forearm should remain straight throughout the drill. The ultimate goal of this exercise is to dribble as fast and as low as you can without the ball stopping. As mentioned in the introduction, you can complete the drill while sitting, down on one knee, or down on both knees.

VI. Advanced Dribbling 137

2. **left hand** -- Was the last drill difficult for you? If not, you are ready to try the left hand. For most of you, this speed dribble will be harder because the left hand is not your dominant hand. If that is the case, work on a six-inch fast continuous dribble instead of the really low speed dribble which may cause you to become discouraged initially. Notice that you do not have to hit the ball hard, a soft, quick touch from the fingertips is what makes this exercise successful.

3. **alternating dribble with both hands – on top of the ball** -- Of all the drills in this book, the ball should travel fastest in this exercise. It will be moving a very rapid speed because both hands will be moving so quickly. Begin by placing your body in the  same position as in the two previous exercises. Alternate your hands dribbling the ball (on top), starting at six inches and working closer to the floor. You will need to develop a soft, quick touch with your fingertips on each hand to keep the ball moving rapidly. Did you realize that the ball moves faster when your thumbs are not used? Thirty continuous seconds of rapid dribbling may wear your hands and fingers out the first few times.

4. **alternating dribble with both hands – side to side** -- In the last drill, all the hand movements were done above the ball. For this one, you will be dribbling the ball quickly from side to side, alternating dribbles between hands. This should sound familiar because these dribbles are actually accelerated crossovers. The ball should bounce low and in the same spot each time with your hands hitting on the side of the ball to keep the dribble going back and forth. The left hand will dribble the ball on the left side and the right hand will hit the ball on the right side. The ball in this drill does not move as fast as when you were dribbling on top because the hand movements are not as quick and the ball has to travel a little farther.

5. **right hand – each finger** -- As indicated by the title of this drill, only the fingers on the right hand will be used. Use only the fingertip of each finger to speed dribble the ball.  It will probably be best to start with the index finger. Speed dribble the ball using just the index finger for at least ten seconds. When you finish with that finger, quickly switch to the middle finger for ten seconds and then move on to the ring finger, the pinky, and finally the thumb. Your goal is to speed dribble the ball for at least ten seconds with each finger. Note that only one finger should be dribbling the ball at any given time.

6. **left hand – each finger** -- Switch the ball to the left hand and speed dribble with your index finger. Continue changing fingers by using the middle finger, ring finger, pinky, and thumb to finish the drill. If you feel that your rhythm is really good, speed dribble longer with that one finger. Also, fifty seconds are the minimum for one complete set using all the fingers (ten seconds with each finger). Try lengthening your sets by changing fingers numerous times.

VI. Advanced Dribbling

7. alternating dribble with each set of fingers -- You may have heard this drill referred to as the "typewriter" or "keyboard" because each finger on both hands is used. This speed exercise is done similarly to the alternating dribble with both hands drill (#3), except you will be alternating dribbles between each set of fingers. Start with only the two index fingers and alternate fingers between dribbles on top of the ball for ten seconds. After ten seconds, switch to the middle fingers, then the ring fingers, the pinkies, and finally the thumbs. Ten seconds will be your goal for each set of fingers. Learn to use all the fingers equally well in order to be able to continuously switch between fingers without the ball ever stopping. This drill will build strong hands and fingers.

8. right fist -- Start by clinching your right hand together to make a fist. You will be dribbling the ball using your hand like a hammer, bouncing it with the bottom of your fist. Begin dribbling the ball about six inches high and continue decreasing the height as you begin to pick up speed. The key to the drill is to use a quick fist and not to hit the ball with force, causing it to bounce up too hard for you to handle. Once you have the speed dribble going, continue for at least fifteen seconds.

9. left fist -- Now try the speed dribble with the left fist. Using short, quick hammer movements with the fist will effectively increase your speed. At least fifteen seconds should be completed once you have the ball dribbling fast. If you can learn to do the right and left fists successfully, the next two exercises will be much easier.

10. alternating dribble with both fists – on top of ball -- Now you will combine the last two exercises, giving you the alternating dribble with both fists on top of the ball. The whole sequence is similar to a speed bag in boxing because of the short, quick alternating hand movements. It would be wise to begin the drill slowly and move up to faster speeds. Start with a higher dribble and work the ball down as low to the floor as you can. Once you develop a comfortable rhythm, thirty seconds will seem easy.

11. alternating dribble with both fists – side to side -- This time the ball is going to travel in a side-to-side direction, much like drill #4. In the last exercise, you dribbled the ball with the fists coming down directly on it. Now "punch" the ball with your fists coming at 45-degree angles making the ball bounce in a "V" pattern. A good rhythm will make the drill run smoothly because the ball does not travel nearly as fast as in the last exercise.

VI. Advanced Dribbling 139

12. **alternating dribble with right fist and left hand** -- This drill and the next one combine exercises #3 and #10 in this section. Alternate each dribble between your right fist and the left hand so the ball is moving swiftly. Begin the dribbling a few inches off the floor and work down as low as possible. Be sure to keep the right hand closed into a fist, resisting the temptation to open the hand.

13. **alternating dribble with left fist and right hand** -- Switch now so you are alternating dribbles between your left fist and right hand. After you have successfully accomplished the drill, combine the last drill with this one so each hand is continuously alternating between a closed fist and an open hand. This should be a challenge for you as you integrate these drills.

14. **alternating dribble with palms** -- Let's try another type of exercise by alternating the palms with every dribble. You are probably so accustomed to using your fingertips exclusively that it will be different with the palms. Open both hands as wide as you can so your fingers are spread apart. Now alternate dribbles between hands using only your palms. Thirty seconds will go quickly. You will be able to dribble the ball much faster than you think. Throughout the book you have been taught to keep the ball out of the palms of your hands while dribbling. Make an exception for this drill and give it a shot.

15. **alternating dribble with sides of hands – chops** -- You probably did not think karate was part of basketball, but here it is! You will be dribbling by chopping at the ball using alternate hands. You will "chop" the ball on the outside part of both hands (next to the pinkies). In fact, you might find that the ball will hurt your hands a little as you are dribbling. To prevent this, use soft and quick "chops" on the ball, which allow you to dribble the ball quickly, but will not be painful for your hands. It is not necessary to hit the ball really hard for the exercise to be effective.

16. **alternating dribble with back of hands** -- This exercise may be the most uncomfortable of all those in this section. Begin by turning your hands over so the palms are facing up; this position will feel awkward. You may dribble the ball with your fingers spread or closed, depending on which is more comfortable; make sure both hands remain flat. Allow the ball do all the work for this drill and use the back of your hands as more of a guide to keep it bouncing. Start out slowly and gradually increase your speed as you become more comfortable using the back of your hands.

VI. Advanced Dribbling

17. **alternating dribble with both elbows** -- If the last drill was the most uncomfortable, this one is the most difficult in this section. All the drills so far have involved using the hands in some form or other. Your ability to be creative will shine as you now alternate the dribble with both elbows. This exercise works best if you position yourself on both knees or down on one knee. Start by placing your arms at 90 degree angles directly in front of you as though you are "putting up your dukes" for a boxing match. Bounce the ball once and then start using your elbows to alternate dribbles. Hit the ball about an inch up the back of your arms so it bounces straight down. Of vital importance, try not to let the ball bounce astray by keeping it positioned around one spot on the floor to help maintain continuity. The speed of the ball is not a factor because you have to dribble much higher when you use the elbows. For this exercise, aim for ten consecutive elbow dribbles, five with each one. Remember this was not meant to be a simple drill; giving up right away is not an option.

18. **down on right knee – alternating dribble under left leg** – This drill and the next are another way to do a low/speed dribble. These exercises are similar to the "down on one knee drills" in Intermediate Dribbling (section B, drills #5 and #6), except now the ball is dribbled much lower and at a quicker pace. Place your right knee on the floor and execute the exercise by alternating each dribble with both hands <u>directly under</u> your left knee, not back and forth under the knee as you performed in the Intermediate Dribbling drills just mentioned. You will have no choice but to do a low dribble due to the lack of space under your left leg. Even though you are alternating hands between dribbles and it is hard to see the ball, try to dribble it in the same spot.

19. **down on left knee – alternating dribble under right leg** -- Switch legs so you are now down on the left knee. Perform the drill by alternating each dribble with both hands <u>directly under</u> your right knee. As in the last exercise, keep dribbling the ball in the same location which will help increase your speed. You will realize that you can dribble the ball very quickly in this position. Much of your success depends on the ability to dribble the ball without seeing it very well.

VI. Advanced Dribbling 141

20. **alternating dribble behind heels** -- Thus far you have been seated, down on one knee, or down on both knees for all the exercises; but this drill and the next two are the only drills in the section in which you will be standing. The ball should move at a very swift pace; that is why this drill is included in the speed dribbling section. Put both feet together and bend your knees far enough so you can place the ball behind your heels with both hands. Now complete an alternating dribble behind your heels, keeping the ball extremely low to the floor. Position your hands so they are near the top of the ball, which will allow you to dribble it straight down instead of side to side. Completing a speed dribble for thirty seconds in this stance will be difficult the first few times.

21. **alternating dribble between legs (reverse)** -- For this exercise you are going to speed up the between the legs dribbles you performed in section A of Basic Dribbling. Start with your feet a little more than shoulder width apart and your knees bent. With the left hand in front and the right hand in back, dribble the ball quickly back and forth between your legs. Continue these fast dribbles for fifteen seconds and then reverse your hands for fifteen more seconds (right hand positioned in the front and left hand in the back). Use a bouncing/rocking motion as you are dribbling to help you get into the drill.

22. **alternating dribble under lifted legs** -- For this drill you have to coordinate the dribbling of the ball with the movement of your legs. Begin with your feet three or four inches part and the knees bent. The exercise works best if you can stay on the balls of your feet while leaning slightly forward; good balance is required. The first bounce will be a crossover dribble from the right hand to the left. As you begin the dribble, lift your right leg (foot) backward (toward the butt area) to allow the left knee to come forward. The ball should bounce under the left knee and up to your left hand. Once you receive the ball, perform a crossover dribble from the left hand back to the right but this time under the lifted right leg. Continue these alternating crossover dribbles back and forth in front of your body under the lifted legs. The opposite leg of the hand that has the ball will be lifted each time (as in a marching motion). Since the ball needs to come <u>under</u> the lifted leg, it is necessary to dribble close to your body and knee high only. Your legs will quickly alternate with every dribble because the ball should be moving rapidly. You can execute a surprising number of these dribbles in thirty seconds. Once you can coordinate all the steps, try the drill without looking at the ball.

VI. Advanced Dribbling

B. Crab Dribbling

Crab dribbling is an excellent dribble because it will improve your balance and agility, it is unique, and it requires you to remain in a good basketball stance. Your stance should be a crouched position with the knees bent and the butt low. Do not hunch your back and do not lean back on your heels. The crab dribble is unusual because you will be reaching your hands behind the legs and then up through the legs to dribble near your toes. Clarification on each kind of crab dribble will be included in the individual drill descriptions. These drills are considered "crab dribbling" because the walking portion (drills #4-#6) of this section has a crab-like look to it when you are moving. All six crab dribbling drills should last a minimum of fifteen seconds. Try to keep your head up when dribbling because this is important for the three walking drills in this section. These are not considered speed dribbles, although they should be dribbled relatively low to the floor.

1. **right hand** – The key to all these drills is the positioning of your arms and hands; let's make sure you get a good understanding in the first exercise. Place your body in the crouched position which was mentioned in the section introduction, with the knees bent and the butt low. Reach the right arm behind your right leg so it is directly behind the right knee. Next, stretch the right arm forward between your two legs to allow you to begin dribbling the ball. Dribble as far as you can out in front of you (near the toe area); this will help in the walking exercises (#4-#6). If your left hand seems to be getting in the way, grab your left ankle with the left hand to keep it from disturbing the exercise.

2. **left hand** – Now reach your left arm behind the left leg so it is directly behind the left knee and stretch it forward between your legs. Dribble the ball as you did in the last drill, now using only your left hand. If necessary, grab your right ankle with the right hand to prevent it from disrupting the drill. Remember, speed is not everything; technique is just as important for a crab dribble. Begin slowly and work towards faster dribbling speeds.

3. **alternating dribble with both hands** – Using both hands for the crab dribble would seem easier, but it is just as difficult. Reach each arm behind each knee and do an alternating dribble using both hands. This dribble will require you to crouch a little lower than the first two exercises. Since your stance is lower, this will allow you to dribble a little faster; also both hands are being used which will also increase your ball speed. Crab dribble in front of you (near the toe area) and in a location where you can reach equally well with both hands.

VI. Advanced Dribbling 143

4. **right hand walking** -- This walking crab dribble adds some movement and coordination to the normal crab dribble you did in exercise #1. Simply crab dribble with the ball in front of you and begin walking, hopefully with your head up to allow you to see where you are going. At first, take short steps but eventually work towards longer strides. Although fifteen seconds is the minimum goal, try for longer times with more dribbles.

5. **left hand walking** -- Shift the ball to your left hand and perform the walking crab dribble with the left hand. Did you realize that the faster you walk, the quicker the ball must be dribbled? Remain in the crouched position the entire time because leaning over with a hunched back will cause you some discomfort.

6. **both hands walking** -- In drill #3, you completed a stationary crab dribble using both hands, but now you are going to do the same while walking. When doing the walking crab dribble, be certain to keep the ball in the middle while performing alternating dribbles with both hands. Keeping the ball dribbled in the middle (between your legs) allows you to reach it equally well with both hands. You need to maintain your dribble throughout the drill to avoid continuously stopping the crab walk. For variety, try to walk in different directions or in a circle.

144 VI. Advanced Dribbling

C. Dribble Lying Down On Back

You may find a few of these drills to be a bit crazy, but that is what makes this section so much fun. The exercises will be more difficult than you may think. With a little practice, you will quickly develop your skills to learn these lying down dribbles. Developing a good dribbling rhythm and maintaining good fingertip control are stressed. All these dribbles provide an excellent method for strengthening your arms, wrists, and fingers. For the first ten drills, lie completely flat on your back with the legs extended straight. The last seven drills are unique; specific instructions about your body position will be included in the description. Complete each drill for at least fifteen seconds unless instructed otherwise in the explanation.

1. **right hand on right side** -- While lying flat on your back, extend your right arm down your right side (at the waist) and dribble the ball with the right hand. The right arm needs a slight bend so it is not completely stiff. As you will find out in all the drills in this section, it is important to dribble on top of the ball and not on the side. This will allow you to have better control of the ball allowing it to bounce near the same spot every time.

2. **left hand on left side** -- Switch the ball over to your left side and dribble the ball with the left hand near the waist area. As in the last exercise, dribble on top of the ball to help keep it continuously bouncing and under control. The ball <u>should not</u> bounce very high or fast like the speed dribbling drills in section A. Develop a good rhythm at the start of the drill and fifteen seconds will pass quickly.

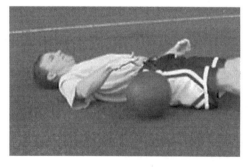

3. **right hand on right side – each finger** -- In section A (drill #5), you performed a low dribble using each finger on the right hand. In this exercise, complete a low dribble with each finger (waist area), while you are lying flat on your back. You may tilt your head to the side to check out your progress, but ultimately you need to look straight up, not at the ball. Dribble the ball for ten seconds with each finger for a total of fifty seconds.

4. **left hand on left side – each finger** -- Switch the ball over to the left side and repeat the last exercise, now using the fingers on your left hand. Dribble a few inches from your waist instead of farther out where it would be difficult to control the ball. Aim for at least ten seconds with each finger and try not to look at the ball.

VI. Advanced Dribbling 145

5. **right hand on left side** -- Let's change things a little and dribble the ball on your left side again, but now with the right hand. You have to reach across your stomach and dribble near your waist with the right hand. Try to remain completely flat the entire time without lifting your right side off the floor.

6. **left hand on right side** -- Place the ball on your right side and dribble near your waist with the left hand while on your back. It will be tempting to look at the ball, but keep your eyes looking straight up. If the left hand is your weaker hand, dribble longer than fifteen seconds to advance your skills.

7. **arm extended behind head with right hand** -- In the preceding drills, you were told to look straight up and not at the ball. You are not going to be able to see the ball at all for the next three exercises. While lying on your back, extend the right arm behind your head to allow you to dribble with the right hand a few inches from the top of your head. You will need to twist the right hand inward so you can dribble on top of the ball. It is essential to dribble on top of the ball in order to control it.

8. **arm extended behind head with left hand** -- This time you will use the left hand to dribble the ball behind your head. Twist the left hand inward to allow yourself a good angle for dribbling. There is no reason to lift your right shoulder from the floor at any time. The whole exercise is based on your ability to dribble the ball without its being in view.

9. **arms extended behind head with both hands** -- Let's combine the last two exercises and perform an alternating dribble just behind the top of your head. Since you are

using both hands, dribble directly behind your head to keep the ball balanced instead of skewed to one side. This drill will allow you to dribble the ball faster and with better control because both hands are being used. Attempt faster speeds once you really get in the flow of the drill.

10. **semi-circle dribble – right side, around head, left side (reverse)** -- The semi-circle dribble is the first lying down drill in which the ball changes locations instead of staying in one spot. Start your dribble on the right side (waist area) with the left hand as you did in drill #6. After a few bounces, dribble the ball up to your right shoulder and then above the head. When you get above your head, switch hands so the ball is

now being dribbled by the right hand (the difficult part of the drill). Bounce the ball past the left shoulder and down to your left side. Once the ball is by your left side (waist area), reverse directions by going back over the head and down to your right side where you began. Three times over and back should be your goal. Attempt to complete the entire semi-circle dribble while lying flat, striving to maintain a continuous dribble the entire time.

11. **underneath butt – alternating dribble** -- This exercise may sound easy but you will discover it is quite difficult. First, lie flat as you have done in all the drills thus far. Next, arch your back so your mid-section is off the floor about a foot. Finally, while your waist is up in the air, complete an alternating dribble with both hands under your butt. Each dribble should be performed on top of the ball, allowing it to bounce in the same spot. Of course, every dribble will be low since there is not much room under your arched back. This dribble will go well in the beginning, but the strenuous part comes when you try to hold the arched position for fifteen seconds.

12. **underneath butt – side to side** -- In the preceding drill, the dribble was done directly under your butt while making a bridge with your body. For this exercise, make a bridge again, but now dribble the ball from one side of your waist so it bounces under the butt and over to the other side of your waist. It may be necessary to lift your butt a little higher since there are many bounces and the ball has farther to travel in this exercise. Try to dribble the ball back and forth from one side to the other at least three times.

13. **circle dribble – right side, around head, left side, underneath (reverse)** -- Let's combine all the lying down drills into this exercise. Begin the drill dribbling the ball by your right side with the left hand (drill #6). Dribble up to your right shoulder, around the top of the head, and then down the left side with the right hand. At this point the dribble differs from the semi-circle dribble (drill #10). Instead of reversing the ball back up around your head, continue dribbling by going under your butt (drill #12) and over to the right side to finish a complete clockwise circle dribble. When you dribble under your butt, you have to start the ball in the left hand and dribble underneath to your right hand. Perform three complete clockwise circle dribbles and then reverse directions for three counterclockwise rotations. For the first few times, work on your hand movements to get an understanding of when to use which hand to execute the circle dribble.

VI. Advanced Dribbling 147

14. **between legs with right hand** -- You probably think this exercise is a cool down from the last drill, but think again. You will be amazed at how much the next three drills stretch your body. Begin the exercise sitting up with your legs spread out. Start dribbling the ball close to your body with the right hand (crotch area). Next, slowly lean backwards (while still dribbling) so your back is eventually flat on the floor. You may need to dip the right shoulder (down) and stretch your right arm forward in order to keep the ball dribbled between the legs. This is not meant to be a speed dribble, but a "controlled" dribble. Begin your goal of fifteen seconds once you are flat on your back and not when you initially start dribbling.

15. **between legs with left hand** -- You are going to start this exercise like the last one, by sitting up while dribbling between your legs (this time with the left hand). Slowly work your way down on your back as you are still dribbling the ball. Dip your left shoulder to get a maximum stretch with the left hand. You will significantly help your cause if you dribble the ball as close to your body as possible (crotch area).

16. **between legs with both hands – alternating dribble** -- Your flexibility will be tested in this exercise. This time, start by spreading your legs as far as you can. Begin an alternating dribble close to your body (crotch area) with both hands as you are sitting upright. While still dribbling, slowly begin leaning back until your back is completely flat on the floor. You will need to stretch both arms out as far as they can possibly go to keep the ball dribbling. Unlike the last two drills, you cannot dip either shoulder because your body needs to remain balanced. If you are having difficulty with the dribble, arch your back for assistance while keeping your shoulders on the floor. Unless you are extremely flexible, most likely you will be using the ends of your fingertips to dribble the ball. Just like the last two drills, start the fifteen second goal once your back is flat on the floor. Yes, this is a difficult drill, but stick with it!

17. **sit-ups – each side** -- In the last three drills you have been sitting upright and then lying down on your back. For this drill, you will come briefly to an upright position and continue the process. These movements obviously sound familiar, a simple sit-up. Dribble the ball with your right hand on the right side of your body (next to your waist). Complete ten sit-ups while keeping the ball dribbled the entire time. After you finish, go to the other side for ten more sit-ups while dribbling with the left hand. This drill could result in soreness, but the sore muscles will go away after performing this exercise a few days. See how many consecutive sit-ups you can do while dribbling the ball next to you. Can you do a hundred?

148 VI. Advanced Dribbling

D. Dribble Lying Down On Stomach

These "lying on your stomach" drills are similar to the "lying on the back" exercises you just finished. Lying down on your stomach while dribbling a ball will be a tough assignment. As you will discover, the drills become more challenging as you progress through this section. These creative dribbling drills will increase your flexibility and strengthen the arms and shoulders. This is another section that requires you to dribble the ball without being able to see it very well or not at all. It is all right to look at the ball when you begin each drill, but not after a few dribbles. While lying down on your stomach, it will probably be best to place your forehead on a towel, shirt, or flat pillow so you can be comfortable. This will allow you to peek out the side, if necessary, to check your progress. For advanced ball handlers, turn your head away from the ball for the first six exercises. Execute each drill for fifteen seconds unless told differently in the drill description.

1. **right hand on right side** – Lie totally flat on the floor (face down) and extend your right hand so you are able to dribble the ball about a foot out from the right side of your waist. Due to the position of your body and right arm, it is better and easier to do a lower dribble than a higher one for the fifteen seconds. This is not a speed dribble, but a controlled low dribble using the fingertips.

2. **left hand on left side** – While still on your stomach, place the ball on your left side and dribble the ball with the left hand. Dribble about a foot from the left side of your waist, not up by the shoulder or down near the knee. Hold your left arm steady, with all the dribbling movements performed with only the hand and wrist.

3. **right hand on right side – each finger** – Stay in the same position as in the two preceding exercises, but now you will dribble the ball with each finger. First, get the ball dribbling with the right hand as you did in drill #1; then switch to using the individual fingers. Dribble ten seconds with each finger for a total of fifty seconds. As you will see, the thumb will be the most troublesome of all the fingers because of the angle of your arm.

4. **left hand on left side – each finger** – Swap sides so you are now dribbling with each individual finger on the left hand. Dribble about a foot away from your waist on the left side. Of course this has to be a low dribble since your arm is already close to the floor. As in the last exercise, complete ten seconds for each finger and fifty seconds for the entire drill. Fifty seconds will challenge your dribbling stamina!

VI. Advanced Dribbling 149

5. **arm extended above head with right hand** -- Exercises #1-#4 were executed down by your waist, but these next three drills will be done above your head. Lie flat on your stomach as you have been doing and position your right cheek on the floor by turning your head to the side. This is done so you will not be able to see the ball at anytime during the drill. Extend the right arm above your head and dribble the ball a foot from the top of your head. This exercise is going to be a little hard on the right shoulder but you can sustain the dribble fifteen seconds.

6. **arm extended above head with left hand** -- Remain in the exact position as drill #5 but turn your head so the left cheek is now on the floor. Stretch the left arm above your head and complete a low dribble with the left hand, using only the fingertips. Be sure to dribble the ball a foot from the top of your head. This will give you sufficient room to extend your left arm, and it will also be close enough to keep the ball under control.

7. **arms extended above head with both hands** -- To begin this drill, place your forehead on the floor comfortably on a towel, shirt, or pillow. Extend both arms above your head and execute a low/speed dribble. Your arms are now situated in a position that allows you to dribble much more quickly than drills #5 and #6. Be certain to keep both arms up during the exercise; <u>do not</u> rest your elbows on the floor.

8. **semi-circle dribble – right side, around head, left side (reverse)** -- Let's now put together all the drills in this section you have accomplished so far. Like the last exercise, place your forehead on the floor so you are incapable of viewing the ball. Begin dribbling down by your right waist with the right hand as you performed in the first drill. Next, advance the ball up towards your head and continue to the top of the head where you will start to dribble the ball with the left hand. Proceed with the left hand dribble down to the left side of your waist, as you achieved in drill #2. Once you have completed the semi-circle (waist to waist), reverse the process and dribble all the way back around your head and down to the right side for one complete rotation. This is not a timed exercise; therefore, finish at least three complete rotations and increase your speed with each new semi-circle dribble.

VI. Advanced Dribbling

9. **between legs with right hand** – If you really want a challenging drill, this is it! These next two exercises are just like drills #14 and #15 in the previous section, except then you were lying flat on your back. Start the exercise on your stomach with both legs spread out as far as possible. Here comes the difficult part. Reach your right arm far back allowing you to dribble the ball between your legs. You will undoubtedly have to dribble up near the top of the legs near your butt (crotch area). You may have to lean your upper body to the right to allow your right arm to reach between your legs to start the dribble. Using only your fingertips will help you keep the ball continuously dribbling for fifteen seconds. This drill will stretch your body, especially your back.

10. **between legs with left hand** – Were you successful with the last drill? If you were able to conquer that one, then this exercise will be a piece of cake! Keep the legs spread very far apart and reach back with your left hand so you can dribble the ball between your legs (crotch area). Use only your fingertips to get the best results. Depending on how flexible you are and your ability to stretch the left arm, try to keep your head on the floor. If you cannot dribble the ball for fifteen seconds, strive to complete as many dribbles in a row as you can and try to better that number each time.

E. Leg Dribbling

This section allows you to dribble the ball using different parts of your leg in addition to the normal hand dribbling. The majority of these drills are challenging and they will require a lot of practice to execute correctly. Do not become frustrated when you have problems; instead, start the exercise over again or come back to it a little later in your workout. Patience and balance are two key elements necessary for this difficult dribbling section. Refer to the individual drill descriptions for the number of required dribbles for each exercise, and read every explanation thoroughly. Since these drills are more complex, the explanations are a little more involved and descriptive.

1. **right foot - continuous** -- These foot dribble drills may seem uncomfortable, but they will help your balance considerably. Begin by dropping the ball from waist level; when it bounces up (about knee high), start dribbling with only your right foot. Use the balls of your feet to dribble the ball instead of your heel or the middle of the foot. After you drop the ball to begin the exercise, neither hand should touch the ball during the drill. If you have problems with a continuous dribble, only dribble the ball with your right foot every other dribble. This will help with your timing and in maintaining your balance. Start with a few high foot dribbles and work your way down to lower dribbles. For fun, see how low you can go with these foot dribbles (quick ankle movements). Try for ten consecutive right foot dribbles, but keep going if you are on a roll.

2. **left foot - continuous** -- Let's give the left foot a workout and try for ten consecutive dribbles. Yes, these foot exercises are awkward because of your stance, which is much like a flamingo. The right foot needs to remain stationary during the whole drill; do not hop up and down. If you are having difficulties with this continuous left foot dribble, only use the foot every other dribble. In addition, use a lot of ankle movement, which will help you keep the ball dribbling at lower heights. Once you drop the ball to start the drill, neither hand is ever used again.

3. **off bottom of right foot** -- While the last two exercises included continuous foot dribbles, the next two drills involve one quick dribble off the bottom of the foot. Begin by dribbling the ball four times in front of you with either hand. When the last dribble hits the floor, bring your right foot on top of the ball so the ball bounces off the bottom of the foot. The ball should not bounce high off the ground before hitting the bottom of your foot. It will almost seem as though you are stepping on the ball! As a result, you must get it to bounce off the foot at an angle to keep the drill going. Once the ball bounces off your foot, retain the ball and perform four more dribbles before attempting another. Strive for five flawless off the foot dribbles; they do not have to be consecutive.

VI. Advanced Dribbling

4. **off bottom of left foot** -- As in the last drill, start with four dribbles in front of you with either hand. On the fourth dribble, place your left foot on top of the ball to make it bounce off the bottom of your foot. Remember to dribble the ball four times in front of you before performing each off the foot dribble. Keep in mind that this is a quick dribble off your foot so you do not have to lift your left leg very high. Try for five sharp dribbles off the bottom of your foot.

5. **off right knee with right hand** -- These next four knee exercises are similar, and of course you need to learn all four. It may be a good idea to read all four descriptions (#5-#8) before trying the drills in order to see how they all connect. Begin dribbling the ball three times with the right hand in front of you. After this third dribble, quickly lift your right foot off the ground so the foot goes behind you and the right knee moves forward. The bounce on the fourth dribble needs to be closer to your body so the ball comes up and hits off the right knee. The dribble off the right knee will happen quickly because the ball does not bounce up as high. Immediately continue dribbling after this knee dribble for three more regular dribbles before attempting another dribble off the right knee. Work on hitting the ball on your knee in the same spot every time, just below the kneecap. Attempt to finish ten right knee dribbles using just the right hand. This exercise is not meant to be done at a fast pace, but at a comfortable speed for you.

6. **off right knee with left hand** -- As you learned in the last exercise, you actually dribble off your knee in the sequence of hand, floor, and then off the knee. Instead of moving over to the left knee, you will now dribble the ball as you did in the preceding drill, except using only the left hand to dribble off the right knee. Remember to lift the right foot backwards so the right knee will bend and give you a target. You need to find a good angle to dribble the ball off the knee, especially since the ball is coming from your left side this time. Do not move your knee to adjust to a bad dribble, which demonstrates the importance of performing an excellent dribble each time. Complete ten dribbles off the right knee with your left hand before you move on to the left knee dribbles.

VI. Advanced Dribbling 153

7. **off left knee with left hand** -- Dribbling with the left knee should not be any more difficult or easier than with the right knee. If you were able to execute the two right knee dribbles, this left hand dribble off the left knee should be a snap. Now you are going to lift your left foot backwards which brings the left knee forward. The ball needs to hit just below the kneecap so it bounces straight down or towards the middle. Let the ball do all the work because the knee is only used as a support for the ball to bounce off. Do at least ten left knee dribbles using the left hand. Remember to complete three regular dribbles before each off the knee dribble.

8. **off left knee with right hand** -- By this time, the off the knee dribbles should not present a problem. Much like drill #4, this dribble comes at an angle since you will use the right hand to dribble off the left knee. To maintain continuity, the dribbles off the left knee need to bounce straight down or towards the middle instead of a carom to the outside. Again, attempt to hit the ball just below the kneecap every time. By now, ten consecutive knee dribbles without an error are a realistic goal.

9. **both knees continuous with one dribble** -- In the last four exercises, you took three regular dribbles between each bounce off the knee. This time you will mix drills #6 and #8 into a continuous exercise with only one dribble. Begin with one regular dribble and then a dribble off your left knee using the right hand. After the ball bounces off the left knee, use your left hand to complete one regular dribble and then a dribble off the right knee, and then start the process over again with the right hand. All of this occurs very quickly because only one regular dribble is involved when the ball changes sides. If you have problems using only one dribble, try two dribbles until you become familiar with the drill. Complete at least ten dribbles (five off each knee).

154 VI. Advanced Dribbling

F. Miscellaneous Advanced Dribbling Drills

Did you think you would ever make it through all the Advanced Dribbling sections? This last section is a hodge-podge of dribbling drills that you will find interesting. These original drills require much practice because they are challenging and require a great deal of coordination and hand quickness. Most of the exercises will have longer descriptions since very few drills are related. The amount of repetitions or timed goal for each exercise will be included in each description. All these drills are different from what you are used to; read the explanations carefully. Do not expect to be able to do all these "miscellaneous" drills the first time. You can complete the first four drills while standing, down on a knee, or sitting.

1. **dribble off ground with right hand** – Usually, you would simply drop the ball to begin any dribbling drill. Now you are going to start with the ball stationary on the floor. With it on the floor, quickly "pop" the ball with your right hand (fingertips) so it bounces about an inch or two off the floor. Once the ball bounces up, execute at least five low dribbles and then place the ball back on the ground. It is essential to "pop" the ball with a hard but quick right hand. This will give the ball some spring

   allowing it to bounce up. The ball you use needs to have plenty of air in it which will make it "jump" off the ground more quickly and easily. You may find you have more luck "popping" the ball with an open hand (the palm) instead of using only the fingertips. Each dribble off the ground and five low dribbles afterwards equal one set. Complete five sets before moving on to the next drill.

2. **dribble off ground with left hand** – Switch to the other side and try a dribble off the ground with the left hand. Remember that the ball needs to be completely stationary each time before you "pop" it. The ball bounces up for just a brief second, so you have to be quick to get going into the dribbling mode. Perform five low dribbles before starting the entire procedure again. Finish five sets before you go to the next exercise.

3. **dribble off ground with right fist** – These next two drills are related to the first two except your fists are used instead of the fingertips or palms. Place the ball on the ground so it is motionless and smack the ball (like a hammer) using the bottom of your right fist allowing it to bounce up. After the ball pops up, immediately open the hand to do five low dribbles. These five low dribbles after the initial dribble ("pop") off the ground are completed with your fingertips, <u>not</u> the right fist. It is not the force of your fist that causes the bounce, but the swiftness of the hand moving on and then quickly off the ball. Finish five sets for this drill and the next one.

VI. Advanced Dribbling   155

4. **dribble off ground with left fist** -- Place the ball in front of you again (stationary) and change fists so you are making each dribble off the ground with the left. Smack the ball using the bottom of your left fist so it bounces up and you can dribble low five times. Remember, the initial "pop" with your fist and five low dribbles equal only one set. Once more, complete five sets before going on to the next drill. Have you noticed that it is harder to dribble off the ground with a fist than it is with an open hand?

5. **crossover slap with right hand** -- The crossover slap is a type of dribble that can certainly be used in game situations. It is similar to the stationary crossover dribbles you learned in section A of Basic Dribbling and the moving crossover in section F of Intermediate Dribbling. Begin in a good basketball stance (crouched position) and dribble the ball four times with your right hand about knee high. After the fourth dribble, slap the ball with the right hand <u>immediately</u> as it bounces off the floor. The ball should come up an inch or two off the floor before you slap it over to the left hand to complete the crossover. Remember this is a quick slap, not the usual crossover dribble. Bring the ball back over to the right side following each crossover slap. Perform ten right crossover slaps before you try the left hand in the next exercise.

6. **crossover slap with left hand** -- The left crossover slap is developed the same way as the right. Dribble four times with the left hand; then slap the ball the moment it bounces up on the fourth dribble. The crossover slap from the left hand to the right hand must stay very low to the floor to be effective. For this reason, be certain to slap the ball <u>immediately</u> as it comes up off the floor. After each slap, bring the ball back over to the left hand to execute another one (for a total of ten slaps). The entire crossover slap happens very quickly, and you will be amazed how fast you can get the ball to travel.

7. **crossover slap - continuous** -- By now, you should be able to do a crossover slap with each hand. Combine the last two exercises so you can continuously complete crossover slaps from side to side. If you are having no problems with the timing of the slaps, use only two dribbles between slaps instead of four. As you are moving the ball back and forth in this drill, pretend you are faking out your opponent to simulate a game situation.

8. **dribble off butt** -- This is another advanced drill that takes practice because not everyone can perform it immediately. While standing, dribble directly behind both legs for a few dribbles with either hand. As one of the dribbles comes up, quickly crouch (squat) down so the ball bounces off the lower portion of your buttocks. This has to hit just perfectly off your butt to keep the dribble going. After the ball bounces off, try doing some trick moves such as a few between the leg dribbles or go behind your back before attempting another dribble off the butt. Do at least five of these "butt" dribbles, and try to have fun with this drill.

VI. Advanced Dribbling

9. **dribble behind head over left shoulder with right hand** – The next two drills involve a fun dribble in which the ball is bounced much higher than usual. Begin by making one hard (and high) dribble with the right hand. When the ball comes up, bring it behind your head and push it over the left shoulder so it bounces near your left foot. Now make a simple crossover dribble from the left hand to the right and perform the steps again. You can also try this while moving forward. Complete ten over the left shoulder dribbles.

10. **dribble behind head over right shoulder with left hand** – Just the opposite of the last drill, start with one hard dribble using the left hand and then bring the ball behind your head and push it over the right shoulder (bouncing near your right foot). Next make a crossover dribble from the right to left hand to begin another. Complete ten over the right shoulder dribbles.

11. **wraparound dribble – right hand and left side** – This drill is called the wraparound dribble because the ball will be "wrapped around" the left side of your body with the right hand. Begin by placing your feet shoulder width apart and bounce the ball once in front of your right foot with the right hand. When the ball comes up, wrap (push) the ball around the left side of your body using the right hand. The ball must travel all the way behind your back and over to your right side (along the right leg). This is similar to a regular behind the back dribble except the ball is coming from the opposite hand. While still keeping your feet planted, you may have to lean your body to the right in order to get the ball around the left side. Once you have quickly regained control of the ball with the right hand, bounce it one time again in front of your right foot and perform another wraparound dribble. The entire drill consists of two right hand dribbles, one in front and one wraparound. Obviously the difficult part is learning to wrap the ball and directing it all the way to the other side of your body. Once you get the hang of it, complete ten "wraparounds" before going to the next exercise.

12. **wraparound dribble – left hand and right side** – In this drill you are going to wrap the ball around the right side of your body using the left hand. Remain in the same position as in the last exercise and bounce the ball one time in front of the left foot with your left hand. Your next dribble will be a wraparound on the right side of your body. It will be necessary to firmly push the ball around your right side to get it to bounce behind your back and over to the left side (along the left leg). Once you complete the wraparound dribble, you must quickly bring your left hand back over to get the ball. Remember that just two dribbles are used to complete the drill, both with only the left hand. Again, your goal is to perform ten "wraparounds".

VI. Advanced Dribbling   157

13. **box dribble – 4 dribbles outside of legs (reverse)** -- Although the next five exercises are related, each is unique in its own special way. When you read the descriptions, visualize the drill to picture how it differs from the others. These five drills are similar to some of the stationary and ball around body drills in Basic Dribbling (part II, sections A and B). This box dribble is well named because the dribbles are done in a box configuration. Stand with your feet a little more than shoulder width apart and your knees slightly bent (all the dribbles will be waist high). Begin the first dribble in your left hand and bounce the ball over to the right hand directly in front of you. The second dribble travels along your right side from front to back with the right hand. The third dribble goes directly behind your back from the right hand to the left. The fourth and last dribble comes from the back to the front along your left side (with the left hand) to where you started the drill. All four dribbles are done outside the legs; the ball <u>never</u> comes between the legs. Each four-dribble set equals one complete box dribble. Execute five box dribbles as just described, and then reverse the direction of the ball for five more.

14. **box dribble – continuous low (reverse)** -- The regular box dribble is not hard once you understand the course that the ball travels. This box dribble requires you to crouch with your knees bent since the dribbles will be performed much lower (instead of waist high). Start with the ball in your left hand in front of you and begin the box dribble as in the last drill, but now use continuous low dribbles. Instead of executing four dribbles to complete one box dribble, you will perform many low dribbles using the box dribbling pattern. This drill is intended to be completed with dribbles in a straight line, not in circle patterns as you have done in other dribbling sections. Perform a total of five box dribbles in each direction, increasing your speed each time.

15. **hourglass dribble – 4 dribbles inside of legs (reverse)** -- If you can visualize the sequence of dribbles in this exercise, you will understand why it is called the hourglass dribble. The ball has the same directional pattern as the hourglass pass you performed in section F of Advanced Ball Handling. Like the last drill, remain in the same crouched position with your feet spread about two feet. This drill is comprised of four short, quick dribbles inside the legs. The first dribble goes from the left toes to the right toes (from the left hand to the right hand). The second dribble moves diagonally from the right toes to directly behind the left heel (right hand to left hand). The third dribble travels across from behind the left

VI. Advanced Dribbling

heel to directly behind the right heel (left hand to right hand). The fourth and last dribble moves diagonally from behind the right heel up to the left toes where you began (right hand to left hand). The ball should never bounce above your knee or move to the outside of the legs. Each four dribble set equals one complete hourglass dribble. Finish five complete hourglass dribbles and then reverse the direction of the ball for five more sets.

16. **hourglass dribble – continuous low (reverse)** – Instead of the four dribble sequence, this drill consists of continuous low dribbles using the hourglass format. This time you will use many low dribbles to go across or diagonally from one side to the other. The low speed dribbles you learned in section A will greatly assist you because you need very quick hands with this type of dribble. All these compact dribbles are performed inside your legs, with a lot of the dribbles occurring directly beneath you. Begin the exercise at your left toes and dribble the ball using the same directions as in the last drill. One set will be complete when you finish the hourglass pattern. Once more, finish five complete hourglass sets and then reverse directions for five more.

17. **butterfly dribble – 4 dribbles (reverse)** – This is a dribble you have probably never seen; you may enjoy demonstrating it to your friends. The butterfly dribble is much like the box and hourglass dribbles except the ball travels in a slightly different path. Stand upright (slight bend in the knees) with your feet spread about two feet apart. Start the ball in your left hand in front of the left foot to begin the first of a four dribble set. The first dribble bounces diagonally between your legs from the left hand to the right hand (behind your right leg). Using only the right hand, the second dribble comes up along the right side past your right leg using only the right hand. The third dribble travels diagonally through your legs from the right hand to the left hand (behind your left leg). The fourth and final dribble comes straight up the outside of your left leg using only the left hand. After the four dribbles, the ball is back in the same spot where you started (in front of the left foot) and ready for you to begin another butterfly dribble. To get a better understanding of the drill, draw the path of the four dribbles on a sheet of paper and you will easily see the butterfly shape. Keep in mind that all the dribbles in this exercise should bounce no higher than your waist. Try to look straight ahead during the drill and finish at least five complete butterfly dribbles in each direction.

VI. Advanced Dribbling

18. **combination dribble (reverse)** -- This last drill combines three different dribble moves you have learned, thus, a "combination dribble." The three different moves you will use are the between the legs dribble, the behind the back dribble, and the double-cross dribble (in that order). Each complete combination dribble consists of these three. To start, dribble the ball between your legs from the left hand (in front) to the right hand (behind you). As soon as the ball reaches your right hand and you have control of it, perform a right hand behind the back dribble over to your left side. Once the ball bounces up along your left side, complete a quick double-cross dribble in front of your body from the left hand to the right hand and then back to the left. When the ball is back in your left hand, begin another combination dribble. Your goal is to complete five complete combination dribbles in each direction. For the reversal mode, you will need to switch the direction of the ball and also change the hands to be used for the different dribbles. The between the legs dribble moves from the right hand (in front) to the left hand (in back). Once the ball reaches your left hand, perform a behind the back dribble over to the right side and then a double-cross dribble in front of your body before starting the whole sequence again. The entire combination drill should happen very quickly, although it is best to begin slowly in order to get a good feel for the drill.

Conclusion of Part VI

– You have just completed the last of the six main parts of this book. Advanced Dribbling contained drills that were beneficial, challenging, and fun. There were probably some drills that you had seen before, but hopefully most of the exercises were brand new to you. This part covered a wide array of different types of dribbles, from speed dribbling to lying down dribbles to dribbling off your leg. Many unique dribbling drills were included, and many of the drills required you to be in positions that were different from the normal standing or crouched position. Strong emphasis was placed on improving your ball control, hand quickness, confidence, and your overall flexibility. Good luck with all the drills you just learned and have fun developing your dribbling abilities. The remaining two parts, Two-Ball Workout and Spinning involve many more creative exercises and are just as challenging. The next part of the book, Two-Ball Workout, will test your ball handling and dribbling abilities; give it your best shot!

VII. Two-Ball Workout

Ball handling drills and tricks are difficult enough with one basketball, so why use two? Drills with two basketballs will greatly improve your hand-eye coordination and concentration because you have to synchronize all your movements so each drill will work properly. This Two-Ball Workout forces you to develop your weak hand because you cannot always watch both balls. This will give you more confidence in your ball handling and dribbling abilities. Also, being able to dribble the ball proficiently with each hand prevents your opponent from overplaying you to one side because they never know which direction you want to go. Most of these two-ball exercises refer to other drills that you have already performed, except now an extra ball has been added. For the Two-Ball Workout to run smoothly, both basketballs must have the same amount of air; otherwise, it would be extremely difficult to get through these drills.

A. Two-Ball Dribbling – Stationary

This section is a good introduction for the Two-Ball Workout because it will show you some basic two-ball dribbles and skills that you can use in the upcoming sections. The first few exercises are not particularly difficult, but they will require coordination and practice on your part to develop them. Many creative dribbling drills are included in this section. Because each drill will have a goal associated with it, read the explanations thoroughly. Be sure to allow yourself plenty of space in order to have room to work. Until you learn all the techniques, the balls may go all over the place, but keep practicing. If you make a mistake, continue dribbling one ball as you retrieve the ball that rolled away.

1. dribble – same time/same height -- If you can learn to do this drill effectively, you are ahead of the game for the rest of the Two-Ball Workout. Simply dribble the balls about waist high in front of you so both balls always hit the floor at exactly the same time. Continue dribbling the balls in this manner for at least fifteen seconds. After dribbling the two balls waist high, alternate the height of the balls by dribbling them low, down near the knees and ankles. For an added challenge, perform stationary speed dribbles with both balls and see how low you can keep them dribbled. Remember always to dribble both balls at the same height during this drill.

VII. Two-Ball Workout 161

2. **dribble – alternating bounces** -- In this exercise you are going to dribble the two balls just the opposite of the last drill. As one of the balls is hitting the floor, the ball in your other hand should be getting ready to be dribbled. Continue this alternating dribbling pattern, and do not let the balls bounce any higher than your waist. This exercise should also be done for at least fifteen seconds, and the fingertips need to be used exclusively.

3. **dribble right hand high, left hand low** -- This will be an unusual exercise because your body is put in an awkward dribbling position. Begin dribbling one ball with your left hand very low to the ground by dipping your left shoulder. Now dribble the other ball with your right hand, but bounce it waist high. You should have two balls dribbling at different heights, one ball about ankle high and the other ball waist high. This drill forces your body in an uncomfortable position because the left shoulder is dipped low and the right shoulder is up much higher. Your goal is to dribble the balls using this style for a total of fifteen seconds. There is no particular sequence for the balls to be dribbled as you were required in the first two drills of this section.

4. **dribble left hand high, right hand low** -- For this drill, you will perform the exact opposite maneuvers as in the last exercise. Start by dribbling one ball waist high with the left hand, and dribble the other ball ankle high with the right hand (right shoulder dipped). Continue to dribble both balls in this manner for fifteen seconds. Neither ball should come to a stop during your fifteen second goal. The drill will become considerably easier once you get the two balls bouncing in a rhythm that is comfortable for you.

5. **dribble off ground – both balls at same time** -- In section F of Advanced Dribbling, you learned to dribble a ball "off the ground," first with the right hand and then with the left hand. In this drill you will dribble both balls off the ground at the same time. You can perform this drill in a sitting position or down on one knee. Begin by setting the balls on the ground about a foot apart. Next, quickly "pop" both balls simultaneously with your hands so the balls bounce an inch or two off the floor. When the balls bounce up, complete at least five low dribbles with each ball, and then place them

back on the ground. As is the case with all "off the ground" dribbles, you must smack each ball with a hard but quick hand to give the balls some spring. Each dribble off the ground and at least five low dribbles afterwards equal one set. Try to finish five sets, although you will find it is much more difficult with two balls than just the one.

VII. Two-Ball Workout

6. **dribble with arms crossed** -- This exercise will introduce you to a type of dribble you have probably not seen before. Start the drill in either a sitting position or down on one knee. Hold a ball in each hand (palms facing up) and then cross your arms at the wrists. Now drop the balls and then quickly turn your hands over to begin dribbling the two balls a few inches off the floor while your arms are crossed. Obviously, the balls are dribbled close to each another. Do not let them collide. It does not matter which arm is crossed over the other because the same result is accomplished either way. If possible, try to have both balls bounce on the floor at the same time, because this will help the drill run more smoothly. You should have no problem completing the required goal of fifteen seconds. You will find this drill to be a good basis for the next exercise.

7. **dribble with crossing arms every other dribble** -- Keep your body in the same position as in the last drill and start the same two-ball dribbles that you just completed with your arms crossed. Once you get the balls going in a comfortable pattern, quickly uncross your arms and complete one regular dribble with the two balls. As soon as that one regular dribble is finished, cross your arms again for another dribble with two balls. Continue this alternating sequence of one regular dribble and then one cross-arm dribble. Your hands must move rapidly to keep up because you do not want a ball to hit the floor without being dribbled. You have to keep the balls relatively close together or it will be difficult to complete the exercise. Try this drill for fifteen seconds but eventually strive for thirty seconds. You will be amazed how quickly your hands will be moving!

8. **each finger – both hands at same time** -- Similar to the last few exercises, you can complete this drill while in a sitting position or down on one knee. Begin dribbling

one ball with only the left index finger and the other ball with only the right index finger. All of the dribbles need to be speed dribbles so keep both balls as low as you can. Use only the fingertip of each finger to help you speed dribble the balls. Continue with the index fingers for ten seconds, and then quickly switch to your middle fingers for another ten seconds. After you finish with the middle fingers, change to the ring fingers, the pinkies, and finally the thumbs. Remember that only one finger on each hand should be dribbling at any given time. Ten seconds for each set of fingers does not seem like a long time, but you will be surprised how hard it is when two balls are being dribbled this low and this fast simultaneously.

VII. Two-Ball Workout 163

9. **side to side dribbles in front – same direction** -- The dribbles in this exercise are just like the side to side V dribbles in Basic Dribbling (part II, section A), except now you  will include another ball. You are going to do a side to side dribble with the right hand (V pattern) so the ball always hits the floor just above the right foot. At the same time, complete a side to side dribble with the left hand (V pattern) so this ball hits the floor every time just above the left foot. Both balls should always be traveling in the same direction and they need to hit the floor at the same time every dribble. Begin with waist high dribbles and work towards knee high dribbles. With your knees bent, complete these simultaneous V dribbles for a minimum of fifteen seconds.

10. **side to side dribbles in front – opposite directions** -- This drill adds a twist to the last exercise. You are going to perform side to side V dribbles in front of you (in the middle) with each hand, but this time the balls will be moving in opposite directions. With your knees bent, dribble one ball side to side (V pattern) with the right hand so the ball hits the floor just above both sets of toes. At the same time, dribble the other ball side to side (V pattern) with the left hand but behind the first ball. The two balls will always be traveling in opposite directions. As one ball is bouncing from left to right, the other ball is being dribbled from right to left (and so on). Begin with waist high dribbles and then work towards dribbling about knee high. Also, try switching around so the left hand side to side V dribbles are in front and the right hand dribbles are behind. Complete these opposite side to side dribbles in front for at least fifteen seconds.

11. **along each side with each hand – same direction** -- This is another drill that was relatively easy with one ball, but now two balls make it more challenging. Position your feet just a few inches apart and bend your knees, much like the stance of a skier. At the same time and moving in the same direction, dribble one ball along the left side of your body (with the left hand) and the other ball along the right side (with the right hand). The balls will bounce a few inches to the outside of each respective

  foot and should be dribbled about knee high. Since the balls move back and forth in a V pattern (push and pull method), be sure to use quick hand movements. This exercise is much easier to do if you can always get both balls to bounce at exactly the same time, because it will allow you to develop a good rhythm. Try to get both balls bouncing simultaneously for fifteen seconds.

VII. Two-Ball Workout

12. **along each side with each hand – opposite directions** – This drill will be much harder than the last exercise, although the drills are very similar. In the last exercise, the balls were synchronized while moving in the same direction with every V dribble. For this drill, you will also perform side to side V dribbles, but the balls will be going in opposite directions at the same time (as one ball is moving forward, the other ball will be going backwards and then vice versa). It may be best to use hand motions without the balls initially in order to develop the necessary movements. While in the skier's stance, dribble one ball along the left side of your body and the other ball along the right side (of course in opposite directions). As in the last exercise, the balls will bounce a few inches to the outside of each respective foot and should be dribbled about knee high. Try to develop a smooth rhythm in order to get both balls bouncing in opposite directions in the V pattern for fifteen seconds. You may be surprised how difficult it is to sustain this dribble for fifteen seconds.

13. **whip dribbles – alternating bounces** – In Intermediate Dribbling (part IV, section A), you performed whip dribbles with one ball using each hand. For this drill, you are going to do the same thing except by adding another ball, you are performing alternating whip dribbles with two balls. Start with the knees bent and your feet in a wide stance in order to keep a firm base with your legs. As you may recall, whip dribbles have only one bounce, and that is always done directly between your legs. For the right side, cradle the ball in your right hand and whip it around the right side of your body (clockwise direction) and bounce it through your legs in order to catch it in front with the right hand. You have to move your right hand quickly around the right leg to grab the ball in front. Just as the ball from your right hand hits the floor, cradle the other ball in your left hand and whip it around the left side of your body

(counterclockwise direction). Throw the ball through your legs so it bounces once and you catch it back in front with the left hand. Continue alternating the balls through your legs for twenty dribbles (ten for each side). This drill involves precise timing because you must coordinate each dribble in order to develop a rhythm. Although upper body movement will be necessary, keep your feet firmly planted.

14. **whip dribbles – both balls at same time** – You may find this variation of the two-ball whip dribbles to be more difficult. Instead of alternating the dribbles, you will bounce the balls through your legs at the same time. Bend your knees and position your feet a little wider for this drill in order to develop a solid base with your legs. Cradle a ball in each hand and simultaneously take the balls around each side of the body and whip them through your legs at the same time. Once you release the balls, quickly bring your hands around the legs to grab the balls in front and continue more whip dribbles. Try to bounce the balls through your legs using this whip dribble technique for twenty dribbles (ten for each side). Your wrists and forearms will get a good workout in this drill.

VII. Two-Ball Workout   165

15. **over/under dribble – standing** – The over/under dribble is a fun drill that requires good coordination and fast hands. It is also a good introduction to the roundabout and cone dribbling drills later in this section. It is important to realize that only one ball is dribbled in the drill, although two balls are used. Stand with your feet shoulder width apart and a ball in each hand. To begin, dribble the ball in your right hand so it bounces up to the left hand (V pattern). As soon as you release that ball, pass the ball in your left hand over to the right hand (which is now empty). Your next move will be just the opposite. Dribble the ball in your left hand to the right hand (V pattern). While that ball is bouncing, transfer the other ball from your right hand to the left

hand. These maneuvers are the basis of the exercise, and you will constantly repeat them throughout the drill. As you can tell from the explanation, one ball is continually handed off back and forth up top, while the other ball is dribbled back and forth underneath. The drill moves rapidly, so get those hands moving! Perform the exercise for a minimum of fifteen seconds.

16. **over/under dribble – sitting** – This sitting over/under dribble requires even faster hands than the last exercise because the dribbles are much lower. You can do the drill in a sitting position, on both knees, or down on one knee. As in the last drill, one ball is constantly handed off from hand to hand up top (over), while the other ball is dribbled back and forth underneath (under). Start by dribbling the ball in your right hand so it bounces to the left hand (V pattern). Immediately after you release that ball, pass the ball in your left hand over to the right hand. The next move will be the reverse of what you just completed. Bounce the ball in your left hand up to the right hand (V pattern), while passing the ball in your right hand back over to the left hand. Continue these maneuvers just described repeatedly because they are the heart and soul of the whole exercise. Since these movements happen so fast, make sure you understand every move or you will become frustrated. Complete the drill for at least fifteen seconds, but also try to see how long you can keep the balls going.

17. **roundabout dribble – standing (reverse)** -- This is a tough two-ball exercise that combines a dribble in front with an around the body drill. Stand with your feet shoulder width apart, a ball in each hand. To begin, dribble the ball in your left hand so it bounces over to the right hand (V pattern). As you release that ball, rotate the ball in your right hand clockwise around your waist and over to the left hand (which is now empty). The ball is simply passed around your waist; there is no dribble involved. You should have a ball in each hand

again. Continue this sequence for at least fifteen seconds, trying to increase your speed each time. The process is more easily said than done and it may take many attempts before you can successfully perform these maneuvers. For the reverse mode, dribble the ball in your right hand over to the left hand and rotate the other ball around your waist counterclockwise from the left hand to the right. Being able to coordinate the timing of each dribble with the rotation around the waist will help.

18. **roundabout dribble – sitting (reverse)** – Like the sitting over/under dribble, this exercise requires quick hands because the dribbles do not bounce very high. You can complete this drill sitting, on both knees, or down on one knee; please find a position that is comfortable for you. Start with a ball in each hand and then dribble the ball in your left hand over to the right (V pattern). At the same time, rotate the ball in your right hand clockwise around your waist and over to the left hand. Once you have a ball in each hand again, you are ready to continue. Remember that the ball moving around your waist is handed off, not dribbled. The hard part is learning to transfer the ball around your waist without losing control of it. When reversing the exercise, dribble the ball in your right hand over to the left and rotate the other ball around your waist counterclockwise from the left hand to the right. Aim for at least fifteen seconds in each direction.

19. **cone dribble – standing (reverse)** – This drill is really neat and you will find it to be a good way to show off your skills. These skills include hand quickness, synchronization of the two basketballs, and dribbling expertise. Start with your feet shoulder width apart and hold a ball in each hand about waist high. Visualize the shape of a cone because that is the pattern the balls will be traveling. Your first move is to dribble the ball in your right hand so it bounces up to the left hand (a V pattern). Immediately after you release that ball, flip (hand) the ball in your left hand over to the right hand to complete the second move. Next, perform the same two moves as above to complete the cone dribble. Now you are back where you began with the same balls in the same hands. Continue this cone pattern repeatedly and increase your speed. Once the balls are moving extremely fast, complete this exercise for at least fifteen seconds. Also, reverse the direction of the balls and execute the drill for fifteen seconds more. When you have mastered this exercise, you will be astonished at how fast you can dribble two balls using this cone format.

VII. Two-Ball Workout 167

20. **cone dribble – sitting (reverse)** -- The last drill was performed with waist high dribbles, but this sitting drill will require much lower dribbles. Try this drill sitting, on both knees, or down on one knee. As in the last exercise, begin with a ball in each hand and dribble the ball in your right hand so it bounces up to the left hand (a V pattern). After you release that ball, flip (hand) the ball in your left hand over to the right hand. Next, perform the same two moves just mentioned to complete the cone dribble. Now you are back where you began with the same balls in the same hands. Try this sequence a few times slowly to acquire a general idea of the ball movements necessary for these low dribbles. Continually increase the ball speed as you become skilled with this sitting cone dribble. You need to complete the drill in each direction for at least fifteen seconds and also see how long you can sustain this sitting cone dribble.

21. **sit-ups with one ball dribbling on each side** -- This is an exercise that is similar to a drill you performed with one ball in Advanced Dribbling (section C, drill #17). You are going to try to finish ten sit-ups while dribbling two basketballs at the same time. Dribble one ball with the right hand next to your waist on the right side of your body. Dribble the other ball with the left hand next to your waist on the left side of your body. These are not going to be speed dribbles, but low and controlled dribbles. Although ten sit-ups are the goal, see how many you can do consecutively without losing control of the balls.

VII. Two-Ball Workout

B. Two-Ball Dribbling – Around Body

The previous section should have given you a good start for the rest of the Two-Ball Workout. Almost every exercise in this section has been introduced at some prior time, but with only one ball. Now you are going to utilize the skills previously learned and apply them to these two-ball dribbling drills around your body. At first, you will most likely have to look at the balls while dribbling. As you become more proficient, try to perform the drills with your head up (a real challenge). Make sure you fully understand all the steps in each exercise before trying them at full speed. Each drill is explained in only one direction because every exercise in this section is also reversed, which means there are really two parts for each drill. Read each description carefully and complete at least five rotations in each direction (clockwise and counterclockwise).

1. **right leg (reverse)** – It is best to begin this drill with a wide stance because you may need the extra room between your legs for the balls to come through. Place your right leg slightly forward and begin dribbling the balls around your right leg with both hands. Start out dribbling the balls around the right leg in a clockwise direction, concentrating on being able to handle two balls successfully at the same time. You do not have to begin with low dribbles but eventually work to increase your speed by dribbling both balls very low to the ground. As mentioned in the introduction, try to complete five clockwise rotations (actually ten with two balls) and then reverse directions for five counterclockwise rotations. You will find the counterclockwise direction more difficult. For a real trick, attempt these dribbles with the balls going in opposite directions. While one ball is traveling around the right leg clockwise, the other one will be dribbled counterclockwise. These opposite dribbles will require a great deal of coordination with your hands.

2. **left leg (reverse)** – Dribbling two balls around the left leg is not significantly different from going around the right leg. This time, place the left leg out front and begin dribbling the two balls around your left leg. You really have to shift both hands quickly to keep the balls moving. Work on coordinating your hand movements at first, and then concentrate on increasing the speed of the balls. This time the clockwise direction will be harder. If you are feeling brave, try to dribble the balls in opposite directions as in the last drill.

VII. Two-Ball Workout   169

3. **dribble one ball out in front, other around right leg (reverse)** -- You may find these next two exercises easier than the two previous drills, although some may find it more difficult. For both exercises, spread your legs out and bend your knees so you are in a comfortable squatting position. Start this drill by dribbling one ball directly out in front of you with the left hand and about ankle high. Next, begin dribbling the

other ball clockwise with the right hand around your right leg, keeping the ball as close as you can to the right foot. After you have dribbled the ball around the right leg five times, reverse directions and complete five more rotations counterclockwise with the right hand. You will notice that dribbling the ball counterclockwise is much more difficult. Of course the ball in your left hand will continually be dribbled out in front when the other ball is being dribbled around your right leg with the right hand. This exercise requires concentration because you are dribbling two balls that are independent of each other.

4. **dribble one ball out in front, other around left leg (reverse)** -- Let's now switch sides and try the opposite of the previous drill. Begin dribbling one ball about ankle high directly out in front of you with the right hand. Now start dribbling the other ball with only the left hand around your left leg. Dribble the ball in your left hand close to the left foot and keep the ball low to the ground so it is not bouncing up to your knee. Complete five rotations with your left hand around the left leg in each direction, while keeping the ball in your right hand bouncing out in front of you. In this drill you will notice that dribbling the ball in your left hand is much more challenging in the clockwise direction.

5. **figure 8 (reverse)** -- Combine the last two drills and you have this two-ball figure 8. Because this exercise is difficult to explain, the description is more detailed. Remain in the same stance as in the two previous exercises, with your legs spread and knees bent. Dribble one ball with your left hand in front of you and dribble the other ball in a clockwise direction once around your right leg with the right hand (like drill #3). When the ball in your right hand comes between your legs to the front, dribble the ball in your left hand counterclockwise once around the left leg. As the ball is going around the left leg, dribble the ball in your right hand in front (like drill #4). Once the ball in your left hand comes between your legs to the front, you have now completed the two-ball figure 8. Continue this figure 8 dribbling pattern five times; then reverse directions for five more rotations. The balls should move rapidly because all the dribbles need to be about ankle high. In the reversal mode, the ball will go around the right leg counterclockwise and around the left leg clockwise. This reversal mode is considerably more difficult.

VII. Two-Ball Workout

6. **both legs together (reverse)** -- For this exercise, put both feet together and bend your knees in order to be in a position to dribble both balls low to the floor. Next, simply dribble the balls around your two legs (feet). If necessary, dribble both balls about knee high at first, but ultimately you should dribble the balls very quickly and low to the floor. Obviously you will be successful in this drill if you can keep both balls dribbled close to your legs.

7. **both legs spread apart (reverse)** -- Spread your legs a little more than shoulder width apart (not a really wide stance) and bend your knees so you are in a crouched position. Dribble both balls around the outside of your legs, never letting either ball bounce between your legs at any time. You will need quick hands to keep up with the balls as they are bouncing around the outside of your legs. Do not forget to reverse the direction of the balls.

8. **two-ball dribbles – one in front, one behind the back (reverse)** -- This drill involves two simultaneous dribbles, a crossover dribble (in front) and a behind the back dribble. Begin with a ball in each hand, your feet shoulder width apart, and knees bent. Next, crossover the ball in your left hand to the right and at the same time, execute a behind the back dribble from the right hand to the left. Each two-ball dribble should hit the floor at the same time to maintain a good dribbling rhythm. To help the drill run smoothly, <u>perform two "same time/same height" dribbles in front of you after each two-ball dribble</u>. For the reverse mode, crossover the ball in your right hand to the left and execute a behind the back dribble from the left hand to the right. Instead of completing five of these two-ball dribbles, aim for ten in each direction.

9. **two-ball dribbles – one in front, one between the legs (reverse)** -- Similar to the last exercise, this drill includes two dribbles performed simultaneously, except now you will execute a crossover dribble (in front) and a between the legs dribble. Start with your feet a little more than shoulder width apart, knees bent, and a ball in each hand. Now crossover the ball in your left hand to the right hand, and at the same time, complete a between the legs dribble from the right hand to the left. Every between the legs dribble for this exercise will be done using the back to front method to assure that the ball is always moving forward to your opposite hand. Each two-ball dribble should hit the floor in unison to keep a smooth dribbling rhythm. Exactly like the last drill, <u>perform two "same time/same height" dribbles in front of you after each two-ball dribble</u>. In the reverse mode the hand and ball movements will be just the opposite. The crossover dribble will be from the right hand to the left, and the between the legs dribble will move from the left hand (in back) to the right (in front). Try to achieve ten of these two-dribbles in each direction rather than only five.

VII. Two-Ball Workout 171

10. **down on left knee – around right leg (reverse)** -- Place your left knee down on the floor and dribble both balls around your right leg (foot) with both hands. Since your body is so low to the ground, the balls must be dribbled very low in order to get them beneath the right leg. You must demonstrate quick hands to keep up with the balls because you have to bounce them very low and as close to the right foot as possible. You will probably find the counterclockwise rotations to be more difficult.

11. **down on right knee – around left leg (reverse)** -- This is like the previous exercise, except now you are down on the right knee. Now dribble the two balls around your left leg using both hands. The drill will run more smoothly if you can execute all your dribbles close to the left foot. This will allow you to have better control of the balls because you will not be reaching out so much. This time the clockwise direction will probably be a little harder for you to handle.

12. **down on both knees around body (reverse)** -- Start the drill by placing both knees together on the floor. Dribble the two balls around your entire body, coordinating both of your hands to keep the balls continuously moving. At first you may have to dribble a little higher until you can successfully do the drill with low dribbles. The hardest part of the dribbling occurs when either ball is behind you, so it is necessary to really stretch backwards. Five rotations in each direction should be difficult, but you can do it!

13. **sitting Indian style around body (reverse)** -- Begin by sitting Indian style (legs crossed) and then dribble the balls around your body using both hands. Since there are two balls involved in such a large dribbling area, you will not be able to turn around easily, so really concentrate on keeping the balls under control. Because it is difficult to dribble the balls very high in the sitting position, there is no choice but to maintain low dribbles. Of course you need to keep each ball within an arm's length because you want to avoid getting up to chase the balls. Do not be surprised if this drill frustrates you somewhat in the beginning.

VII. Two-Ball Workout

C. Two-Ball Dribbling – Moving

Some very difficult two-ball dribbling drills while walking/running are included in this section. These drills are similar to the stationary and around the body drills in the first two sections of the Two-Ball Workout, except now there is movement involved. The first two drills are basic but the last seven are quite challenging. Coordination and concentration are necessary for properly executing these exercises. Every drill will have either a timed goal or a certain number of court lengths to complete. Each drill will have one of these goals associated with it. Give yourself a test to see if you can do all these two-ball moving drills with your head up throughout the entire exercise. For additional challenge, try these two-ball dribbles while moving backwards.

1. **dribble – same time/same height** -- Try to recall the first two-ball drill because here it is again in a walking format. You are going to dribble both balls waist high in front of you as you are walking. The balls need to hit the floor at the same time in order to have synchronized dribbles when you are moving down the court. If you have no problems with the waist high dribbles, change heights and try two-ball dribbles down near your knees or even ankles. Start the drill by walking slowly; then walk more quickly, and finally work your way up to dribbling the two balls while running (speed dribbles). Your goal is to use this "same time/same height" dribble for two court lengths.

2. **dribble – alternating bounces** -- For this exercise, dribble both balls down the court using alternating bounces as you performed in drill #2, section A. As one of the balls is hitting the floor, the ball in your other hand should be at your fingertips ready to be dribbled. Continue alternating the dribbles and use bounces that are waist high throughout the drill. Since you are moving forward, keep an eye on what is around you to be sure no hazards are in your path. Start this dribble by walking slowly; then gradually increase your speed until you are moving rapidly (speed dribbles). Complete two court lengths using this alternating dribble.

3. **figure 8 – walking (reverse)** -- This drill has the same ball movements as the two-ball figure 8 in the last section. Start with your legs spread and your knees bent so you are in a crouched position. Dribble one ball with your left hand in front of you and dribble the other ball in a clockwise direction once around your right leg with the right hand. When the ball in your right hand comes between your legs to the front, dribble the ball in your left hand in a counterclockwise direction once around the left leg. As the ball is going around the left leg, dribble the ball in your right hand in front. When the ball in your left hand travels around the left leg and between your legs to the

VII. Two-Ball Workout 173

front, you are ready to begin another figure 8. The actions just described are the basis for the ball movements, but you also need to be walking forward simultaneously. This is certainly the slowest moving exercise in this section because you have to take such small steps. Begin with slow dribbles and work your way up to swift ankle high dribbles. Bear in mind that the faster you dribble the ball, the faster you will be walking. Instead of the two-court lengths goal, complete this drill for a minimum of fifteen seconds; then reverse the direction of the balls for at least fifteen seconds more.

4. **two-ball dribbles – one in front, one behind the back (reverse)** -- Like exercise #8 in the last section, these "two-ball dribbles" combine a crossover dribble (in front) and a behind the back dribble. Start this exercise dribbling both balls three times using the moving "same time/same height" method you performed in the first drill of this section. Next, crossover the ball in your left hand to the right hand and execute a behind the back dribble from the right hand to the left hand. These two-ball dribbles just explained happen simultaneously and must be perfect each time to maintain continuity. <u>Complete three "same time/same height" dribbles between each of the two-ball dribbles</u>. Your goal is to go two court lengths while continually performing the techniques just mentioned. This drill can be done in a walking mode or you can move a little faster and run down the court while doing the two-ball dribbles. In the reversal mode, you will crossover one ball from the right hand to the left hand and execute a behind the back dribble from the left hand to the right hand with the other ball. Complete two court lengths again using the reversal mode.

5. **two-ball dribbles – one in front, one between the legs (reverse)** -- This drill is identical to #9 in the last section except you will execute the two-ball dribbles in a moving fashion. Begin with a ball in each hand and perform three "same time/same height" dribbles in front of you. Next, crossover the ball in your left hand to the right, and at the same time complete a between the legs dribble from the right hand up to the left. Remember to use the back to front technique when dribbling between your legs to guarantee that the ball is always moving forward. <u>Complete three "same time/same height" dribbles between each of the two-ball dribbles</u>. You will execute all these dribbles while moving forward down the court. Start out walking slowly and then gradually move to faster speeds. As in the last drill, your goal is to go two court lengths while completing these dribbles. For the reverse mode, the crossover dribble will be from the right hand to the left, and the between the legs dribble will travel from the left hand up to the right. Aim for two court lengths again using the reversal method.

6. **over/under dribble – walking** -- Recall from the standing over/under dribble in the first section that only one ball is dribbled in this drill, although two balls are used. Begin with a ball in each hand; then dribble the ball in your right hand so it bounces up to the left hand (V pattern). As soon as you release that ball, pass (hand) the ball in your left hand over to the right hand, which is now empty. Your next move will be the opposite. Dribble the ball in the left hand up to the right hand (V pattern). At the same time, transfer the other ball from your right hand to the left hand. Continue the two moves just described repeatedly as you are walking down the court. To help you

VII. Two-Ball Workout

with this drill, remember that one ball is constantly handed off back and forth up top (never dribbled), while the other ball is dribbled back and forth underneath. Although this is a walking exercise, you can eventually move quickly down the court. Complete this exercise for thirty seconds rather than two court lengths. At first you may find it difficult not to look at the two balls as you are walking.

7. **roundabout dribble – walking (reverse)** – The walking roundabout dribble is identical to the stationary one you learned in section A. Start by dribbling the ball in your left hand over to the right hand (V pattern). As you release that ball, rotate the ball in your right hand clockwise around your waist and over to the left hand. Keep repeating these two simultaneous maneuvers as you are walking down the court. Recall that when the ball is rotated around your waist, it is passed from hand to hand and is never to touch the floor. The balls simply change directions for the reverse mode, a right hand to left hand dribble and a counterclockwise rotation around your waist from the left hand to the right. Your hands need to be moving rapidly during the entire drill. Although the title says this is a walking exercise, you can eventually progress to a running speed. Aim for fifteen seconds and then reverse the direction of the balls for an additional fifteen seconds.

8. **cone dribble – walking (reverse)** – This drill has the same ball movements as the standing cone dribble (section A), except now you will be moving forward (walking). Always think of a cone shape, because that is the pattern in which the balls will be traveling. Begin walking and your first move is to dribble the ball in your right hand so it bounces up to the left hand (in a V pattern). Immediately after you release that ball, flip (hand) the ball in your left hand over to the right hand to complete the second move. Next, perform the same two moves again to finish a complete cone dribble. Continue dribbling the balls using this cone pattern while walking down the court for at least fifteen seconds. Also, reverse the direction of the balls and complete the drill for at least fifteen seconds more. Start out moving slowly and gradually increase your speed. When you become proficient with this walking cone dribble, complete the exercise with your head up the entire time.

9. **dribble ball off stationary ball placed on floor** – A great deal of coordination is necessary to complete this difficult drill. Place one ball on the floor (stationary) and then drop the other ball so it hits the ball on the ground and bounces back up to you. When the ball pops up, push it back down and continue bouncing it off the other ball on the floor. Basically you are dribbling a ball but having it bounce off another ball instead of hitting the floor. In the beginning, it is best to try just one bounce at a time before attempting continuous dribbles. You have to hit the bottom ball just right or the top ball will bounce wildly away from you. If you want to get fancy, try to complete this drill while walking forward. This will require you to hit the bottom ball at an angle, forcing it to roll forward. Try to perform this challenging dribble for at least fifteen seconds.

VII. Two-Ball Workout 175

D. Ball Handling With Two Balls

While the first three sections of the Two-Ball Workout involved dribbling, this section deals with drills in which the balls never touch the ground. An assortment of balancing and flip drills is included to improve your overall coordination. You have probably never seen most of these exercises. The drills are relatively easy to learn but will take considerable effort to perform correctly. Each exercise has a goal associated with it; try to equal or exceed the suggested goals.

1. **balance balls on top of each other with both hands** -- The title states clearly the purpose of this drill. While standing, position your feet so they are shoulder width apart. Hold one ball in your right hand (fingertips only) with the palm facing up. Put the second ball on top of the first ball with the left hand and hold the ball in place. Now you should have one ball sitting on top of the other. Next, quickly remove the left hand from the top ball and place it on the lower ball (of course, each hand should be placed on the sides of the lower ball for better balancing). Your goal is to balance the top ball on the lower ball using both hands for at least ten seconds. If possible, balance the balls while remaining stationary and keep the balls at least a foot away from your body. This drill and the next two are excellent for developing your concentration and improving your balancing abilities.

2. **balance balls on top of each other with right hand** -- This exercise has the same basic concepts as the previous drill but the balancing will be done with only the right hand. Remain in the same position and hold one ball in your right hand with the palm facing up. With the left hand, place and hold the second ball on top of the first. Now remove the left hand so you are balancing one ball on top of the other with only the right hand. The left hand is never used except to position the second ball on top of the first. The goal is to balance the top ball for at least five seconds. This does not seem long, but it will be difficult to accomplish at first. Balancing the balls in this fashion tends to move you all over the place, but make a strong effort to remain stationary throughout the entire exercise.

3. **balance balls on top of each other with left hand** – Switch hands so you are now holding the lower ball with your left hand (palm facing up). Place and hold the other ball on top of the first with the right hand. Now quickly remove the right hand so the left hand is doing all the balancing. If you need to, put the right hand behind your back after you have positioned the second ball on top to avoid the temptation of using the right hand. Try to balance the top ball for at least five seconds while keeping the balls about a foot away from your chest.

VII. Two-Ball Workout

4. **hold one ball with both hands, bounce other one on top** -- In the last three drills you balanced a ball on top of another ball, but for this drill you are going to <u>bounce</u> a ball on top of another. Start by using the same balancing techniques used in drill #1 of this section (balancing with both hands). After you have the top ball balanced for two seconds, push it up in the air about six inches and then start bouncing the ball off the lower one. Continue these bounces with your feet firmly planted to remain stationary. Try to complete ten bounces in a row.

5. **leapfrog -- up and under** -- Now you will demonstrate your balancing skills and combine them with quick hands. The ball will travel in an up and under pattern much like the leapfrog game. Begin by balancing one ball on top of the other with both hands as you did in the first exercise in this section. Now lift both balls up in the air about a foot and release your hands from the bottom ball. Once you let go of the ball, quickly grab the top ball and bring it under the other one so you are balancing one ball on top of the other again. What you have actually done is switch positions of the balls by making the top one now the bottom ball. Your hands have to be extremely quick to grab the top ball each time or the drill will not work. Your goal is to complete five consecutive leapfrogs, which will not be easy!

6. **two-ball quick switch** -- This is a drill that is more difficult than it may seem. With your knees slightly bent, hold one ball at waist level in front of you with your right hand. Hold the other ball at waist level behind your back with the left hand. Make sure both balls are out an inch or two from your waist, do not lean the balls against your body. Next, toss (flip) the balls straight up at the same time about two or three inches. After you release the balls, quickly switch hands by bringing the right hand to the back and the left hand to the front to catch the balls. Now you are going to reverse the process using the same movements. Toss the balls up again and bring the right hand back to the front and the left hand around to the back to catch the balls. You should now have your hands and both balls in the same position as when you began the drill. Try to complete ten consecutive two-ball quick switches (five each way). Remember that the balls should only touch your hands and are not to hit any other part of your body.

VII. Two-Ball Workout   177

7. **toss both balls high in the air, catch in same hand at same time** -- To begin, hold one ball in each hand and toss the balls about three feet straight up. When the balls come down, catch them with the same hand used to do the tossing. The importance of a good toss cannot be overstated because a poor toss with either hand ruins the entire drill. Each throw must be very accurate to enable you to catch both balls at the same time. Continue to toss the two balls simultaneously in the air, increasing the height each time. The goal is to see how high you can toss the balls and still catch both of them. Of course you should try this drill outside or in a place that has a high ceiling, like a gymnasium.

8. **throw balls over head, catch in same hand behind back** -- This is the first of two drills in which some action will take place behind your back. You will also see a variation of this exercise later when you get into the two-ball spinning section. Begin by holding one ball in each hand in front of you. Next, throw both balls at the same time about two feet directly over your shoulders. As soon as you release the balls, quickly move both hands behind your back to catch a ball in each hand (catch in the same hand that did the toss). Both balls need to be thrown perfectly because there is little room for error when catching two balls behind your back since you are unable to see them. It is important to catch the balls with your fingertips instead of catching them in the palms of your hands. Complete five successful throws and catches that are two feet over your shoulders. Also try to see how high you can throw the balls and still catch both of them behind your back. It is strongly suggested that you attempt this drill outside in order not to break anything!

9. **lying down – toss both balls up, catch in same hand at same time** -- While lying flat on the floor, hold a ball in each hand by your shoulders. Simultaneously push both balls about four feet straight up. The balls should be completely synchronized; they need to leave your hands at the same time, tossed to the same height, and caught simultaneously. The tosses are similar to shooting a ball (slight backspin, good wrist action, etc...), except now you are lying down. You may need to practice these on each side with one hand before trying them with both hands. Staring at one ball may cause you to miss or even get hit by the other one. Looking straight up in the air will allow you to see both balls at the same time. Complete ten of these synchronized tosses and then see how high you can toss (shoot) the balls still catching both of them.

VII. Two-Ball Workout

10. **two-ball behind the back passes with partner or off wall (reverse)** -- This exercise is similar to the behind the back passes off the wall in Advanced Ball Handling (section F), except now two balls are used. Stand straight with your feet firmly planted and shoulder width apart. Start by standing six to ten feet from your partner or the wall and hold a ball in each hand. Begin by taking the ball in your right hand around your back from the right side to the left, letting go to complete the behind the back pass. Once you release the ball, quickly shift the ball in your left hand over to the right hand. As the first ball is reaching your partner or hitting the wall, the second ball will be coming around your back (from the right hand again). Each time you catch a ball, quickly pass it behind your back because the other ball is coming right behind it! If you are working with a partner, he/she will continually catch the balls and bounce them back to your right side. If you are using a wall, pass the balls off it at an angle in which they will bounce up to your right side. Try to hit the same spot on the wall each time to help the drill run smoothly and to prevent having balls bounce all over the place. The importance of perfect bounces off the wall cannot be overemphasized; strive to perfect this aspect of the drill. Standing sideways to your partner or the wall might work better for you because you do not have to bring the balls all the way around your back. For the reverse mode, change directions and pass the balls around your back from the left side to the right side. Complete a total of ten passes in each direction. Once you have the balls really moving, see how long you can sustain the action.

Conclusion of Part VII – Do you realize that you have just completed some of the most difficult ball handling and dribbling drills and tricks? It is hoped that the Two-Ball Workout helped develop your weak hand and improved your coordination and concentration. Continue practicing these two-ball drills because they will be beneficial for increasing your overall ball handling and dribbling skills. Now that you have completed the Two-Ball Workout, it is time to move on to something equally challenging, spinning a basketball.

VIII. Spinning

A. One Ball

Spinning a basketball is one of the greatest ball handling drills because learning to spin a ball will give you great confidence. Besides learning the basic spin, the advanced part of these drills will increase your ability to toss, catch, control, and maneuver a spinning basketball.

Two key elements of spinning a ball are balance and coordination. When you get the ball spinning, let it do all the work because that is when balance comes into play. Balancing a ball successfully allows you to maintain the spin for long periods of time, especially if you are changing the ball between your fingers or hands. It is very difficult to spin a basketball without coordinating the movements between the ball and your hands. To help all the spinning exercises begin smoothly, it is extremely important to develop the initial spin (more on this later).

Start each drill by spinning the ball either clockwise or counterclockwise, whichever is most comfortable for you. It does not matter if you are left handed or right handed because spinning with either hand will work. You will initially be taught to use a clockwise spin; therefore, perform the opposite movements if you are spinning the ball counterclockwise. If you become frustrated with these spinning drills, go back to some of the ball handling or dribbling drills and then come back to try the spinning drills again. Spinning a basketball is not an easy task, especially in the beginning, but you will enjoy what you can learn to do with a spinning ball. Each drill explanation will include a suggested goal. This section includes an extensive list of drills, but there may be other spinning exercises that you have seen and would like to try. Be creative and invent some of your own drills because spinning a basketball will bring you great satisfaction in your workouts. Good luck!

VIII. Spinning

1. **each finger on both hands** -- Although the ultimate goal of this drill is eventually to learn to use all five fingers on both hands, you are going to start out spinning the ball on only the right index finger. In time, you will need to learn to begin the drills by twisting the ball with only one hand. This one hand twisting skill will be important to develop in order to complete the two-ball spinning drills in section B. For now, let's start by spinning (twisting) the ball in a clockwise direction using both hands. After you have twisted the ball an inch or two up in the air with both hands, quickly place your right index finger directly under the ball so it lands on the tip of the finger while still spinning. It is easier to spin a ball and keep it balanced when your finger is in a vertical position. Continue to keep the spinning ball balanced on your index finger until you feel the ball starting to lose speed (which only takes a few seconds). This phase of the drill is the most difficult; be patient as you try to improve your twisting and balancing skills.

   Next, you will begin "fanning" the ball by slapping the left side of the spinning ball with your left hand. (Note: fanning is sometimes referred to as "waving" or "brushing" the spinning basketball). It is important to frequently fan the ball to increase the spin speed until you get the ball back to a comfortable speed. Of course the faster you can get the ball moving, the longer you can maintain the spin. When you are fanning the ball, barely tip the ball so you do not knock it off your right index finger. Try to maintain the spin as long as you can on the index finger and then stop the ball to switch to the middle finger on the right hand. Complete the same procedures as just described with the middle finger before moving on to the ring finger, the pinky, and finally the thumb. A minimum of five seconds should be completed for each finger. The pinky is a little more difficult to do because the finger is weaker and the weight of the ball will tire the finger sooner. All the movements that were just described were done on the right hand with the left hand doing the fanning. Use the same technique for the left hand by twisting the ball in a clockwise motion with both hands and then quickly placing the left index finger directly under

the ball. Now fan the ball with the right hand by slapping it in a clockwise motion. Learn to spin the ball on all five fingers on the left hand, spinning it as long as you can on each finger (minimum of five seconds). Do not be surprised if you are unable to spin the ball correctly for a while because it takes practice to learn to spin a basketball. If you know someone who can spin a ball well, have them place a spinning ball on top of your finger. This will help you get an idea for what a spinning ball feels like and it will improve your fanning of the ball.

Note: The description for this opening exercise was long because it explains the basics for spinning a basketball. These spinning basics will no longer be repeated in the rest of this section; it is now assumed that you can spin the ball successfully using all fingers on both hands. It will be very difficult to continue this section until you have mastered the fundamentals of spinning.

VIII. Spinning 181

2. **each finger on each hand – continuous** -- Switching fingers while the ball is spinning is considered a difficult task. In this drill, you are going to replace each finger with another finger on the same hand while the ball is continually spinning. You will have to fan the ball periodically to maintain a constant spin speed throughout the exercise. Begin by spinning the ball on your thumb for five seconds. After the five seconds, quickly replace the thumb with your index finger and spin the ball for another five seconds. Continue spinning the ball by replacing the index finger with the middle finger, the ring finger, and then the pinky. Once you finish the pinky, reverse the process by completing the five second spin again on the ring finger, middle finger, index finger, and finally the thumb. After you have done the exercise for five seconds on each finger, complete the same sequence but now keep the ball spinning on each finger for just one second before moving to the next. This "one second series" happens very quickly as the spinning ball starts on the thumb and moves down the hand on each finger and then back up to the thumb. You will need to spin the ball rapidly on the thumb to start this "one second series" because there will be no time to fan the ball! Remember that this is a continuous drill; the ball should never stop spinning until you have spun it on all fingers. Once you finish spinning the ball on one hand, do not forget to change over to the other hand and complete the same steps.

3. **alternate hands with each set of fingers** -- This will be the first exercise in which you switch the spinning ball between hands. Begin spinning the ball on your right index finger and then fan the ball a few times to increase the spin speed. Next, exchange hands by replacing the right index finger with the left index finger. When the ball is on the left index finger, fan it a few more times to build up speed and then switch back over to the right index finger. Exchange the ball back and forth three times with the index fingers, spinning the ball for five seconds after each exchange. Once you complete the index finger, move on to the middle fingers, the ring fingers, the pinkies, and finally the thumbs. When you are proficient in exchanging the ball between each set of fingers, try switching the ball every two seconds instead of five. This will require you to exchange the ball back and forth quickly and also to spin the ball rapidly.

4. **each knuckle on both hands** -- Spinning a basketball on your knuckle can be very tricky. This spinning exercise will take some practice, so try to do the best you can. Spin the ball as you regularly do to begin the drill. Then quickly let the ball slide down your finger so it rests on your knuckle and you can continue spinning the ball. It may sound easy, but this exercise is more complicated than you may think. You will find that the thumb will be the easiest because none of the other fingers will get in the way. Try to spin the ball a minimum of five seconds on each knuckle, <u>both</u> hands.

5. **flip spinning ball from one hand to the other hand – each finger** -- The key word for this exercise is "flip" instead of exchange. Thus far the transition between fingers has been a simple replacement of fingers while the ball is spinning. Now you will flip the ball from one hand to the other (easier said than done!). Start by spinning the ball on your right index finger for a few seconds. Next, flip the ball up in the air (with it still spinning) and catch it on the left index finger to continue spinning. Keep on flipping the ball from one index finger to the other until you can complete the flip successfully each time. Try the middle fingers next and then attempt the flip with the ring fingers, the pinkies, and finally the thumbs. The pinky is the most difficult because the force of the ball makes it challenging to catch on top of the finger and still keep the ball spinning. Each flip does not have to be high in the beginning, but eventually every toss should be one to two feet up in the air. Learn to complete these flips with all the fingers, not just the index fingers.

6. **flip spinning ball high up in the air** -- This drill will have a similar ring to the last exercise because the spinning ball is flipped up in the air and caught while still spinning. Begin spinning the ball on any finger; then flip it high into the air and catch it on the <u>same finger</u> to continue spinning. The drill works best when you have the ball spinning very rapidly before flipping it. This will guarantee that the ball will still be spinning at a decent pace when you catch it. See how high you can toss the ball and still catch it spinning!

VIII. Spinning 183

7. **hit off back of hand** -- This is the first of six drills in which you will hit (knock) the spinning ball off a part of your body and then resume the spinning when you catch it. Begin by spinning the ball with either hand (any finger). After that, flip (push) the ball up a few inches with your finger and then hit it off the back of your hand. Try to knock the ball so it pops straight up about six inches, which is just enough time to get your finger in a set position to catch it and resume spinning. If you are having no problems, attempt this drill with the other hand so you are able to complete the exercise with either. Strive to finish three hits off the back of each hand.

8. **hit off fist(s)** -- Hitting the ball off your fist is comparable to the back of the hand exercise you just completed. Start spinning the ball with either hand (any finger) and then flip (push) the ball up a few inches so you can make a fist to punch it up in the air. Hit the ball just hard enough to pop it about a foot or two straight up. When the ball comes down, quickly place your finger under the ball to "catch" it on the finger to keep it spinning. Do not hit the ball hard with your fist because you may lose control. Attempt this drill with each hand, although using your weaker spinning hand could be difficult the first few times. Complete three successful "punches" with each hand. You can also try hitting the ball with alternating fists instead of just one before catching the spinning ball. At first, try these two-hand alternating punches without the spin because this technique requires perfect hits each time and a good amount of coordination.

9. **hit off elbow** -- If you can hit the spinning ball off your fist and catch it, why not try the elbow also? Start the drill by spinning the ball with any finger on your right hand and then toss (push) the ball about a foot up in the air. As soon as you have released the ball, quickly lift your right elbow so the spinning ball drops and hits an inch or two below it. When the ball bounces off the elbow, immediately "catch" it by placing your finger under the ball to keep it spinning. Complete three of these "hits" off the right elbow, using the right hand to spin the ball. Next, try to do three more using the left hand and the left elbow. It is imperative to hit the ball off the elbow so it bounces straight up; the drill will not work if the ball caroms off to the side. As an alternate method, try hitting the ball off the elbow by flapping your arm out like a chicken wing once the ball has been released. Perform three "chicken wings" with each elbow.

VIII. Spinning

10. **hit off head** -- Here is a twist to drill #6 in which you flipped the spinning ball high in the air and caught it on the same finger. Start spinning the ball on any finger and then flip it a foot or two directly above your head. The ball should then hit off the top of your head and bounce forward so you can "catch" it on your finger and continue spinning. Be sure to hit the ball forward off the head and not to either side or behind you, because the bounce off the head is the most difficult part of the exercise. Complete three successful "hits" off the head with each hand.

11. **hit off knee(s)** -- Hitting the spinning ball off your knee and keeping it going is not an easy assignment. Begin spinning the ball on any finger and then flip it about a foot in the air. As the ball starts to descend, lift your right leg straight up so the ball comes down and hits just above the knee. When the ball pops up, place your finger under the ball to keep it spinning. Strive to hit the ball successfully off the right knee three separate times and then use the left knee for three more. It does not matter which hand the ball is spun on; try a finger on each hand to see which one will work best for you. For advanced ball handlers, try hitting the ball off your knee(s) three consecutive times before catching it on your finger. You may find these successive hits off the knee(s) difficult to control. You have probably seen this move performed by soccer players (of course without the spinning element). It is strongly suggested that you perform this drill and the next one outside, where you would have more room and to avoid breaking anything!

12. **kick off foot** -- Hopefully you had no problems with the last exercise because this drill also uses a part of the leg to hit the spinning ball. Stand with your feet together and begin spinning the ball with a finger on either hand. Next, simply release your finger so the ball drops straight down. As it starts to descend, lift your right foot to kick the ball straight up. When the ball pops back up, place your finger under the ball to "catch" it and keep it spinning. It would be a good idea to practice a few kicks without the spin before putting all the steps together. The kick itself determines the outcome of this exercise. When you are kicking the ball, be sure to have it hit off the top of the foot so it comes straight up to your finger. Try to complete three of these "kicks" with each foot, although it will be more difficult when you use your weaker foot. Like the last drill, it does not matter which hand you use to spin the ball; try a finger on both hands to see which one will work best for you. As previously mentioned, you are probably going to need quite a bit of room to do this exercise, especially the first few times or until you can keep your kicks under control. Yes, this is a difficult drill!

VIII. Spinning 185

13. **spin after bouncing ball on floor** -- At this point you should have a good command of spinning tricks. Starting with this exercise, the rest of the section will include some very challenging drills. Begin spinning the ball very fast with any finger. Next, remove your finger so the ball drops straight to the floor. When it bounces back up, place your finger under the ball in order to start spinning it again. It is important to start fanning the ball <u>immediately</u> to keep it spinning. You will be amazed how much spin the ball loses when it makes contact with the floor. Drop the ball from a height equal to your own height so the ball will bounce up near your chest. This will make the exercise a little easier because the ball will be in a workable position for you. Your goal is to correctly complete three bounces in a row using any finger.

14. **spin ball on floor, pick up spinning** -- This is another difficult drill that is going to take you a few tries to complete correctly. Twist the ball very fast on the floor, much as you would spin a top. Be sure to twist the ball in the same direction that you are used to spinning the ball on your fingers, either clockwise or counterclockwise. After you have twisted the ball, place your finger under the ball and pick it up off the floor so the ball is still spinning as you are lifting it up. Begin fanning the ball as soon as you get it balanced to maintain the spin. You can use any finger to pick up the ball, but the drill seems to work better if you use the index or middle finger. It is best to twist the ball very quickly to start the drill so you do not lose a lot of spin when you pick it up and before you start fanning. Try to complete three successful pickups in a row with each hand.

15. **throw spinning ball over head, catch behind back with both hands** -- These next two exercises should have a familiar ring because they are similar to some of the flip drills in the coordination section of Advanced Ball Handling (part V, section B). Start spinning the ball with any finger on your right hand. Next, throw (flip) the spinning ball at least two feet over your head. As the ball is traveling over your head, quickly move both hands behind your back to catch it (of course the ball stops spinning once it has been caught). You will be surprised at how difficult it is to catch a spinning ball, especially when you are unable to see it. Complete six "throws" and "catches," spinning with the right hand three times, then using the left hand for three more.

16. **throw spinning ball over head, catch behind back with same hand** -- This exercise is a little trickier than the last one because you are catching the spinning ball with only one hand. Begin spinning the ball with any finger on your right hand. After that, throw the spinning ball at least two feet over your head and quickly move the right hand behind your back to catch the ball. Keep your left hand down by your side because it is not used for the toss or the catch. Attempt to catch the ball without trapping it against your back. Complete three throws and catches with only the right hand and then use just the left hand for three more. See how high you can throw the spinning ball and catch it behind your back with the same hand.

VIII. Spinning

17. **spin between legs – switch hands (reverse)** -- Spinning a ball between your legs will require much coordination because of precise movements you must make. Begin with your feet spread at least two feet apart (knees bent) and spin the ball with any finger on your right hand. Keep the ball spinning (by fanning) and bring it down to your knees. Now reach behind your left leg with your left hand so you can switch the spinning ball between your legs from the right hand to a finger on the left. After you have changed hands, bring the ball around the left leg (to the front) and then back through your legs in order to transfer it back to the right hand. You may have noticed the entire drill works like the figure 8 you learned in Basic Ball Handling, except the ball is passed while spinning instead of simply handed off. The hard part occurs when you have to bring the spinning ball down and then behind your legs. Finish three of these complete figure 8 rotations, which is equal to six different exchanges between hands. Reverse directions by starting the spinning ball from behind the right leg and passing it through your legs to the left hand in front. Complete three more rotations using this reverse figure 8 method. The whole drill is done slowly because the ball is spinning the entire time and the exchanges between hands have to be perfect. Since the drill does take some time to complete, there will be times where you have to fan the ball to maintain the spin. It is very difficult to complete three figure 8 rotations without having to stop briefly once or twice to fan the ball. Without a doubt, this is one of the most challenging spinning tricks you will learn; do not give up on it right away!

18. **spin behind back – switch hands (reverse)** -- Switching a spinning ball from hand to hand behind your back is a difficult move to execute. Start spinning the ball with any finger on your right hand and slowly take it under your arm and around your right side (hip). As the ball is moving toward the middle of your back, bring your left hand behind the back so you can switch the spinning ball from hand to hand. When the ball is safely spinning on the left hand, bring it around the left hip and back to the front. Next, pass the spinning ball off to the right hand to begin another rotation around your back. As you can probably tell, the exercise was just described with the ball moving around your back in a clockwise direction, but learn to reverse directions allowing you to go counterclockwise. Your goal is to complete three rotations around your back in each direction without any errors. This exercise can be challenging since you are unable to view the switch of the spinning ball between hands behind your back.

VIII. Spinning

19. **spin between legs, flip ball up, catch spinning in front** -- This is a variation from the spin between legs exercise you previously completed (drill #17). As you learned in that drill, it is not easy to spin a ball at low heights because the angle of your finger has to change so your palm is facing up. Start with your feet spread at least two feet apart and begin spinning the ball in your right hand. Bend down and bring the ball behind your right leg so you have it spinning between your legs. Once you have the spinning ball balanced, quickly flip (push) it up near your waist. Bring the right hand back around to the front <u>immediately</u> after you toss the ball so you can catch it spinning in the front on the same finger that was used for the flip. You will need to toss the ball at least waist high to give yourself enough time to move the right hand around to the front. The higher the flip, the easier it will be to catch the ball on your finger to keep it spinning. Try to complete three of these with your right hand and then attempt to accomplish three with the left hand behind the left leg. If initially you are having problems getting the spinning ball between your legs, try lifting a leg off the floor and bringing the ball under it. You may find this to be a better method for flipping and catching the spinning ball.

VIII. Spinning

B. Two Balls

This section includes five spinning exercises in which you will be using two balls. You may think that using two balls would be twice as difficult, but that is not true. These two-ball drills require much coordination and balance. Developing the basic one-ball spinning technique is vital for achieving success in these more complicated drills. Each will include a specific goal; read the descriptions carefully.

1. **spin one ball in right hand – dribble other ball with left hand** -- These first two exercises are a good introduction to this two-ball spinning section because they involve two things you know how to do very well, dribbling and spinning. Thus far you have probably started your spinning drills using both hands, but now you must learn to begin each spin using only one hand. This allows your other hand to be free to allow you to do two things simultaneously. Spinning the ball with one hand is not that much more difficult than starting your spin with both hands. To begin, hold a ball in each hand. Place your right hand under the ball and twist the ball quickly in the direction you are used to spinning, either clockwise or counterclockwise. Position your finger immediately below the ball to start your normal spin routine. For this exercise, begin by spinning the ball in your right hand with the one hand technique just mentioned. Once you get the first ball spinning, start dribbling the other ball waist high with your left hand. This is not a low or a speed dribble, just a normal waist high dribble directly in front of you. To keep the drill continuous, fan the spinning ball with your left hand. This will require you to let the ball you are dribbling continue to bounce while you quickly fan the spinning ball in your right hand a few times before resuming your dribble. Try to maintain this spin and dribble combination for at least fifteen seconds, but see if you can keep it going for a full minute.

2. **spin one ball in left hand – dribble other ball with right hand** -- This drill should not be too difficult unless you have trouble keeping the ball spinning in your left hand. First, get one of the balls spinning very fast on a finger on your left hand, using the one hand spinning technique you learned in the last exercise. As the ball is spinning rapidly, begin dribbling the second ball directly in front of you with the right hand. Continue spinning and dribbling for at least fifteen seconds, but aim to keep the drill going for a full minute. Recall from the last exercise how to keep the drill uninterrupted. You will need to let the ball you are dribbling bounce once or twice while you quickly move your right hand over to fan the spinning ball in the left hand.

3. **spin one ball in each hand at same time** -- This is the first drill in which you will have two balls spinning simultaneously, which may cause this drill to be a little tricky. You can start by holding one ball in the left hand and placing the other ball between your knees (legs close together). Spin the ball extremely fast on your left hand by fanning the ball many times with your right hand, increasing the spin speed. As the first ball is spinning in your left hand, grab the second ball from between your knees and twist

VIII. Spinning 189

it in your right hand using the technique you learned in drill #1 of this section. Keep the balls balanced on your fingers until they stop spinning, hopefully for at least ten seconds. Try to keep your feet stationary while spinning the balls, avoiding unnecessary movement. Once you become an accomplished spinner, you can try this drill using the one hand twisting technique for each ball.

4. **throw spinning balls over head, catch in same hand behind back** -- This drill combines the last exercise with drill #16 in the previous section in which you flipped only one spinning ball over your head to catch behind your back. Begin this drill by spinning both balls at the same time as you completed in the previous exercise. Once you have both spinning balls balanced, throw them at the same time about two feet over your shoulders. As soon as you release the balls, move both hands quickly behind your back to catch a ball in each hand (catch in the same hand that did the toss). Both throws must be absolutely perfect or the entire exercise will fail. Practice your throws a few times without the balls spinning so you can get an idea of how the tosses and catches should feel and work. These practice throws are exactly like the two-ball flip drill in section D of the Two-Ball Workout (drill #8). Try to catch the balls with your fingertips instead of in the palms of your hands. Your goal is to complete five successful throws and catches with the spinning balls. Please remember this is a very complicated exercise.

5. **spin one ball on top of a stationary ball** -- As pointed out in the Spinning introduction, balance and coordination are key elements for spinning a basketball and this exercise definitely requires both skills. To start this drill, begin spinning one of the balls very quickly on your right hand (index finger) and then grab the other ball in your left hand and hold it with the palm facing up. Once you have the ball spinning rapidly, place it on top of the stationary ball in your left hand and begin fanning the ball with your right hand to prevent its falling. Continue fanning the ball to keep it spinning and try to balance it on top of the stationary ball in your left hand for at least five seconds. The difficult part of the drill occurs when you position the spinning ball on top of the stationary ball. You must have a smooth transfer from your index  finger to the top of the stationary ball or the spinning ball will slide off. If you are unable to transition the spinning ball from your right index finger, try starting the drill by balancing one ball on top of another in your left hand as you did in the Two-Ball Workout (section D, drill #3). Once you have the top ball balanced, begin fanning it with your right hand and keep it spinning for at least five seconds. You may find this alternate method to work better so give it a try. When you have successfully balanced the ball using either one of the steps just mentioned, switch sides and begin spinning the ball in your left hand; then place it on top of the stationary ball in your right hand (keep spinning for at least five seconds). Balancing a spinning ball on top of another ball with just one hand may be harder than you think.

VIII. Spinning

Conclusion of Part VIII – You have just completed some of the more challenging ball handling drills and tricks. Spinning a basketball is not an easy task and it can take many hours to grasp all the skills and maneuvers. Some basketball fans associate ball handling tricks with spinning because the drills are very different and fun to watch. It is hoped that you will continue to develop your spinning skills and create some of your own spinning drills and tricks.

Conclusion

As mentioned in the introduction, *Just A Basketball* was designed for you to reach your potential and have fun in the process. Hopefully you have greatly increased your ball handling and dribbling skills to make you a better all-around player. This book has included many types of drills to help you improve your various ball handling and dribbling abilities. Given that almost every drill in this book can be done individually, all you need are a few good basketballs and the desire to become a better ball handler. *Just A Basketball* is only a guide; you have to make it happen to become an outstanding ball handler.

You can officially call yourself a ball handling "wizard" if you have successfully completed all of the drills in *Just A Basketball*. Yes, some of the exercises were very challenging and probably frustrating at times. Some players develop skills more quickly than others. If you had a few difficulties, keep practicing and practicing because eventually you will be able to perform all of the drills in *Just A Basketball*. Excellent ball handling and dribbling skills create confidence to help you in other phases of the game and to allow you to compete at a higher level. You must continue to set goals for yourself and work hard to attain them. Your achievements will depend on your having a positive attitude and a commitment to become the best ball handler that you can possibly be. Best of luck for continued success and fun as you work to develop your ball handling, dribbling, and spinning skills.

About the Author

Like most players, **Andy Hart** started out in recreational leagues at an early age to learn basic basketball fundamentals. As he got older, Andy played on competitive traveling teams and then four years of high school basketball in Northern Virginia. A few years later he coached youth basketball teams in Western North Carolina and eventually worked his way up to the high school level back in Virginia.

Andy has frequently attended basketball camps and clinics to share and also learn ball handling and dribbling drills and tricks. Watching hundreds of games, talking with other players and coaches, and reading numerous basketball books have also helped him to understand and appreciate the game. He is especially known for his ball handling creativity and basketball knowledge. In 2001, Andy was chosen as a National Semi-Finalist in a nationwide "Freestyle" basketball contest. He has also performed at a number of school and talent events to showcase his abilities.

Being able to find a multitude of individual ball handling and dribbling drills in one place can be rather difficult. As a result, Andy decided to consolidate many of the drills he learned and created into one comprehensive book. Ball handling and dribbling were always his specialty as a player and coach so he decided to develop a list of drills regarding these skills. Many of the drills in *Just A Basketball* were created by Andy to help players with their coordination, ball control, strength, and quickness. People like the fact that Andy is just an everyday person who enjoys the game of basketball and wants to share his ball handling and dribbling knowledge and secrets with others.

Besides basketball, he also enjoys tennis, softball, cycling, and running. Andy resides in Springfield, Virginia, with his wife, Candace, and their sons, Ryan and Kyle.

Contact the Author

Please send your comments, suggestions, success stories, or other words of ball handling and dribbling wisdom to me by email: dribble4fun@aol.com. I would love to hear from you!

Made in the USA
Middletown, DE
25 March 2021